"In this erudite and articulate book, Edgar offers an embodied account of human existence in terms of hunger, dependence, desire, and intersubjectivity. He does so by means of a sincere and subtle development of Merleau-Ponty's ontology. As such, he fleshes out the deep philosophical meaning of incarnation that has relevance for both epistemology and Christian theology. He diagnoses and overcomes the dualisms that still haunt the contemporary imagination. We do not realize how Cartesian we are."

—PHILIP GOODCHILD, Professor of Religion and Philosophy, University of Nottingham

"*Things Seen and Unseen* is a welcome and elegant contribution to the recovery of Merleau-Ponty's 'incarnational' phenomenology for theology. It will be read with value by those interested in theological aesthetics and philosophy of religion as well."

—JANET SOSKICE, Professor of Philosophical Theology, Faculty of Divinity, University of Cambridge

"Merleau-Ponty's philosophy is at last beginning to receive the attention it so richly deserves. It remains one of the most fertile sources in recent thought for reshaping the way we think about knowledge, time, and embodiment—a reshaping made all the more urgent by the political and ecological disasters of our times. It is also a style of thought with obvious theological resonance, a question that has long been in need of the kind of careful, insightful, and creative attention that Orion Edgar provides in this really admirable study, which brings Merleau-Ponty's analyses of bodily existence together with central themes of the Christian imagination—incarnation and sacrament—in a deeply original and fruitful way."

—ROWAN WILLIAMS, Master of Magdalene College, Cambridge

"In this sophisticated first monograph, Orion Edgar reexamines the philosophy of Merleau-Ponty from the perspective of the Catholic faith that always lapped at the edges of his thought. Once Merleau-Ponty's notions of 'flesh' and 'depth' (in particular) are thus freshly illuminated, his striking relevance for a contemporary theology of the incarnation becomes apparent. Edgar's analysis is both philosophically insightful and theologically rich, and this study makes a significant contribution to Merleau-Ponty scholarship."

—SARAH COAKLEY, Norris-Hulse Professor of Divinity, University of Cambridge

"*Things Seen and Unseen* confirms the significance of Maurice Merleau-Ponty as one of the principal philosophical voices deserving contemporary theological attention. It also confirms Orion Edgar's significance as a voice in Christian philosophical theology. The *Veritas* series has its genesis in the Radical Orthodoxy movement and, since its beginnings, that movement has pointed to, and explored, the centrality of mediation to the Christian intellectual vision. This book is a further substantial contribution."

—ANDREW DAVISON, Faculty of Divinity and Corpus Christi College, University of Cambridge

"This is, quite simply, the most magnificent account of Merleau-Ponty's phenomenology ever written. Edgar brings to life, in the fullest possible terms, the genius of Merleau-Ponty—the Church should be truly grateful."

—CONOR CUNNINGHAM, Associate Professor in Theology and Philosophy, Department of Theology; Co-Director, Centre of Theology and Philosophy, University of Nottingham

Things Seen and Unseen

VERITAS
Series Introduction

"... the truth will set you free" (John 8:32)

In much contemporary discourse, Pilate's question has been taken to mark the absolute boundary of human thought. Beyond this boundary, it is often suggested, is an intellectual hinterland into which we must not venture. This terrain is an agnosticism of thought: because truth cannot be possessed, it must not be spoken. Thus, it is argued that the defenders of "truth" in our day are often traffickers in ideology, merchants of counterfeits, or anti-liberal. They are, because it is somewhat taken for granted that Nietzsche's word is final: truth is the domain of tyranny.

Is this indeed the case, or might another vision of truth offer itself? The ancient Greeks named the love of wisdom as *philia*, or friendship. The one who would become wise, they argued, would be a "friend of truth." For both philosophy and theology might be conceived as schools in the friendship of truth, as a kind of relation. For like friendship, truth is as much discovered as it is made. If truth is then so elusive, if its domain is *terra incognita*, perhaps this is because it arrives to us—unannounced—as gift, as a person, and not some thing.

The aim of the Veritas book series is to publish incisive and original current scholarly work that inhabits "the between" and "the beyond" of theology and philosophy. These volumes will all share a common aspiration to transcend the institutional divorce in which these two disciplines often find themselves, and to engage questions of pressing concern to both philosophers and theologians in such a way as to reinvigorate both disciples with a kind of interdisciplinary desire, often so absent in contemporary academe. In a word, these volumes represent collective efforts in the befriending of truth, doing so beyond the simulacra of pretend tolerance, the violent, yet insipid reasoning of liberalism that asks with Pilate, "What is truth?"—expecting a consensus of non-commitment; one that encourages the commodification of the mind, now sedated by the civil service of career, ministered by the frightened patrons of position.

The series will therefore consist of two "wings": (1) original monographs; and (2) essay collections on a range of topics in theology and philosophy. The latter will principally be the products of the annual conferences of the Centre of Theology and Philosophy (www.theologyphilosophycentre .co.uk).

Conor Cunningham and Eric Austin Lee, *Series editors*

Things Seen and Unseen

The Logic of Incarnation in Merleau-Ponty's
Metaphysics of Flesh

ORION EDGAR

CASCADE *Books* · Eugene, Oregon

THINGS SEEN AND UNSEEN
The Logic of Incarnation in Merleau-Ponty's Metaphysics of Flesh

Veritas 17

Cascade Books
An Imprint of Wipf and Stock Publishers
199 W. 8th Ave., Suite 3
Eugene, OR 97401

www.wipfandstock.com

ISBN 13: 978-1-4982-0261-9
HC ISBN 13: 978-1-4982-0263-3

Cataloging-in-Publication data:

Edgar, Orion

Things seen and unseen : the logic of incarnation in Merleau-Ponty's metaphysics of flesh / Orion Edgar.

Veritas 17

xii + 264 p. ; 23 cm. —Includes bibliographical references.

ISBN 13: 978-1-4982-0261-9
HC ISBN 13: 978-1-4982-0263-3

1. Merleau-Ponty, Maurice, 1908–1961—Criticism and interpretation. 2. Phenomenology. 3. Theology. 4. Human body. I. Series. II. Title.

B2430.M3764 E241 2016

Manufactured in the U.S.A.

For Joan

Contents

Contents

Acknowledgements

IT IS A CENTRAL thread of this work that thought is essentially embodied: it belongs not to the inner workings of an individual mind but to a bodily person located in a complex web of relations, to other people, to a world, and to the fundamental *logos* of that world. To compose a list of persons without whom my work could not be what it is would be an unending task; but I'd like to thank a few of whose influence I have been most keenly aware.

My greatest debt is to my wife, Sharon, whose support for me has been unfailing. You have shared the discipline and the suffering of this project and have borne much of its strain on our life together. You deserve its rewards and the joy of its completion as much as I do. Thank you.

The prudence and generosity of Andrew and Elaine Phipps gave us both the freedom to spend several years in study, for which I am deeply grateful.

I am indebted to my friend Ben Pollard, with whom I have shared the delight of intellectual sparring in both serious and silly modes for many years, and who has long appreciated and encouraged my philosophical instincts. Many other friends have held me up and been a source of comfort and levity in times when I have been most deeply lost in my work: Sam and Ronnie McDermid, Lionel and Rachel Miller, Max and Beth Edgar, Rich Johnson, Laurie and Ann-Marie Ison, and Paul and Jen Prigg are among them. Lizzie and John Lacey provided both encouragement and a place to stay in my final weeks of writing up the doctoral thesis on which this work is based: John's death is a great loss to many, keenly felt here. Without the detailed and focused conversation I have had the pleasure of sharing with Jennifer Good, I could not have learnt as much as I have about many things, not least about vision.

I wish to thank my teacher and friend Philip Goodchild, from whom I have learnt so much, and who has often helped me to see what it is I am really trying to say. Komarine Romdenh-Romluc was instrumental in introducing me to Merleau-Ponty's philosophy, and has continued to help me to think through it in productive ways, as has Conor Cunningham, under whose guidance my search for the theological significance of Merleau-Ponty's philosophy has been significantly shaped. The late Denise Inge's encouragement and conversation is greatly missed. Christopher Cocksworth and Br. Ian Mead both provided encouragement and help in learning to hold together serious thought with deeply-lived faith. I owe special thanks to John Inge for encouraging me to get on with turning my doctoral thesis into this book.

I also owe a great deal to my student colleagues, especially to Anthony Paul Smith, who, with great generosity, tried to help me see what is of value in even my worst ideas; to Alex Andrews, who continued to bring to my attention thoughts and perspectives I could not otherwise have encountered; and to Stuart Jesson, whose careful questioning of philosophical and theological ideas has often given me both pleasure and encouragement. Aaron Riches encouraged me at a crucial time near the beginning of this project, and first brought some of its central theological sources to my attention. David Rowe and Rich Johnson provided invaluable feedback as readers of early drafts of the text, and Dylan Trigg, Marika Rose, Ruth Jackson, and Simon Ravenscroft all gave detailed feedback during the preparation of the manuscript. Erin Clark and Sam Kimbriel both saved me from significant errors at the proofreading stage, and have both fed my thought in deeper ways.

I am grateful to the communities of faith who have nourished me for the past nineteen years—to my friends from St. Albans Vineyard; Trent Vineyard; St. Catherine's, Arthog; St. Cynon's, Fairbourne; All Saints Worcester; and Westcott House. My special thanks go to the Brothers and Sisters of Mucknell Abbey, whose generous silence was succor to me at a crucial point in its development. To all of you, and to the many others who have contributed to the formation of my thinking along the way, thank you.

INTRODUCTION

The Logic of Incarnation in Merleau-Ponty's Ontology

MY AIM IN THIS book is to explicate the ontology that Maurice Merleau-Ponty was developing throughout his work, the final and most complete expression of which comes to us in the unfinished work published as *The Visible and the Invisible*, and to show how this ontology points towards a metaphysical completion grounded in the logic of the Catholic tradition in which Merleau-Ponty received a long formation. I will argue that the progression of Merleau-Ponty's thought is not well characterized by a turn from an early phenomenological philosophy of consciousness to a later, more consistent ontological philosophy of *flesh*. Rather, Merleau-Ponty's thought follows a trajectory (within each text and in his whole corpus) towards an incarnational understanding which is never brought to completion but which is continually reworked and refined, each time bringing to clearer expression something of the fundamental insight that is present from the beginning.

My conviction is that Merleau-Ponty's ontology participates in a radical movement of thought that seeks to liberate the thinker from dissipative dualisms by identifying the common source of their elements in an *intertwining*, that is, in a chiasmatically structured prior whole from which we make analytic abstractions. In modernity these abstractions remain determinative for thought; they impair a synthetic, intuitive understanding of structured wholes in the very same moment that they enable an analytic, atomic understanding of the elements of the experienced world. The analytic function well established, we are left with a glut of problems of integration that characterize the weakness of modern thought: the problems of mind and body, form and matter, ideal and real, thought and things, freedom and causation, instinct and desire, animal and environment, body and world, telos and genesis, humanity and nature, and so on.

Merleau-Ponty's logic is *incarnational* in the sense that it takes as its icon the flesh, a supposed "union of opposites" which, inasmuch as it succeeds in uniting them, announces their originary indivision and the possibility of their transformation. This ontological story scandalizes our already-existing stories and our established categories, and this should come as no surprise; the clear separation of things, the making of these distinctions, initiated a great advance in human understanding of which it remains the fundamental basis. The search for knowledge depends on taking things apart to understand them. But if knowledge is not to supplant wisdom, if *scientia* is not to spurn its ancient concern with life and living, with integrating such knowledge into the world of thought, of values, and of relationships, it must learn to put things back together.

There is in Merleau-Ponty's thought, then, a kind of methodological commitment to a coherentism both narrow and broad: his fundamental impulse "to understand the relations of consciousness and nature"[1] arises from dissatisfaction with the chasm left between them by Cartesian thought. What perception furnishes us with must make sense in its own terms, and if the phenomenological reduction means excising what we cannot fit into a predetermined set of terms, then it is of no use. As Merleau-Ponty tells us in the introduction to the *Phenomenology of Perception*: "The most important lesson of the reduction is the impossibility of a complete reduction. [. . .] If we were absolute spirit, the reduction would not be problematic. But since, on the contrary, we are in and toward the world, and since even our reflections take place in the temporal flow that they are trying to capture [. . .] there is no thought which encompasses all of our thought."[2]

My aim, then, is also to draw out those aspects of Merleau-Ponty's ontological thought that are of interest to Christian theology. In the use of the notion of *incarnation*, in the repeated deployment of sacramental language, of the notion of the centrality of faith, and in a continued dialogue with Christian thinkers, Merleau-Ponty is always drawing on and reflecting on the Christian tradition, and to the reader sensitive to this world of thought it is clear that he is deeply marked by his Roman Catholic upbringing, operating very much within a sacramental imaginary.[3]

1. Merleau-Ponty, *The Structure of Behaviour*, 3.

2. Merleau-Ponty, *Phenomenology of Perception*, lxxvii–lxxviii. Except where specified, references to the *Phenomenology of Perception* are to the 2012 edition, translated by Donald Landes.

3. On Merleau-Ponty's connection with Christian thought, see Simpson, *Merleau-Ponty and Theology*; Kearney, *Anatheism*, especially 85–100; and "Merleau-Ponty and

Merleau-Ponty grew up as a Catholic and had an unusually happy childhood.[4] He broke with Catholicism in his twenties, partly in response to the shelling of working-class parts of Vienna by the Catholic "Christian Socialist" government of Engelbert Dollfuss, and he alludes to this event in the 1946 essay translated as "Faith and Good Faith." But, as Graham Ward says, "he never manages to shake off his Catholic imagination."[5] Merleau-Ponty's thought does not by any means require a Christian commitment to make sense. But it does draw on a set of ideas that an understanding of Christianity will help us to elucidate, and my contention will be that it is also informed by an essential strand of the Christian tradition, namely its incarnationalism, which gives the ontology that Merleau-Ponty was developing a singular significance for Christian thought and that demands a theological interpretation.

My emphasis will remain on Merleau-Ponty's philosophy and its implications for ontology and for theology. I do not seek here to stage an encounter between Merleau-Ponty and theology in general or any particular theologian. This work has been begun by others; but I focus here on understanding and developing the *internal* logic of Merleau-Ponty's trajectory, understanding him in his intellectual and religious context, and attempting to tease out the implications of his thought with as little outside determination as possible. To stage an encounter would place us under the burden of focusing on how Merleau-Ponty's thought differs from Christian Orthodoxy, as it surely must. But such an exercise can easily miss what each can learn from the other, and as such I intend to develop Merleau-Ponty's thought in its theological sympathies, seeking not to Christianize Merleau-Ponty's philosophy but to draw out theological implications already present there. This will involve, in chapter 6, a dialogue between key theological ideas and Merleau-Ponty's work—a dialogue that, I claim, his later work anticipates, particularly through its engagement with incarnation as both a philosophical and a theological concept.

---

the Sacramentality of the Flesh"; Saint Aubert, "L'incarnation change tout"; Milbank, "The Soul of Reciprocity Part Two: Reciprocity Granted"; Nordlander, "Figuring Flesh in Creation" and "The Wonder of Immanence"; and Whaite, "'Suspending the Material.'"

4. Sartre writes, "One day in 1947, Merleau told me that he had never recovered from an incomparable childhood. He had known that private world of happiness from which only age drives us. Pascalian from adolescence, without even having read Pascal, he experienced his singular selfhood as the singularity of an adventure." Sartre, *Situations*, 228.

5. Ward, *Christ and Culture*, 71 n. 25.

In addition to these few interventions, a handful of commentators on Merleau-Ponty have attended to the theological dimension of his thought,[6] and many more theologians have seen fit to make use of his thought in passing.[7] Although theologies of the body have abounded in recent years, and especially in the wake of Pope John Paul II's 129 lectures on "Theology of the Body" between September 1979 and November 1984, these have tended to focus not on embodiment *per se* but on issues associated with the human body, and particularly on sexuality, where "body theology" has been a site of the battle between conservative approaches to sexual morality and the more progressive positions emerging from feminism and queer theory. Theoretical approaches to the body have tended to focus on the questions brought up by the facts of bodily difference, and as such the body has been territorialized and instrumentalized. This has diverted attention away from the body as precisely the ground that human beings share with each other and with the material world, and so often the question of what it is to be a body that is structured in *this particular* way, shared by human beings, that incarnates me in the world and grounds my relationships to others in concrete intersubjectivity, has been put aside in favor of questions of difference. Such questions are important, but to approach questions of bodily difference without a well-founded understanding of embodiment in general may be to put the cart before the horse. I attempt here to elucidate an ontology that understands the body in terms of *flesh*; following Merleau-Ponty, we start with perception, which draws us into an understanding of intersubjectivity, hunger, dependence, and desire, clarifying an account of vision liberated from the Cartesian scopic regime, and ultimately determining fleshly incarnation in terms of expression, institution, and historicity. In this way I attempt to offer an account of what it is to be an incarnate person by focusing on the irreducible structures of embodiment, which always already install us in a world of coexistence with others, a world in which love, hunger, suffering, and transformation carry metaphysical significance and are not simply epiphenomenal. Thus, the questions of the politics of the body, and the discussion of what it might mean for God to have assumed a body, find their much-needed systematic grounding in a logic of incarnation.

There is not a "Merleau-Ponty and Theology" industry in the way that there is for theological interpretations of Heidegger or Wittgenstein for example. For some time there have been occasional excursions into the field of engagement between Merleau-Ponty's thought and Christian theology, but

---

6. See, for example, Rabil, *Merleau-Ponty*; Bannan, "Merleau-Ponty on God"; Bernet, "The Subject in Nature"; and Hamrick and Van Der Veken, *Nature and Logos*.

7. See, for example, Pickstock, *After Writing*, 107–16; Cox, *The Secular City*, 5; Arnould, "Theologians Wanted!," 368; Blond, "Theology and Perception."

this remains a territory for the most part unexplored, and I here develop a fundamental route into that region on the basis of Merleau-Ponty's thought and its theological resonances, both latent and readily perceived.

What, then, is the importance of Merleau-Ponty's ontology? From the first, it proposes to move beyond entrenched dualisms. It is a refrain of my work here that we do not realize just how Cartesian we are. It is for this reason that I seek to develop Merleau-Ponty's ontology: to expose our assumed dualisms, to call them into question, and to find ways to overcome them. Of course, many others have sought to do this before me. I can hardly hope to succeed where they have failed. But this is not a question of finding the solution to the problem of dualism. We are interrogating the mystery of the fleshly connections of human beings and nature, of nature and God; where a rigid rationalism is challenged by the reconciliation of things, dualisms are not simply replaced by unitive monisms; rather, thought is challenged to come to terms with identity within difference. As I understand it, this is the basis for the progression of Merleau-Ponty's thought. Renaud Barbaras writes, "I am inclined more and more to think of Merleau-Ponty's final philosophy as not having fully cast off the presuppositions of the philosophy of consciousness and as faltering because of a lack, rather than an excess, of radicality."[8] Nevertheless Barbaras thinks it justified to keep on returning to Merleau-Ponty's thought; this thought proposes to help us to think our way out of a dualism *that we are in*, and not to dictate from without an entirely new ontology. In this sense, the ontology of the flesh is the goal of our philosophical exercise, and is neither a complete truth already somewhere expressed nor a final answer to the problem of ontology awaiting its definitive expression. To be truly expressed, it must be lived. I attempt to show here why, and how this is possible, by developing the ontology of the flesh in its implications for theology and for the practice of Christianity.

My anticipation is thus that Merleau-Ponty's ontology, to come to full expression, must be brought into dialogue with the world of *praxis*: in the flesh, philosophy is related to history, to action, and to nature. I *do not* think, nor claim, that Christian theology is the only realm in which Merleau-Ponty's ontology can come to a fuller expression. But there must be *a* field of practice and reflection on practice for such fuller expression to be attained, and the field of Christian life and sacramental practice is the one I have seen most clearly implied in his thought, and have settled on. I also see in Christian thought fertile ground for the development of a non-dualistic ontology. The religion of God incarnate, of the *logos* made flesh, has a long tradition of thinking of the intertwining of thought and action, of soul and body, of

---

8. Barbaras, *The Being of the Phenomenon*, xxiv.

heaven and earth, of God and human beings, of self and others, of nature and history. This tradition is sometimes covered over by the influence of a sclerotic scholasticism, by simplistic thinking, by our daily failures in the difficult task of understanding and holding the two poles together.

My guiding questions, then, will be: How can Merleau-Ponty's ontology be developed in light of Christian life and thought? And what implications does this development have for philosophy and for theology?

Such an investigation will, I hope, serve as a guide to theologians who are interested to make use of Merleau-Ponty's thought. In philosophical terms, this book seeks to show how a compelling reading of Merleau-Ponty, which begins without a commitment to methodological atheism, quickly reveals a convergence between Merleau-Ponty's thought and Christian theology. Merleau-Ponty, though not a Catholic Christian in any straightforward sense after he lost his faith in his mid-twenties, was no more straightforwardly a secularist or an atheist. The question of faith and its commitments remained with him, and that he received a Catholic funeral is no surprise, resonating as it does with his ongoing and ambiguous relationship to the faith he inherited and its deep thought-structures.

Developing Merleau-Ponty's thought in these directions will perhaps begin to elucidate a kind of natural theology. Natural theology after Descartes has always led in a basically deist direction. But, when we properly call into question the modern view of the world and its attendant mechanical picture of nature, natural theology begins to look like a rather different kind of exercise. A phenomenological starting-point, leading into the thick ontology of flesh that I will expound in chapters 5 and 6, ultimately points to a God intimated at the depths of the world, a world that bears subtle witness to its own created nature. This makes room for a metaphysics that escapes an objectivizing onto-theology, that affirms the contingency of the world. Such an investigation shows how faith necessarily goes "all the way down" in reason—and as such, this natural theology is always already in a sense revealed. There is no hard divide between the book of nature and the book of Scripture; revealed truth is forever intertwined with the truth of reason. As such, this is not a natural theology that would seek to establish by reason one or another kind of prerequisite for faith—to attempt, for example, to prove the existence of God or establish the coherence of theodicy. Rather, I seek to show how Merleau-Ponty's philosophy justifies a logic that is consonant with that of Christian faith, that must be committed to openness to it (though it cannot justify the claim that *only* this particular kind of theology can ultimately make sense of the ontology of flesh). Merleau-Ponty's philosophy coheres remarkably well with the Christian vision of God and creation correctly understood—but it cannot establish it with the force of law.

I will take several steps on the way. First of all, I explicate Merleau-Ponty's ontology of flesh with detailed attention to its genesis in his understanding of perception. I emphasize the centrality of a fundamental perceptual faith, and show how vision is grounded in its relationship to eating: perception is essential to life as crucial for nutrition, for meeting our appetitive needs. But in human beings perception exceeds the world of needs, as appetite is transformed in *hunger*, which is the imaginative development of desire.

Secondly, I offer an account of perception that affirms vision as the central and pre-eminent sense, but also as rooted in the body and the imbrication of the senses, as dependent on a perceptual faith which is basic, thus moving beyond the impasses of Cartesian perspectivalism and the postmodern antioculocentrism that is its inversion. On the basis of this account of vision I develop an understanding of transcendence as *depth*, which points to a conception of God as knowable at the same time that God must always elude our grasp and exceed every attempt at comprehension.

Thirdly, I show more clearly the roots of Merleau-Ponty's thought in an incarnational and sacramental logic whose source is Christian, and I develop the ontology of flesh with reference to this incarnational logic in theological thought, paying attention to sacramental practice. I show how Merleau-Ponty's notion of institution reveals that ontology and anthropology are intertwined; both a *philosophy of consciousness* and a *philosophy of nature* must be refused, understanding nature as "soil" for ontological flesh. Refusing to reduce God to consciousness or to nature provides a corrective to Spinozist pantheism and to an Idealist conception of God as *penseur absolu du monde*. This philosophical development will build towards an ontology that insists on an account of God that is grounded in Christian theology's deepest logic: that of incarnation.

In Part One I develop the groundwork for a Merleau-Pontyan ontology of *flesh* through an interrogation of perception. In the first chapter, I introduce Merleau-Ponty's fundamental insight, on the basis of his thought in the *Phenomenology of Perception*, situated within and drawing on the whole current of his philosophy. I offer an exposition of his opposition to the atomism of sensationalism and to the objective thought of idealism and empiricism. I explain his notion of the structured *gestalt* of perception and show how the idea of reversibility introduces the problem that the observer (scientific or philosophical) cannot stand outside of the world she observes. I show how the Cartesian problem of illusion drove a wedge between the mind and the world, and how a kind of perceptual faith is basic for Merleau-Ponty, a prerequisite for perception. This grounding of perception in life enables us to develop a sense of subjectivity in the midst of things, fundamentally situated with regard to objects and the world. The fundamental dimension of perception is the existential dimension of depth, and this is allied to *meaning*, made clearer by the French word that Merleau-Ponty uses, *sens*, which implies not only *meaning* or *sense* but also *directedness* and *orientation*. Thus perception is grounded in the life of the moving body. But to fully understand perception in its existential dimension, an account of seeing is not enough. So, in chapter 2, I turn to the question of eating as perception to develop a thicker understanding of perception in general. Rather than beginning with the question of "taste" and the metaphorical use of that concept in the aesthetic philosophy of the eighteenth century, I begin with hunger, contrasting the simple animal appetite, whose drive maintains nutrition and growth, with hunger properly speaking, which is not simply appetite but also its imaginative development, that takes hunger beyond the simple expression of a lack or a need towards the expressive development of possibilities. This typifies the *lability* of human beings in which they transcend the operation of the purely given. I then turn to a consideration of the sense of taste as an example that helps us to develop an understanding of perception as contact with the world that does not depend on the construction of a mental theatre of representation in which the world is re-created "inside my head." Taste thus transforms the Cartesian epistemological question, of how I can know that I am not being deceived by an illusion, into a new form of epistemological question: how can I know a world of which I am only part and to which my access must necessarily be partial? This epistemological reformulation opens onto and is bound up with further questions, of the nature of subjectivity and of ontology: what is it to be a perceiving being, incarnate in this world? The answer to this question begins with an anthropology of the human as a *hungry* being, that is, as dependent and desiring, as willing matter, subject to a world which he also transforms through his desire, charged not only with *conatus* and the instinct for survival but with an openness to his own remaking and thus to the transformation of the world.

Chapter 3 marks a crossing point between Part One, in which I have laid my groundwork in an account of perception, and Part Two, in which I develop the ontology of flesh. I assess what I have called "the old ontology" of Descartes, paying special attention to his account of visual perception as presented in the *Optics*. That text constitutes a crucial moment in the history of ontology insofar as it reifies a universal geometrism into a mathematized conception of space, which is consummated in its imagined joining to a totally abstract principle of subjectivity with which it can never remain in contact. Mind is excluded from a mathematized nature, and the human being as desiring body is rent asunder.

Part Two begins in earnest in chapter 4, where I begin to develop an ontological alternative to the Cartesian scene on the basis of a renewed understanding of visual perception, which escapes the absolute distance of the Platonic cave, the chasm of Cartesian *mathesis*, and the paranoid hostility of Sartre's neo-Cartesianism. Merleau-Ponty's positive account of vision, especially as expressed in his late essay "Eye and Mind," establishes *depth* as the fundamental dimension of perceptive intertwining with the world, in which sight organizes our perceptive knowledge, including our tactile sensations, in such a way that we can "have the world at distance": that is, we are installed among things, in contact with them, without coinciding with them in full presence. As such, we perceptually interrogate and explore a world that massively transcends us, and sight is understood in its fundamental dependence on movement and intersensoriality. The "thickness" of the things sight perceives in this fuller account can reveal their meanings in our intersubjective relation to them and a richer materiality of color and melody, not just of line and instantaneity, with which our engagement is necessarily simultaneously passive and active, that is, interrogative. This interrogation refuses an absolutely passive illumination of a clear and distinct vision of the world, and as such suggests an incarnationalism that embraces ambiguity and that refuses to withdraw from the transcendence that we encounter in immanence but that ultimately escapes us.

In chapter 5, I re-install this account of vision in an ontology of flesh and draw out the implications of incarnational thought in both philosophical and theological terms. I develop an understanding of transcendence as *depth* rather than as height, of the *logos* of things, which appears in their depths as revealing an orientation not to God conceived as utterly outside, as *penseur absolu du monde*, nor to a pantheist God who is convertible with nature, but rather to a God at work within nature, refusing a rationalist deism as well as a romanticist spiritualism, and revealing God "on the other side of things." In this conception, nature is the soil of meaning, neither as given in pure ideality nor as constituted by a thinker, but as instituted by the thinking subjects that are grounded in it. I develop in detail Merleau-Ponty's logic of institution as presented in his 1954–55 lectures on that theme, showing how the later lectures establish Nature as a ground of meaning that is beyond objectivity. As such, a philosophy of nature is as much a failure of ontology as is a philosophy of consciousness; the ontology of flesh demands that both poles are understood in terms of their intertwinement with one another, and I develop this incarnationalism by showing how Renaud Barbaras misunderstands it as the insertion of consciousness into nature and how Michel Henry evacuates all life from the world in a Manichaeism that refuses the humility of humanity.

In chapter 6 I go on to develop the sacramental implications of this intertwining of humanity and nature, suggesting that an understanding of *epiphany* grounds the relation of the logic of incarnation we have been developing to the continual transformation of history and thus the advent of historical time: for Merleau-Ponty, "sensation is, literally, a communion."[9] A certain *logos* is made known in and through material things, which announces and to some extent presents a transcendent *beyond*. We have called this beyond "God," but the question of its nature passes beyond the limits of philosophy. What Merleau-Ponty's incarnationalism has taught us is that the difficulty and ambiguity of this *beyond* must not be neutralized by attempts to determine it beyond its presentations; it must not become an attempt to explain away the world, suffering and joy, but to look upon the truths present in them.

Where theology has been dismissed in modern thought, it has been on the basis of the flat, objectivized ontologies that we have here called into question. Naturalism supplanted an explanatory theology with its inverse. Merleau-Ponty's critique of Christianity, based on a view of God as the *ens realissimum*, seeks to guard against such a flat ontology and a dissolution of mystery. A properly incarnational theology returns us to the God who is not *ens realissimum* but *ipsum esse subsistens*—the uncreated ground of existence, beyond determination but known in self-revelation, who is the metaphysical source that assures freedom and contingency in a nonetheless ordered world. An ontology of the flesh calls into question the division between natural and supernatural; its sacramentality is not an assertion of the supernatural but an interrogation of nature that takes seriously the notion that *logos* appears within nature and thus makes a question of nature. This makes possible a metaphysics that is grounded in the perceived world, that affirms a reason that dwells in the contingency of things and does not demand a Spinozistic determinism nor a Leibnizian rationalism for which everything is necessarily as it must be. For the one who finds God made known in the flesh, in nature and history, sacramentality institutes and expresses God's self-revelation by continued participation in it. Such participation does not simply repeat that revelation but also brings it into dialogue with the world and with its own history, so that the Eucharist always fractures and sends out those who are gathered, so that *mass* must always also be *mission*.

---

9. Merleau-Ponty, *Phenomenology of Perception*, 219.

PART ONE

Perception

1

Merleau-Ponty's Embodied Philosophy

I N THIS CHAPTER I introduce Maurice Merleau-Ponty's thought. I
show how his developing philosophy provides an avenue for thinking
about the human person, the world, and knowledge beyond fundamental
(though often latent or unnoticed) dualisms in contemporary philosophy.
Thinking with Merleau-Ponty, and the embodied mode of philosophy of
which he is a key source, we will see that our understanding of perception
is crucial for the formation of a paradigm for viewing the relation of the
human person with the world around him: for, in perception, the domain
of causes, of physical events, is connected to the domain of reasons, or
mental events; things are connected to thoughts. Philosophy has tended to
conceptualize perception as internal visual representation, making central
the question of how an internal "picture" of the world is formed, and how
we can know *how much* and *in what ways* that picture is in accord with
the external world of causes, and so asking how the individual senses are
connected to one another. These are the classical questions of epistemology.
We will see how Merleau-Ponty's account of perception may dispel this
picture, which, according to Wittgenstein, "held us captive."

In the following chapter I will go on to propose a richer account of
perception which will ask instead how our originary common sense of the
world is analyzed into the five individual senses, and will take the more
concrete (and more inextricably intertwined) senses of taste, smell, and
touch, in their primordial relation to the more abstract senses, as primary.
If we form our paradigm for perception in light of the act of eating, we
can form a robust idea of perception beyond the epistemological picture,
as the communion of persons with the world, which are not two basically

incommensurable categories. We will see that the human being is from the beginning at the heart of things, not a spirit alien in the world, but rather an incarnate, bodily subject of an objective world. This conception of human being will lead to a reconsideration of the concept of nature as implied by the notion of a domain of causes, and of the concept of freedom as implied by the domain of reasons, leading to a conception of nature that has situated freedom at its heart, and opening onto the investigation of an incarnational ontology of flesh in the latter part of this book.

Merleau-Ponty's Gestalt Phenomenology

In the *Phenomenology of Perception*, Merleau-Ponty traces out a conception of the human subject that is opposed to the problematic and too abstract conceptions of human being in the philosophy of his time. He begins by analyzing the accounts of the perception of objects offered on the one hand by the scientifically-minded Empiricists, and on the other by rationalist Intellectualists, starting with the idea of sensation.

Both the realist Empiricist and the idealist Intellectualist account for the object in terms of its atomic components in perception—pure sensations. This seemingly common-sense starting point already governs the trajectory of such accounts in a problematic direction, by misconceiving the relationship of the object of perception to its subject.

For the empiricist, perception offers access to the world as it is, and this is in part because the world is composed of deterministic entities that stand in observable relation to one another; consciousness, then, must be another thing in the world, and perception a theoretically observable relation between things. By contrast, for the intellectualist, we can only come to know the world-as-experienced, and consciousness cannot be accounted for as part of that world, but is the experiencer that constitutes the world as experienced. Nevertheless, the world as experienced is, for the Intellectualist, composed of determinable entities that stand in relation to one another, which is to say a reductive analysis of it is possible.[10]

Merleau-Ponty's dual-headed attack on these two positions focuses on what they share—the thought that the world, whether real or experienced, is analyzable into determinate parts whose relation to one another can be reduced into determinate constituent elements. This is the significance of his notion of *gestalt*. In the long introduction (comprising the first four

10. I owe this formulation of the Empiricist and Intellectualist position to that given by Komarine Romdenh-Romluc in lectures at the University of Nottingham and in Romdenh-Romluc, *Guidebook to Merleau-Ponty.*

chapters) to *Phenomenology of Perception* Merleau-Ponty opposes this ge-staltist view to the reductive view, which supposes sensations as atomistic units of perception and which asserts the "Constancy Hypothesis"—that is, that these sensed units are part of a simple one-to-one correspondence between sensory stimuli and perceived qualities, so that a mental represen-tation of the world corresponding to these stimuli, is built up out of these atomic units.

The notion of sensation is problematic because we perceive not just sensations, but things, persons, and, indeed, a world. These perceptions, on the model of objective thought, must be produced in some way by the combination of sensations in the space of mental representation. But if, as the realist might prefer to say, they are combined according to a manner determined by the object itself (that is, individual sensations refer to the object, and provide the principle according to which they are combined into the object that is the source of the stimulus), then the notion of "sensation" must be excluded, for the simple property is *not* sensed, but rather a *thing* with certain analyzable properties is sensed—the sensations are artificial abstractions from the prior reality of intentional perception.

Alternatively, if sensations are not combined in a manner given by the object, they must be combined according to some principle internal to me, and there is in fact no reason to think that our perception refers to the world at all: I may happen to combine certain kinds of sensation in certain ways but there is no rule by which such combinations could be compared to real objects and affirmed or rejected as veridical or illusory.

For the empiricist, the subject must combine sensations into perceived objects according to a principle given by the objects themselves. Thus con-sciousness is simply part of a causal chain, and just another thing in the world. It is, though, hard to see in what sense there is truly a pure and neu-tral "sensation," in this case—it seems that perception must already have intentionality, must already refer to a perceived "thing," or else the manner in which sensations are combined into objects must not be according to the principle given by the thing itself, in which case it is hard to see how percep-tion can refer to anything at all. For the intellectualist, it is clear that sensa-tions are combined according to a principle given by consciousness, which constitutes the world as perceived. In this case, sense experience would seem to be understood as a form of judgment, which erases the common-sense distinction between judgment and perception, making it very difficult to understand what it means for things to "seem" one way (as in many opti-cal illusions, for example) when we in fact know that they are another way.

Otherwise, if perception is not already a form of judgment for the intellectualist, then their account will fall foul of the same problems as the empiricist account—either perception of the object is given according to the object, or there is no reason to think that perception represents the real world at all. The second part of this faulty theorization of perception, the Constancy Hypothesis, is equally easily shown to be false, according to Merleau-Ponty. For him, it

> enters into conflict with the givens of consciousness, and the same psychologists who posit it also acknowledge its theoretical character. For example, the intensity of a sound lowers its [perceived] pitch under certain conditions; the addition of auxiliary lines renders two objectively equal shapes unequal [in the Müller-Lyer illusion]; and a colored area appears uniformly colored even though the chromatic thresholds of the different regions of the retina ought to make it red here and orange there, and in certain cases even colorless. [. . .] When red and green presented together give a resulting gray, it is conceded that the central combination of stimuli may immediately give rise to a sensation different from what the objective stimuli would require. When the apparent size of an object varies with its apparent distance, or when its apparent color varies with the memories we have of it, it is conceded that "sensorial processes are not impervious to central influences." In this case, then, the "sensible" can no longer be defined as the immediate effect of an external stimulus.[11]

Merleau-Ponty's arguments here do not carry the force of deductive certainty. Nevertheless, they open up, in the pages that follow, a way of viewing the world that makes good sense of the human situation. In the preface to the *Phenomenology of Perception*, Merleau-Ponty has told us that

> Because we are through and through related to the world, the only way for us to catch sight of ourselves is by suspending this movement, by refusing to be complicit with it (or as Hussserl often says, to see it *ohne mitzumachen* [without taking part]), or again, to put it out of play. This is not because we renounce the certainties of common sense and the natural attitude—on the contrary, these are the constant theme of philosophy—but rather because, precisely as the presuppositions of every thought, they are "taken for granted" and they pass by unnoticed, and because we must abstain from them for a moment in order to awaken them and to make them appear. Perhaps the best formulation of the reduction is the one offered by Husserl's assistant Eugen Fink when he spoke of a "wonder" before the world.[12]

11. Merleau-Ponty, *Phenomenology of Perception*, 8, translation modified.
12. Ibid., lxxvii.

And soon after he writes that, "The most important lesson of the reduction is the impossibility of a complete reduction."[13] As Stephen Priest notes,[14] for Merleau-Ponty, as for many post-Husserlian phenomenologists, the reduction is no longer considered completable. Where Husserl's reduction sometimes seems like the attainment of a certain state of mind, an "attitude" that contrasts with the natural one, Merleau-Ponty's conception of the reduction is a much more concrete and pragmatic one—he attempts to perform a reduction, by argument, on that dominant scientific rationalism, which undermines a view of the world that looks on at it in wonder.

The criticism of the constancy hypothesis and more generally the reduction of the idea of *the world* opens up a *phenomenal field*, which then has to be more accurately circumscribed, and suggests the rediscovery of a direct experience which must, at least provisionally, be assigned its place in relation to scientific knowledge, psychological and philosophical reflection.[15]

Merleau-Ponty's arguments against empiricism and intellectualism are an attempt to dislodge the reader of the *Phenomenology of Perception* from this complacent naïve realism so as to be able to confront perception as it is, without the artifices imposed on it by the confusion between the perception and the thing perceived that is revealed in the notion of "sensation." For him, the idea that sensation as a concept is self-evident is based not on phenomena themselves but on "the unquestioned belief in the world [*le préjugé du monde*]." Where we assume that sensations are prior, and that we know what it is to hear, to see, and to feel, our experience of things in fact offers us first precisely *things*, in all their primordial meaningfulness as relevant to our lives as they are lived, and their analysis into component perceptions can be seen to be derivative.[16]

For Merleau-Ponty, the basic picture of perception as constituting an inner mental representation of an outer world must be challenged. *What if* what we see is not a set of mental images viewed by a soul or subject that is something like a little man in my head, but is rather the world itself? Our standpoint on the world would then not be that of an inner subject but of a *body*-subject, a material subject of the world. Experience reveals that the problem of perception is only possible against a background of perceptual faith. And this structure, of the object of investigation against a background, is itself central to perception: for Merleau-Ponty, perception always involves

13. Ibid., lxxvii.

14. Priest, *Merleau-Ponty*, 22.

15. Merleau-Ponty, *Phenomenology of Perception*, 47–48.

16. Ibid., 5.

a *gestalt* or figure-ground structure.[17] Hubert Dreyfus puts it thus in his introduction to Merleau-Ponty's *Sense and Non-Sense*:

> Merleau-Ponty starts his analysis from the Gestaltist principle that whenever I perceive, I perceive a figure on a ground. A spot on a page appears to be *on* the page, i.e., the paper is perceived as present behind the spot. Whatever appears suggests in its very appearance something more which does not appear, which is concealed. For this reason the figure can be said to have meaning since—unlike a brute datum, and like a linguistic expression or a work of art—it refers beyond what is immediately given. For example, when I perceive an object, such as a house from the front, the back is involved in this perception not merely as a *possible* perception which I judge could be produced if I walked around the house, nor as a *necessary* implication of the concept "house." Instead, the back is experienced as *actually* co-present—concealed but suggested by the appearance of the front.[18]

So, as for Levinas and Heidegger, though in different ways, phenomenology here reaches beyond itself, toward a reality that is fuller than that we have immediate access to, and that "fulfills" our perception, for the most part. The spacing of bodies in a world is revealed by the fact of depth in perception, the spatiality of perception, which is closely tied to movement and perception as a *lived* act, which tends toward optimal perspective, optimal grip on the world that is always already presupposed.

This bodily conception of the human subject is clearly set out in opposition to an analytic and atomistic conception that ultimately derives from Descartes. Although Descartes's goal is to securely ground knowledge of extended things, he ends up by leaving us with a deeply impoverished conception of the subject as the space of internal intellectual representation of an outside world, the relationship of the two being the subject of the questions of traditional epistemology. He leaves us with the pure subject considered as a *res cogitans*, as a thinking thing, and no longer with the human being, the living, reasoning material being who essentially acts in and on the world. This picture—with the attendant problems of the relationship between self and world, or between knowledge and known object—tends always to resolve the two terms into one or the other; that is to say, either to a materialism or to an idealism. To overcome the problems of the deep

17. Ibid., 3–12.

18. Dreyfus and Dreyfus, "Translator's Introduction" (to Merleau-Ponty, *Sense and Non-Sense*), xi.

dualism between subject and object that Descartes sets up, philosophy has tended to attempt to translate one into the other without remainder.

Reversibility and the Perceptual Faith

The overcoming of this dualism, through an attentive investigation of perception, introduces a crucial implication of perception for Merleau-Ponty, that he later calls "reversibility." Reversibility is first presented by Merleau-Ponty, in its nascent form, in the *Phenomenology of Perception*, where he speaks of the alternation of the touch of a person's two hands, touching one another.[19] What is crucial here is that while objectivity and subjectivity never coincide, neither are they radically separated, since either hand is in principle both touching and touched. Mike Dillon emphasizes the crucial role of this "identity-within-difference" in Merleau-Ponty's ontology.[20] In *The Visible and the Invisible* Merleau-Ponty names this concept "reversibility," and explores the notion further. There is a fundamental asymmetry to reversibility that is revealed when we take, as a further example, the hand touching the table—I cannot feel the table touching me in the same way that I feel my hand touching the table.[21] The table is clearly not a part of my body, and neither is it sentient as I am. This asymmetry is extended as Merleau-Ponty applies the concept of reversibility to vision. Reversibility is grounded in, and characteristic of, my body precisely to the degree that my senses are common. The perspective given to me in perception finds its "zero degree" in touch, as I can touch what I see and vice versa. This zero degree is enabled by the fact of my moving around, my tactile investigation, in which changes in visual perspective accompany the exploration of touch.

> Every movement of my eyes—even more, every displacement of my body—has its place in the same universe that I itemize and explore with them, as, conversely, every vision takes place somewhere in the tactile space. There is a double and crossed situating of the visible in the tangible and of the tangible in the visible; the two maps are complete, and yet they do not merge into one.[22]

19. Merleau-Ponty, *Phenomenology of Perception*, 95.

20. Dillon, *Merleau-Ponty's Ontology*, 159. In this discussion of reversibility I follow Dillon's argument on pp. 157–61.

21. Merleau-Ponty, *The Visible and the Invisible*, 133.

22. Ibid., 134.

This perspectivism is closely tied to the notion, which Merleau-Ponty insists on, that vision is reversible. Vision, for Merleau-Ponty, is not taken to be a one-way movement of light reaching our eyes. Rather, vision is constituted by our looking, by our moving around in the world that we see, rather than by a passive reception of data.

> Between my exploration and what it will teach me, between my movements and what I touch, there must exist some relationship by principle, some kinship, according to which they are not only [. . .] vague and ephemeral deformations of the corporeal space, but the initiation to and opening upon a tactile world. This can happen only if my hand, while it is felt from within, is also accessible from without, itself tangible, for my other hand, for example, if it takes its place among the things it touches, is in a sense one of them, opens finally upon a tangible being of which it is also a part.[23]

Although Merleau-Ponty seems so often to take vision as paradigmatic for perceptual experience, it is clear here that his model for seeing is a kind of "visual palpation," a "feeling" of the world that gives knowledge in a way that is substantial, that matters. The body as ground of common sense gives a clearer meaning to this "visual palpation," which is not a mysterious property of sight that goes to the things themselves, but rather the fact of vision's *embodiment*, of its belonging to a body that moves and endures and finds its zero degree in touch. It seems Merleau-Ponty is trying to reveal vision in this way, as reversible, so that when I see, I know myself not only as a seer, but also as visible, as seen. The embodied subject as such is grounded in a dualism (object/subject, seen/seer, material/mental), which it overcomes without reducing it to one of its terms. There is no "third term" between these pairs—rather, they must be "suspended." If we decline to separate the whole into parts, the whole cannot then be accounted for (at least not by any method that would account for it by dividing and categorizing it in any way). The same is true for any account that would overcome a dualism by simply excluding one of its terms, as in a vulgar materialism that cannot speak of matter in any way that would reveal it, that would account for its essence, genesis, or even its existence.

In his late, unfinished work *The Visible and the Invisible*, he writes:

> The flesh is not matter, is not mind, is not substance. To designate it, we should need the old term "element," in the sense it was used to speak of water, air, earth, and fire, that is, in the sense of a *general thing*, midway between the spatio-temporal

23. Ibid., 133.

individual and the idea, a sort of incarnate principle that brings a style of being wherever there is a fragment of being. The flesh is in this sense an "element" of being.[24]

Here Merleau-Ponty returns to the notion that is central to this chapter of his unfinished work, the notion of "flesh." The chapter is entitled (in its English translation) "The Intertwining—The Chiasm," and this elemental flesh *is* the intertwining, the "crossing" after which it is named. The theologian John Milbank writes in *Theological Perspectives on God and Beauty*,

> The entire series of sensed things to which the body belongs forms one continuous surface that Merleau-Ponty (following Aristotle, though he does not say so) names "flesh." At the point of "bodies," flesh somehow folds back upon itself, becomes "for itself" as well as "in itself," and in being able to touch itself is also able to touch the whole series of fleshly things.
>
> However, this is no simple materialism. The flesh is as much spiritual as it is material, because the showing of a depth of possibility that is spirit is constitutive of everything.[25]

This "depth of possibility," which constitutes everything, is related to, though not limited to, the depth revealed in perception. Phenomenology reaches beyond itself. That is, careful attention to the phenomena reveals that they intimate the presence of a depth that is more than they can fully reveal.

If philosophy's historical dualism has led gradually but inevitably to the disenchantment of the world, to the "natural attitude" that conditions our very perception, and that the phenomenological *epoché* is an attempt to overcome, then Merleau-Ponty's philosophy might be read as the movement of the *Vorzauberung der Welt*, the (re-)enchantment of the world. Merleau-Ponty's philosophy has restored what might seem like a more primitive view of the world, a view that is prior to the natural attitude (or perhaps the "scientific attitude"). We are no longer ephemeral conscious subjects with access (as if "from above") to an outside world. The body is no longer an indescribable mediator between the mental and the physical. There is no longer any hard divide between thought and things. Consciousness is restored as a characteristic of the lived world, and perception gives access to things that disclose themselves as both unpredictable and familiar, as stable yet in motion, as subject-objects.

24. Ibid., 139.
25. Milbank, "Beauty and the Soul," 12.

> The flesh of the world is not *self-sensing* (se sentir) as is my
> flesh—It is sensible and not sentient—I call it flesh, nonetheless
> [. . .] in order to say that it is a *pregnancy* of possibles, *Welt-
> möglichkeit* (the possible worlds variants of this world, the world
> beneath the singular and the plural) that it is therefore abso-
> lutely not an ob-ject, that the *blosse Sache* mode of being is but a
> partial and second expression of it.[26]

The reversibility of perception finally implies that the world itself is flesh, and though of course I do not expect to engage in conversation with the trees, such always remains within the realms of possibility. Just as I recognize that the organization of this flesh is a property of the organs proper to it, I do not expect to be addressed by a tree, as I do not expect to be seen by a hand. But the organization is never final in its arrangement, and my understanding of it is never complete, is never beyond the possibility of revision, and as such I still feel *seen* by the trees as I see them—as Dillon says, their visibility to me is forever linked to the possibility of my being visible to them. The ontology that takes perception as primary is founded on reversibility as characteristic of perception.

So, the method of a philosophy that takes perception as primary leads us, by the reversibility of such perception, to a world in which we are involved. If we think our own embodied perception as *flesh*, the world also is flesh, although that is not to say that it is sentient through and through. It reveals us, as bodily things present to the world, as always potentially and partly visible, without depending on the actual presence of another seer, and without reducing us to what might appear in our visibility.

For Merleau-Ponty the problem of illusion, the wedge that Descartes drives between appearance and reality, depends on a more basic affinity between them. It is only on the basis of *further perceptions* that a perception is found to have been illusory. While the oneiric quality of a dream may not be immediately apparent to the dreamer, when he wakes up it is not difficult for him to discover the difference between the dream and his everyday life. Without the basic parity between the things and their appearances, which Descartes must *at once* assume *and* call into question, there would be no determinable experience to speak of at all.

For Merleau-Ponty, perception then is not a passive reception of impressions whose authenticity must be tested and to some degree found wanting. Rather, the subject of perception is a bodily subject whose looking constitutes a two-way interaction with the object and with the world

---

26. Merleau-Ponty, *The Visible and the Invisible*, 250.

in which it is situated. The abstract, conceptual element of perception is grounded in a much more basic lived engagement with the world.

For an embodied perspective, the unity of the world cannot be an *a priori* possibility to be realized to some degree by contemplation, though this classical view may not be so far from the truth. Certainly the unity of the world cannot be constituted by something like identity with the unity of the transcendental world-subject, which is why this line of thought degenerates into the monadology of Leibniz or the reduction of selfhood to an illusory and conventional status in Hume, for whom the unity of the world still remains to be grounded.

Rather, as embodied thought shows through these investigations, the unity of the world is a *de facto* possibility grounded in embodied life. No abstract or logical assurance can be given against the possibility of another, totally foreign world. But the body co-ordinates experience in such a way as to assure the unity of the world *not* from "on high," in the realm of the forms, nor from an absolute requirement that all that is is commensurable, as in eliminative materialism, but from a given position: a place within the world, by which a person is given to relate to a world of which they are a part but which is not theoretically delimitable.

The unity of the world is grounded, then, in a sense, by what Merleau-Ponty calls *la foie perceptive*, the perceptual faith. This is a concept that comes up repeatedly in *Phenomenology of Perception*, and persists throughout Merleau-Ponty's thought, such that in his unfinished work posthumously published as *The Visible and the Invisible*, it has become the organizing concept.

In some ways the idea of the perceptual faith names an opening onto the givenness of things, of objects and of the world. That things are the ground of our subjective, perceptive determinations of them is not something that can be established in the Cartesian manner. But even if the perceptual faith might be taken to open onto the world as a gift, it is *not* to be understood as any kind of religious faith. The perceptual faith is common, *in fact*, though not by any necessity, to human beings. Even the scientific realist must start in perceptual faith if he is to have any world to investigate.

The idea of perceptual faith also refers to the coherence of things, that is, to the possibility of the unity of the world, the object, and of the subject. Even though sight discloses a visual field, and touch a tactile field, we find that what can be seen can in fact also be touched, and so on, so that what is given to the perceiver is not an arrangement of sensations making up a consciousness but an array of connected fields that make up a world. As well as being interconnected, these fields are grounded in my subjective body: where for the empiricist, vision is a movement of light reaching my eyes, for embodied philosophy, it is constituted by our looking, by our moving around in the world that we see, rather than by a passive reception of data.

So, although Merleau-Ponty very often takes vision as paradigmatic for perception, and offers primarily visual examples, it is clear that his understanding of seeing is a kind of "feeling" of the world in a way that locates the seer in the world in her full bodiliness—the seer is always also a hearer and a toucher. Merleau-Ponty speaks in his later work of "visual palpation," and it is clear in *The Visible and the Invisible* that the developing ontology of flesh is grounded in the idea of a body-subject that depends on this perceptual faith in the aspects I have outlined—that its senses have a fundamental unity that corresponds to the unity of the world, that the senser is actually installed in that world and active within it, so that our motility, our moving around in the world, is as much a part of our vision as light or color.

Merleau-Ponty uses the famous example of one hand touching another to illustrate how the body can be both subject and object, first in *Phenomenology of Perception*, though he returns to the example in his later work. If I feel an object with my left hand, and then feel my left hand with my right hand, the hand exists both as subject and as object of tactile perception, and indeed, both hands and my whole tactile body are shown up as potentially both toucher and touched. For him, the tactile is a kind of "zero degree" of the perspective given to me in vision, so just as I am both touchable and touched, I can in principle see what I touch and touch what I see—indeed, when sight offers objects that seem indeterminate or unsubstantial, the activity of perception is led quite soon to tactile investigation.

So there is a fundamental duality in the body-subject, but one in which the terms (object and subject, perception and action, material and mental) are brought together without reducing one to the other. At the point where the Cartesian perceptual doubt calls into question the veracity of the senses, as a result of Descartes's methodological concern to find a secure foundation on which to build, and in so doing tears the human subject asunder, Merleau-Ponty's perceptual faith re-installs the living body at the center of philosophy.

In the first part of this chapter, I have focused on expounding Merleau-Ponty's philosophy on the basis of the perceptual interrogations that are most basic to his thought, throughout the *Phenomenology of Perception* and beyond. In the latter part, I will bring Merleau-Ponty's work more fully into dialogue with later thinkers, particularly Charles Taylor, Samuel Todes, and David Morris, to expound an embodied philosophy that I take to be a development of Merleau-Ponty's work, and of that stream of thought which found a crucial moment of its expression in his work and which continues to express itself and to refine its expression. I am not particularly concerned to ascertain whether Merleau-Ponty himself would have supported these developments, but rather to seek fidelity to the trajectory of the philosophy of flesh that speaks itself in his work, and for this reason will continue to return to his thought and to refer to him. In thus situating Merleau-Ponty's thought and the trajectory of its developments by others after his death, I hope to prepare the way for further developments based on his account of perception and his later, more explicitly ontological, philosophy, in the second part of this book.

Physicalist Cartesianism

Speaking about the epistemological problem whose source is found in Descartes, Charles Taylor notes that "Descartes is not in fashion these days. He is rejected as a dualist, as too rationalist, as clinging to an outmoded psychology, and for many other reasons."[27] But despite this, the chasm between the inside and outside, between the human person and the world, is a structure that "goes on influencing much of our thought and other elements of our culture, even though many of its elements are changed."[28] This structure, with which Taylor is concerned in epistemological terms, reaches much further than simply the domain of knowledge. Indeed, it is the centrality of this incommensurability of the subject with any object, and her radical removal from any worldly term, including her own body (which does not escape Descartes's radical doubt), that ensures the centrality of epistemology to contemporary philosophical projects.

Physicalist philosophical perspectives, which have garnered favor among the advocates of a perspective closely aligned with the natural sciences, inherit this Cartesian dualism, and simply drop one side of it. So the impoverished view of matter that sees it simply as stuff with extension, with *res extensa*, is totalized—for the physicalist, this bare stuff is all there is. Of course, since the physicalist is also an embodied, thinking human subject, or, in other words, because the physicalist is both embedded in a physical situation and situates himself as a neutral observer of the situation, this point of view cannot be carried to its conclusion. In a long passage in which Merleau-Ponty suggests a narrative of the historical encroachment of science and scientifically-minded philosophy into the human understanding of self and world, he writes:

27. Taylor, "Merleau-Ponty and the Epistemological Picture," 27.
28. Ibid., 27.

> The entire concrete content of "psychic states" resulting from a universal determinism according to the laws of psychophysiology and of psychology was integrated into the *in-itself*. There was no longer a genuine *for-itself*, except for the thought of the scientist who perceives this system and who alone ceases to have a place therein. Thus, while the living body became an exterior without an interior, subjectivity became an interior without an exterior, that is, an impartial spectator. The naturalism of science and the spiritualism of the universal constituting subject, to which reflection upon science leads, share in a certain leveling-out of experience: standing before the constituting I, the empirical selves are merely objects.[29]

But if any physical effect must have a physical cause, then any purportedly mental causation must really be, at bottom, physical. If thought is taken to be something categorically different from "bare stuff," then it cannot *as such* cause anything physical, but must produce the illusion of doing so; it is simply epiphenomenal, a distraction from the real matter. It is clear that the Cartesian bias is here maintained, since the question of separating appearances from realities remains foundational. This conception of the world derives ultimately from substance dualism. Substance, in the Cartesian sense, is what the physicalist refers to as matter. The physical is conceptualized on the model of the *res extensa*. Of course, the *res cogitans* is denied any separate reality; this seems to be nothing but a dualism that has sublated one of its terms, and it seems necessary to take up such a dualism to explain physicalism: all that is can be accounted for in terms of physics, including consciousness (or subjectivity, thought, human persons). For Merleau-Ponty, "given these requirements, the living body could not escape the determinations that alone made the object into an object, and without which it could not have had a place in the system of experience. [. . .] Thus [. . .] subjectivity became [. . .] an impartial spectator."[30] Reductive perspectives hide deeply dualistic ontologies because lived experience offers not only things but selves, experience of our own subjectivity, as identified with, but not simply reducible to, our bodies. Continental philosophy has sometimes preferred to sublate the material term of the dualism—to deny bare stuff and think all of reality as a pure plane of thought. This "immanentist" idealism falls foul of the same problem—it seeks to escape Cartesianism but ends up locked in a perverse modification of Descartes's problematic.

29. Merleau-Ponty, *Phenomenology of Perception*, 56, translation modified.
30. Ibid., 55–56.

All this is in a sense the result of the Cartesian *cogito*. For Merleau-Ponty, this movement of doubt has taken philosophy on the wrong course, and the remedy is in some ways an act of faith—*La foie perceptive*. As Taylor points out, the motive of the Cogito stems from the fact

> that the foundationalist argument required the stabilization of doubt in a clearly defined issue [i.e., the veracity of my perception and the ideas that derive from it]. We can't be left reeling under the cumulative effect of all the possible sources of error, where the ancients abandon us with the injunction to cease the fruitless quest for certain knowledge.[31]

Descartes's method of doubt leads him immediately, in the first meditation, to wonder if at any time he might be dreaming or, subsequently, subject to illusion. By proposing a purely intellectual doubt as his method, Descartes has already presupposed *sum res cogitans*; the divide between body and soul is present in incipient form at the very beginning of his philosophy. And there seems to be very little reason that can be given for this method of doubt. It is clear that this is a crucial moment in the divorce of philosophy from the concerns of life, which sets philosophy for many centuries on a path of investigation that is blind to its own significance or relevance. In the hope of establishing knowledge in a kind of certainty that matches this purely intellectual conception of the subject, Descartes tells us: "today I have expressly rid my mind of all worries and arranged for myself a clear stretch of free time. I am here quite alone, and at last I will devote myself sincerely and without reservation to the general demolition of my opinions."[32] Real life must not impinge on this project. But Descartes's failure to adequately establish knowledge against all possibility of doubt is well known. This alone might be enough to imply to us that knowledge is *not* in fact purely intellectual, and that abstracted from bodily life, intellectual knowledge amounts to nothing at all.

For Taylor, Descartes's requirement for a manageable criterion for doubt, which arises at the birth of modern philosophy, is the source, ultimately, of the hard divide between the space of self-certifying thought, or reasons, and that of causes, of things, which is always subject to illusion. The soul/body divide, then, arises as an accident from methodological concerns. For him, "what takes place is a kind of ontologizing of proper method."[33] Merleau-Ponty's re-reading of the Cogito, what he calls the *tacit cogito*, avoids this absolutizing dualism. According to Taylor, the tacit cogito,

31. Taylor, "Merleau-Ponty and the Epistemological Picture," 42.
32. Descartes, *Meditations*, 17.
33. Taylor, "Merleau-Ponty and the Epistemological Picture," 43.

that is, the fundamental dimension of our experience, which the *cogito* as explicit argument tries to articulate, is "myself experienced by myself." [. . .] It is, indeed, independent of any particular thought, but it is also in its unformulated state not really a bit of knowledge. To become this, it must be put into words. [. . .] This predicament rules out absolute, that is, complete and self-evidently incorrigible knowledge. The nature of our opening to the world, of our contact with it, makes this impossible. But this contact also rules out total error. It can turn out that our grasp on things was wrong in this or that respect. Yet it cannot be entirely wrong, and for the same reason that it can't ever be guaranteed to be totally right. The inseparability of inner and outer means that there is no realm of inner certainty, but it also means that perceiving, thinking, feeling cannot be totally severed from the reality it bears on.[34]

To get beyond the deep ontological divide, Taylor recognizes, is to reengage with "our bodily commerce with the world,"[35] and to put this back at the center of philosophy. But Taylor quite correctly observes:

Our humanity also consists, however, in our ability to decenter ourselves from this original engaged mode; to learn to see things in a disengaged fashion, in universal terms, or from an alien point of view; to achieve, at least notionally, a "view from nowhere." Only we have to see that this disengaged mode is in an important sense derivative. The engaged one is prior and pervasive, as mentioned earlier. We always start off in it, and we always need it as the base from which we, from time to time, disengage.[36]

As Taylor observes, the Cartesian dichotomy between what is perceived and what is thought is born in an attempt to find a sure epistemological foundation, on which certain knowledge can be built.[37] But this notion that I can be sure of what I am thinking, whilst perception may always be subject to illusion, is wrong-headed. Perception is from the first only ever found to be illusory on the grounds of *further perceptions*, so its rejection as unreliable depends on the assumption that it is basically reliable.

For Merleau-Ponty, this Cartesian hiatus between thoughts, which are indubitably known, and observations, which must always be regarded as

34. Ibid., 48.
35. Ibid., 46.
36. Ibid., 46.
37. Ibid., 42.

possibly illusory, is responsible for the dualistic and atomistic tone of much contemporary thought, and the notion of sensation is one of its effects; such thought he refers to as "objective thought," of which both empiricism and intellectualism are species.

> Objective Thought, or thought applied to the universe and not to phenomena, knows only dichotomies; beginning from actual experience, it defines pure concepts that are mutually exclusive: the notion of *extension* (which is that of an absolute exteriority of parts) and the notion of *thought* (which is that of a being gathered together into itself); the notion of a vocal *sign* (as a physical phenomenon arbitrarily linked to certain thoughts) and that of *signification* (as a thought entirely clear to itself); the notion of *cause* (as a determining factor external to its effect) and that of *reason* (as a law of the phenomenon's intrinsic constitution). Now as we have just seen, the perception of one's own body and external perception offer us the example of a *non-thetic* consciousness, that is, of a consciousness that does not possess the full determination of its objects, the example of a *lived logic* that does not give an account of itself, and the example of an *immanent signification* that is not clear to itself and only knows itself through the experience of certain natural signs.[38]

Though we have explained the perceptual faith in conceptual terms, I argue that the *content* of perceptual faith is not intellectual: it is not faith in the truth of a proposition or set of propositions. Although we can specify it in some ways, the perceptual faith has no creed. This is precisely why Descartes had to do away with the perceptual faith, which up until his time had been taken for granted: it could not offer intellectual grounds for the veracity of perception, and from the first moment Descartes had excluded all the aspects of life that could not be intellectually thematized, i.e., all that which is given to the embodied subject.

Merleau-Ponty writes:

> We see the things themselves, the world is what we see: formulae of this kind express a faith common to the natural man and

---

38. Merleau-Ponty, *Phenomenology of Perception*, 50. Translation modified—the Landes translation makes a serious mistake in the last line here, writing of "an *immanent signification* that is clear to itself," which entirely misses the point of what Merleau-Ponty is saying: that lived thought, consciousness of the life-world, is not perspicacious. Cf. *Phénoménologie de la perception*, 61: "une *signification immanent* qui n'est pas claire pour soi."

the philosopher—the moment he opens his eyes; they refer to a deep-seated set of mute "opinions" implicated in our lives.[39]

The significance of the idea of "mute" opinions is not that these opinions are unspoken; rather, it is because there is a sense in which these opinions are expressed (through their implication in our lives) that there can be said to be a perceptual faith: there is no purely representational mental content for Merleau-Ponty. The perceptual faith, then, is not established by argument; rather it is the ground of the very possibility of argument insofar as the world we investigate, those with whom we might argue, and the language we use to do so are all inaccessible without it. It is a deeply-rooted aspect of our bodily engagement with the world.

The Unity of *Sens*

For Merleau-Ponty, to conceive of our perception as an aggregation of data from the various senses, so that the perceiver links the sound of a dropped glass shattering with its appearance, for example, in a perceptual judgment, would be to make a similar mistake to that which objective thought makes when it thinks that perceptions of objects are built up from atomic sense-data, from combining the individual patches of bright shininess into the visual perception of the broken glass. This is to fail to see that perception, grounded in embodied life, reveals to us a world in which the senses are *given together*, and in which the shards of glass look not only shiny but sharp, and almost weightless, and in which it is given in our perception of them that they would be painful if we stepped on them and should be avoided.

For Merleau-Ponty, the unity of the senses is analogous to the unity of vision, which is itself given by two separate organs, the two eyes, yet is uncontroversially experienced as a single visual field. He gives an example in which if I look into the distance, something very close-up is seen double (for example, if while looking into the distance I lift my finger very close to one eye). If I shift my gaze to the close-up object, it comes into focus as a single object. But this is clearly not the operation of an intellectual judgment, since I can judge that there is only one finger there even when I see two.

He says:

> One passes from double vision to the unique object not through an inspection of the mind, but when the two eyes cease to function in isolation and are used as a single organ by a unique gaze. The synthesis is not accomplished by the epistemological

---

39. Merleau-Ponty, *The Visible and the Invisible*, 3.

subject, but rather by the body when it tears itself away from its dispersion, gathers itself together, and carries itself through all of its resources toward a single term of its movement, and when a single intention is conceived within it through the phenomenon of synergy.[40]

In this example it is important to notice, too, that the focusing of the double image into a single one has a deeper significance. In the diplopia, the juxtaposition of monocular images makes the thing look insubstantial as well as unclear. Though I see a rather indeterminate "something," in a blurry way, when I lift my finger close to my eye, I also seem to see through it. When I bring it into focus, I perform a sort of prospective activity, and the "something" is brought into focus as my finger. This bringing into focus is almost like the knowledge of the Meno paradox—there is a perceptual "something" that is "known" indeterminately, which my further act of bringing it into focus aims at making determinate—though what is to be made determinate cannot be known prior to making it so. My perceptual act aims at something, though what that something is cannot be specified in advance. But despite this, such perceptual acts can be fully satisfied—when I bring the blurry something into focus my perception reaches its goal, which was to reach beyond the blur to the thing itself, to my finger. I achieve contact, it seems, with the real world. I don't simply line up or superimpose two competing images, but I proceed from these two monocular images to a grip on the thing itself. All this applies to the situation with the senses in general—their complex interplay is, in normal perception, *prior* to their analysis into individual senses, although such analysis can be effected for a certain restrictive "analytic attitude." Merleau-Ponty writes of synaesthetic perception (that experience in which the visual is heard, the auditory felt, and so on) as the result of a psychological abnormality or as an effect of mescaline, saying,

> Synaesthetic perception is the rule and, if we do not notice it, this is because scientific knowledge displaces experience and we have unlearned seeing, hearing, and sensing in general in order to deduce what we ought to see, hear, or sense from our bodily organization and from the world as it is conceived by the physicist.[41]

Synaesthetic experience is a problem for the scientific attitude, which has to postulate some exception to the normal explanation of perception to

40. Merleau-Ponty, *Phenomenology of Perception*, 241.

41. Ibid., 238.

account for it, whereas for his account of perception it is, in a sense, always already present. It is because we perceive *things*, rather than simple sensations, that we can see the woolly-whiteness of the rug, hear the cold brittleness of the glass, and taste the warm redness of a wine.

Imagination and Perception

Samuel Todes, in his 1963 thesis published as *Body and World*, makes a similar argument for a new set of categories, and Todes puts his argument forward in Kantian terms. For Todes, Kant's valuable work in the *Critique of Pure Reason* is fundamentally compromised by the problem that he "imaginizes" perception. Imagination, Todes observes, constitutes a world that is fundamentally dependent on, and wholly accessible to, the imaginer. Kant constructs his synthetic *a priori* in these terms, and as such the categories he offers are those of the faculty of *imagination*. This all fails to account for the human relation to the world in its deepest sense, since this relation depends not primarily on imaginative constitution but on perception. Unlike the imagined world, the perceived world is not perceived as dependent on the faculty of perception; perception does not offer the world as fully disclosed or even as theoretically disclosable; we are subjects of a perceptual world in a very different way to that in which we are subjects of an imaginative world: perception assumes already that we are of one and the same stuff as the perceived world. Merleau-Ponty notes this in the observation that "Cartesianism, like Kantianism, would seem to have fully seen the problem of perception, which consists in its being an *originary* knowledge [*connaissance* originaire]."[42]

For the Merleau-Ponty of *The Structure of Behavior*, there is a certain inevitability of duality—not a substantial dualism, but a positional duality like that which Taylor observes in the human ability to remove oneself from situatedness in a certain sense, though this possibility depends on that situatedness.

> There is always a duality which reappears on one level or another: hunger or thirst prevents thought or feelings; the properly sexual dialectic ordinarily reveals itself through a passion; integration is never absolute and it always fails—at a higher level in the writer, at a lower level in the aphasic. [. . .] But it is not a duality of substances; or in other words, the notions of soul and body must be relativized: there is the body as mass of chemical components in interaction, the body as dialectic of living being

42. Ibid., 45, translation modified.

and its biological milieu, and the body as dialectic of social subject and his group; even all our habits are an impalpable body
for the ego of each moment. Each of these degrees is soul with
respect to the preceding one, body with respect to the following
one. The body in general is a set of paths already traced, of powers already constituted; the body is the acquired dialectical soil
upon which a higher "formation" is accomplished, and the soul
is the sense which is then established.[43]

It seems that the fundamental duality may be expressed as that between nature and consciousness. This duality resists reification into a dualism of the Cartesian kind, or reductive resolution into an empiricist or
idealist monism, because I am, as an embodied being, already both of these
things—both a conscious thing and a natural thing. So these two terms,
"nature" and "consciousness," already describe not two opposites but two
aspects of the kind of thing that I am. Not only this, but they also necessarily
describe the kind of world in which I live, which is neither totally natural
nor totally conscious, but always both of these things. The middle term
between subject and world in this ontology, the object, is the same—both
natural and conscious, both material and mental, as a worldly thing and
an object of my perception or knowledge and a more or less meaningful
part of the human world. For Merleau-Ponty, "ultimately, the question is
to understand what is, in us and in the world, the relation between *sense*
[*sens*] and *non-sense*."[44] For him, reality has a richly variegated texture with
varying degrees of significance and insignificance, which are not grounded
in the *Sinngebung* (sense-giving) of the self in a manner which attributes
meaning in a "centrifugal" manner purely to consciousness, nor are objects
themselves, and the whole world, inherently sense-making. Rather, meaning and sense arise in the relationship of consciousness to the natural world,
and such relationship is grounded, for the human being, in his natural and
conscious body. For Merleau-Ponty, "We say that events have a sense when
they appear as the realization or expression of a unique intention."[45]

In philosophy's misconstrual of the sense of things as that of an essential, simple unity or a pure plurality lies the inability of contemporary
thought to think God beyond conception as a deterministic puppetmaster
(on whom the sense of everything rests); or of human beings as a manifold
of little such gods (organizing the world in accord with the operation of
their pure, individual wills in the absence of any such God—and so leading

43. Merleau-Ponty, *The Structure of Behavior*, 210.

44. Merleau-Ponty, *Phenomenology of Perception*, 452.

45. Ibid., 452.

to interminable and inevitable conflict, as in the Hobbesian conception of humanity.) As I attempt to show, Merleau-Ponty's conception of a world open to sense-making yet not without a fundamental sense opens the door to a logic of incarnation that does not reduce the created world to an idea whose workings can be read as a system of laws and boundary conditions, but takes seriously the embodiment of *sense* within *non-sense* and the recognition of an invisible *logos* of the visible. As such, human beings are made free to make sense of the world in ways that may acknowledge the created world as the gift of God who is its source, but may also fail to do so. Merleau-Ponty's conception of the world as variegated scene of sense and senselessness avoids kitsch utopianism, on one hand, in which it must be asserted that all that is makes sense and is as things must be, and, on the other, a tragic nihilism that denies that there is any fundamental sense other than those fragments of sense that individual human beings make for themselves.

Merleau-Ponty tells us that "*signification* is only revealed if we look at [things] from a certain point of view, from a certain distance and in a certain *direction* [*sens*], in short if we put our involvement with the world at the service of the spectacle."[46] Such "collusion with the world" is precisely our assumption (though perhaps not recognition) of a fundamental grounding of sense in our relationship to the world in which we live:

> There could be no actual movement, and I would not even possess the notion of movement if, in perception, I did not leave the earth—as the "ground" [*sol,* "soil"] of all rest and all movement—beneath movement and rest, because I *inhabit it*; and similarly, there would be no direction without a being who inhabits the world and who, by their gaze, traces out the first direction-landmark [*direction-repère*].[47]

For Merleau-Ponty, then, the world, even the earth, is "the homeland [*la patrie*] of all rationality."[48]

In *The Sense of Space*, contemporary philosopher David Morris picks up on the complex interplay of meanings established by the polyvalence of the word *sens* in Merleau-Ponty's French.[49] In English, the word "sense" already reflects a link between perceptual sensation and meaningful sense; the sense that language has is linked to the sense that perceptions have, and to perceive is always already to make sense of things. But the French *sens*

46. Ibid., 453.
47. Ibid., 453, translation modified.
48. Ibid., 454.
49. Morris, *The Sense of Space*, 24.

captures these meanings as well as the notion of direction or orientation; a one-way street is signed *"sens unique,"* and *"être dans le mauvais sens"* is to be the wrong way round. For Merleau-Ponty, the sensitive body is the ground of sense, but this sense does not refer to the body alone but belongs to its directedness to the world.

This duality is perhaps best thought of in terms of a depth of being—as the above quote from Lawlor and Toadvine shows, "body" and "soul" may be relativized as terms whose meaning is, in a sense, positional. Thought, in this conception, does not so much supervene on the physical as arise from its depths, and the two orders meet and form a continuum, but not one that can be meaningfully explicated in only one of its terms. The objective world, it is clear, is the ground of the subjective world. But it is also dependent on the subjective world—with no subjects, there are not things, just flux.

Taylor's exposition of Hegel's philosophical position reveals a similar overcoming of the subject/object dichotomy, which is also the human/ nature dichotomy, and places this in continuity with romantic thought and with Aristotle's understanding of human being:

> Hegel restored the sense of the continuity of living things which was damaged by Cartesianism. But there is not just continuity between ourselves and animals; there is also continuity within ourselves between vital and mental functions, life and conscious- ness. On an expressivist view these cannot be separated out and attributed to two parts, or faculties, in man. Hegel agrees with Herder that we can never understand man as an animal with rationality added; on the contrary, he is a quite different kind of totality, in which the fact of reflective consciousness leaves noth- ing else unaltered; the feelings, desires, even the instinct for self- preservation of a reflective being must be different from those of other animals, not to speak of his bearing, bodily structure, the ills he is subject to, and so on. There is no other way of looking at things for anyone who sees living beings as totalities.[50]

So in Merleau-Ponty's thought, as I read it, there remains a duality. A dualism of *substance* it is not, but a mode of thinking that refuses to reduce the understanding of things to a single plane of thought. This approach stands in a tradition stemming from Aristotle, for whom the ontological duality is between Form and Matter, both of which are indispensable to the reality of any thing. This point of view is necessary from the standpoint of a philosophy that starts with consciousness. It is also necessary, as we will argue in chapter 5, for a philosophy that starts with nature; and since

---

50. Taylor, *Hegel and Modern Society*, 19.

philosophy must begin somewhere, duality is inevitable, and it is this duality that demands that we refuse any reduction to a pure monism. For Emmanuel Mounier, the personalist philosopher with whom the young Merleau-Ponty was associated, understanding the human person depends on this essential unity of the spiritual and the material in the human body:

> Man is a body in the same degree that he is a spirit, wholly body and wholly spirit. His most fundamental instincts, eating and reproduction, he has elaborated into the subtle arts of gastronomy and courtship.[51]

Nevertheless, in Merleau-Ponty's early works, the specter of dualism still looms large, and it is only as the fundamental intuitions progress through a certain dialectical development towards his later work that the full force of the insights already latent in them comes to expression. We will be pursuing that development in the final part of this book.

The possibility of detachment—which Taylor, as we saw, recognizes, and on which Mounier's "subtle arts" depend—is also recognized by Dreyfus in his introductory essay for Todes's *Body and World* (the sole published work of this phenomenological philosopher of the latter half of the twentieth century.)[52] In this essay, Dreyfus recognizes in modern thought the same consequence as was suffered by Kant, of the covering-over of the centrality of the body in relating the objects of perception to the objects of conception, or, as Todes himself puts it, the "imaginizing" of perception: "McDowell, like Kant, can conceive of only two alternatives: either perception is so radically nonconceptual as to be totally outside the space of reasons and therefore blind, or, if it is to enable us to form beliefs and make inferences, it must be as conceptual as thought itself."[53] In the end, in a philosophy that fails to assess correctly the necessity of the body for thought, the world must become either the blind workings of nature, or conscious through and through. Todes has shown, drawing on and developing the embodied philosophy he inherits from Merleau-Ponty, that objects of perception are a part of the world of the living and thinking body in everyday interaction, held in their orientation by the body as it holds itself in balance, and in significance by the body's poise to deal readily and thoughtfully with a continually changing situation, without being conceptually articulated or even entering reflective consciousness at all. *Contra* Descartes, almost all of what we think about we are unaware of thinking about, and we certainly do not

51. Mounier, *Personalism*, 3.

52. Todes, *Body and World*.

53. Dreyfus, "Todes's Account of Nonconceptual Perceptual Knowledge and Its Relation to Thought," xxv.

think about riding a bike, cooking a meal, or praying by formulating and manipulating concepts. A detached, spectatorial position can be achieved by the reflective consciousness, but this is not to be taken as paradigmatic for thought: it is, rather, a limit case.

The *Sens* of Action

On Merleau-Ponty's analysis, as we will see, perception is always bound up with movement. Henri Maldiney, in an investigation of Merleau-Ponty's notion of flesh, sees in movement and perception "one act and not two operations. 'The movement is not included in the perception as a conditioning factor: the perception *is* auto-movement.' The mutual imbrication of perception and of movement implies their 'reciprocal dissimulation.'"[54] And, referring to Husserl's famous example used to elucidate the notion of apperception and the transcendence of the thing itself, he says

> Consisting of the simultaneity of its six sides, the cube "itself," always given in the sides and never seen altogether, is irreducible to all the perspectives on it. It *is* beyond all its profiles, transcending its mode of appearing; without this "beyond" I would not be able to recognize it as an independent being; it would not be distinguished from a certain multiplicity of conscious lived experiences where it would figure as an index. It *is* therefore only for a gaze without viewpoint, "for an unsituated gaze, for an *operation* or an inspection of mind seating itself at the center of the cube, for a field of *Being*—and everything one can say about the perspectives upon the cube do not concern it."[55]

Where for Husserl apperception gives an indication of the transcendence of the object—allows it to be given in a perspective as "the thing itself"—for Merleau-Ponty I am not a transcendental onlooker but a body in a fleshy world, and my perspective on the cube tells me as much about *myself* as about the cube, it confirms my inherence in things, allowing the perceptual object to be "in-itself-for-us,"[56] as Dillon says.

In *The Incarnate Subject*, a lecture course on Malebranche, Maine de Biran, and Bergson, it becomes clear that Merleau-Ponty was profoundly influenced by Biran's work.

---

54. Maldiney "Flesh and Verb," 59.

55. Ibid., 63.

56. Dillon, *Merleau-Ponty's Ontology*, 53.

> Biran did not reduce consciousness to motility but he identified motility and consciousness. The primitive fact is consciousness of an irreducible relationship between two terms irreducible themselves. It is not a consciousness becoming movement, but a consciousness reverberating in movements. It is neither an interior fact nor an exterior fact: it is the consciousness of self as relationship of the I to another term. Therefore it is not a question of an empirical philosophy which would fill consciousness with muscular phenomena, but a philosophy which recognizes as fundamental a certain antithesis, the antithesis of the subject and of the term which bears its initiatives.[57]

Movement and perception are contemporary with one another and neither grounds the other, it seems, for Merleau-Ponty. In these lectures Merleau-Ponty cites Biran's work criticizing Condillac, and his essentially Cartesian insistence on the priority of sensation. For Biran, sensation amounts to nothing if does not present any facts, and this is of course the motive for the notion of sensation, that it allows for and makes some sense of those cases in which what is sensed and what is later found to be the case do not coincide (i.e., cases of perceptual illusion). As Merleau-Ponty sees it, "Biran, for his part, starts with a thought, and in this sense he is Cartesian. [. . .] But beginning with this notion of fact, his position deviates from Descartes's position."[58] He cites Biran:

> There is a fact for us only to the degree that we have the feeling of our individual existence and the feeling of something, object or modification, which confirms this existence and is distinct or separated from it. Without this feeling of individual existence that we refer to in psychology as *consciousness (conscium sui, compos sui)*, there is no fact that we can say is known, no knowledge of any sort: for a fact is nothing if it is not known, that is to say, if there is not an individual and permanent subject who knows.[59]

So perception, if it indeed offers *facts*, also refers strongly to its subject. For Biran and Merleau-Ponty, perception can no longer be seen as the causal chain that leads to a purely internal, mental event, a "mental image," which would seem to require an internal observer and lead to a chain of *homunculi* in an infinite regress. Neither is perception a fundamentally physical event

57. Merleau-Ponty, *The Incarnate Subject*, 64.

58. Ibid., 66–67.

59. Ibid., 67. The quotation is from Maine de Biran, *Essai sur les fondements*, Introduction, II.

that simply carries on a chain of physical causes and effects. Rather, perception fundamentally refers to the perceiver, the subject of perception, as the subject of a world of which she is a part. There is "a fact only for a witness," Merleau-Ponty observes, and this consciousness is a "for-itself," although for Merleau-Ponty this is "a notion that Biran rediscovers free from any Hegelian influence,"[60] which I take to mean that this consciousness is not at all a *pure* for-itself whose ipseity amounts to self-consciousness, but rather a consciousness that is situated, that is becoming-conscious against a background that is biological, geographical, historical, social, and political. Any conscious fact, then, is a relationship rather than an event or a state. Again, Merleau-Ponty quotes Biran:

> Every fact implies necessarily within it a relationship between two terms or two elements which are thus given in connection, without any one of these terms being able to be conceived in itself separately. Thus the *self* can know itself only in an immediate relationship with some impression which modifies it, and, reciprocally, the object or whatever the mode can be conceived only under the relationship to the subject which perceives or which feels. This is the origin of the very expressive title of *primitive duality.*[61]

Thus for Merleau-Ponty, "This duality is irreducible: 'any evocation of the two elements to unity is absurd and implies a contradiction.'"[62] That this is a move that "gets behind" the problems that we ascribe to the Cartesian paradigm to a way of thinking with ancient parallels may be seen in the sixth- and seventh-century eastern theologian Maximus the Confessor:

> Every thought certainly expresses several or at least a duality of aspects, for it is an intermediary relationship between two extremes which joins together the thinker and the object thought of. Neither of the two can completely retain simplicity. For the thinker is a subject who bears the power of thinking in himself. And what is thought of is a subject as such or dwells in a subject, having inherent in it the capacity of being thought of, or else the essence whose faculty it is which formerly existed. For there is no being at all which is by itself a simple essence or thought to the extent of also being an undivided monad.[63]

60. Ibid., 67.

61. Ibid., 67. This quotation is also from Maine de Biran, *Essai sur les fondements*, Introduction, II.

62. Ibid., 67.

63. Maximus, *Selected Writings*, 143–44.

For Samuel Todes, this reflects the classical conception, for which "the human subject had been regarded as moored in the world by his body. As a direct consequence of the *cogito* argument in which he discovered the conceptual form of human necessity, Descartes cut this mooring."[64]

The body, then, is the principle that mediates this irreducible duality—it inhabits both the space of causes (in perceptive sensitivity) and of reasons (in active motility); it is both subject and object. These two realms can never be absolutely separated, precisely because the living body that we are combines them and *is* our access to both of them. This will play out in Merleau-Ponty's account of perception and motility as fundamentally intertwined. As Stephen Priest puts it

> The central phenomenological ground for the rejection of the clear mental interior/physical exterior distinction is the postulation of the body-subject. Crucially, "the body of another, like my own, is not inhabited." This is not just a repudiation of Cartesian mind-body dualism (though it is that), it is also the thesis that there is nothing mental that, so to speak, occupies the body. It is not as though finding out that and what other people think could take the form of making discoveries about a mind that is hidden inside a body, or hidden "behind" the physical exterior of a body.
>
> On the contrary, the body is a physical subject, that is, a psycho-physical whole that cannot be reduced to the mechanical object of materialist and behaviourist psychology, yet which does not resist this reduction through being "occupied" by a Cartesian consciousness.[65]

Samuel Todes shows clearly the shortcoming of Descartes's method. With the procedure of radical doubt, he brought into question any belief that could be doubted, with the foundationalist motive to find a foundation for thought that is beyond doubt. He sought "to discover that about the human subject which is required by the very attempt to reject it, and is thus invulnerable to the subject's attempt to dispense with it intellectually."[66] The problem is that Descartes did not think to extend this procedure beyond beliefs; that is, he did not try to discover what else might be indispensable to the human subject's knowledge. "Instead, he concluded that whatever could be dispensed with in a purely intellectual way was not philosophically

---

64. Todes, *Body and World*, 13.

65. Priest, *Merleau-Ponty*, 186. The citation is from Smith's translation of *Phenomenology of Perception* (407 in the 2002 edition); Cf. Landes's 2012 translation, 365.

66. Todes, *Body and World*, 13.

necessary to the human subject, that it was not 'of the essence' of the human subject."[67]

Prior to doubt lies a perceptual faith, which crucially cannot be reduced to purely intellectual, conceptual content, but is rather already engaged with the world. This faith is not a faith in some specified conceptual content that resists doubt. Rather it is the "what else" to which Todes refers, the indispensable ground of human knowledge that is not itself knowledge in the conceptual sense. At the very beginning of *The Visible and the Invisible*, Merleau-Ponty offers a pointer to it, saying

> We see the things themselves, the world is what we see: formulae of this kind express a faith common to the natural man and the philosopher—the moment he opens his eyes; they refer to a deep-seated set of mute "opinions" implicated in our lives.[68]

As we have said, such a faith cannot be grounded on firm foundations, because it is *itself* the first ground of knowledge. Its necessity must refer not only to philosophy but to the philosopher himself, that is, in some sense, to life as it is lived.

Depth and the Bodily Subject

If the body-subject is the central term for conceptualizing subject and object, and the relation between what I have called the "space of causes" and that of reasons, how do we go about describing the body? Edith Stein, in the generation of phenomenologists before Merleau-Ponty's, writes

> The distance of parts of my living body from me is completely incomparable with the distance of foreign physical bodies from me. The living body as a whole is at the zero point of orientation with all physical bodies outside of it. "Body space" [*Leibraum*] and "outer space" are completely different from each other. Merely perceiving outwardly, I would not arrive at the living body, nor merely "perceiving bodily" [*leibwahrnehmend*], at the outer world. But the living body is constituted in a two-fold manner as a sensed (bodily perceived) living body and as an outwardly perceived physical body of the outer world. And in this doubled givenness it is experienced as the same. Therefore,

---

67. Todes, *Body and World*, 13–14.
68. Merleau-Ponty, *The Visible and the Invisible*, 3.

it has a location in outer space and fills up a portion of this space.[69]

The body that mediates to us the irreducible duality has its own duality that must be resolved in living itself. For Merleau-Ponty, one crucial element of this lies in the active nature of perception. Another line of investigation is that of the problem of depth. The perceptual faith that is implicated in the notion of the body-subject grounds an existential conception of depth that may begin to help us to grapple with the question of what a body *is*. Merleau-Ponty explicates this in *The Visible and the Invisible* in a way that opposes it to the skeptical impulse.

> The illusion of illusions is to think now that to tell the truth we have never been certain of anything but our own acts, that from the beginning perception has been an inspection of the mind, and that reflection is only the perception returning to itself, the conversion from the knowing of the thing to a knowing of oneself of which the thing was made, the emergence of a "binding" that was the bond itself. We think we prove this Cartesian "spirituality," this *identity* of space with the mind, by saying that it is obvious that the "far-off" object is far-off only by virtue of its relation with other objects "further off" or "less distant"—which relation belongs properly to neither of them and *is* the immediate presence of the mind to all; the doctrine finally replaces our belongingness to the world with a view of the world from above.[70]

This "view of the world from above" is precisely the view that cannot understand things in their *depth*. In *Phenomenology of Perception* Merleau-Ponty already anticipates this, drawing on his initial critique of the notion of sensation. For him, "Classical conceptions of perception agree in denying that depth is visible."[71] For Berkeley, the problem is one of how depth could ever be given to a sight that depends on the flat projection of an image on the retina, and for analytical reflection, even if depth could appear, it would have to be synthesized in a representation. "In both cases, depth is tacitly assimilated to *breadth considered in profile*, and this is what makes it invisible."[72] So,

69. Stein, "On The Problem of Empathy," 232–33.

70. Merleau-Ponty, *The Visible and the Invisible*, 37.

71. Merleau-Ponty, *Phenomenology of Perception*, 265.

72. Ibid., 266.

> In order to treat depth as a breadth considered in profile and to arrive at an isotropic space, the subject must leave his place, his point of view on the world, and think of himself in a sort of ubiquity. For God, who is everywhere, breadth is immediately equivalent to depth. Intellectualism and empiricism do not give us an account of a human experience of the world; they tell us what God might think.[73]

The element of depth, which is fundamental to perception, begins to reveal the place of the body-subject. The body is, first of all, a kind of "zero point" of the dimension of depth in which the world is revealed to us. Rather than as constituting an absolute divide between "inner" and "outer" at the (underspecified) point of interaction between the body and the mind in the Cartesian paradigm, the body locates the human subject in the world at the nearest limit of the dimension of depth. My body locates me amongst things, and persons, in the world. "Depth is born before my gaze because it attempts to see *something*."[74]

It is striking that in Merleau-Ponty's work on the senses he is satisfied to focus for the most part on sight, while showing how sight is closely connected to touch. He rarely speaks of hearing, or of those most concrete senses of smell and taste. Indeed, a phenomenology of taste, even of eating, seems like it would provide great insight into the ontology of the body-subject and her relation with the world.

There seem to be two points to be made here that arise as consequences of the understanding of perception we have outlined. The first is that, just as what can be seen can also be heard and touched, so it can in principle be eaten. A human's relationship with the world around is not that of a passive spectator; Merleau-Ponty has shown us that it is one of active engagement with the world. But it is not only that—a human is a hungry being, dependent, like the animals, on their natural environment for food, but also able much more radically than they to order his or her world toward the meeting of this hunger, and the hunger of others. The human being is in fundamental interchange with the world, not just situated in it, not even just having a fundamental likeness to it, but actually composed of it, and without the right kind of food he or she wastes away.

Secondly, this hungry being is also an endangered being—just as to see is to be capable of being seen, so it must be that to eat is to be edible. The human being knows himself as dependent on his body for his life. What else

---

73. Merleau-Ponty, *Phenomenology of Perception*, 266–67, translation modified. (*Phénoménologie de la perception*, 295–96.)

74. Ibid., 274, translation modified.

can be the significance of the fact that a body can be eaten? Well, it would seem that an element of normativity found in perception would come into play here—my own body and human bodies generally are not usually seen as potential food, and to see them as such would seem to be to fail to achieve a proper focus on them, to fail to see them as *lives*.

The life of conscious bodily experience co-ordinates phenomena into a world in perception and action, or absorbed coping. This function of the body in many ways finds its epitome in the experience of eating, by which I mean not simply the moment of consumption, but the whole set of human actions implicated in that moment—from working the land, hunting, foraging, trading, preparing, cooking, serving, tasting, digesting, and dealing with the resultant waste, and all of these in their complex and varied social implications. Eating is intertwined in a dense complex of projects grounded in the lived body, and attention to these may help us to return attention to life as the interdependence of humanity and the natural world. Such relationship raises question about appetite, hunger, and the nature of desire, to which we turn in the next chapter.

I have argued here that Merleau-Ponty's account of perception grounds an ontology that overcomes the analysis of being offered by Descartes's dualism. This ontology holds together mind and body, and thought and matter, attempting to understand them on their own terms, not reducing one to the other, but neither fully divorcing them from one another nor making them radically incommensurable. This holding-together is possible precisely because of the centrality of the sentient, moving human body to our understanding, and it is as such the embodied human person who provides the epistemological grounds and ontological example for understanding the world. This attempt to overcome the traditional philosophical analysis that still holds so much sway makes room for a richer account of perception, to be developed in the next chapter. Both the negative moment (undermining Cartesian dualism) and the positive (laying out a constructive account of *what there is* that reconnects perception to movement, and mind to matter, by taking the body as its central term) serve to modify our conception of the person, and his relationship to the world of nature. Humanity is, by this account, that part of nature that most strongly displays the characteristic of *lability*; that is, it is powerful to mold and re-shape itself and its surroundings, which re-shaping is always sensitive to those surroundings, but it is not strictly determined by them. Humanity is, then, naturally free, and this freedom cannot be understood purely in terms of the workings of nature.

2

"Taste and See . . .": Eating as Perception

Appetite or desire, not DNA, is the deepest principle of life.[1]

IN THE PREVIOUS CHAPTER, I argued for an embodied account of perception on the basis of Merleau-Ponty's philosophy, paying particular attention to the *Phenomenology of Perception*. In this chapter I seek to locate Merleau-Ponty's account of perception in relation to the history of philosophy, and to deepen our understanding of the imbrication of the senses in our bodily unity and dependence through an account of eating, which, as a central thread of human life (but one that is sometimes taken for granted in thought) has formed a kind of hidden, subterranean theme for philosophy.

Hunger, Appetite, and Imagination

We begin our analysis of eating with an investigation into its natural preliminary, hunger. I will argue here that hunger is a significant meeting-point of nature and culture, of thought and matter, which helps to show us what sort of thing a body is, and what sort of thing a person is, as well as giving us insight into the nature of desire and human need, of knowledge, of what kind of nature human persons may be thought to have, and of what human goodness consists in. As Raymond Tallis observes, where life is a complex and highly ordered state in any individual case, it must always be snatched from the clutches of the second law of thermodynamics:

1. Kass, *The Hungry Soul*, 48.

> At the root of hunger is the fact that living organisms are very highly ordered systems and are, consequently, improbable. They have what the physicist and prophet of molecular biology Erwin Schrödinger called "negative entropy." They are intrinsically unstable. Their endurance, unlike that of a rock, consequently has to be *earned*: their order has to be actively maintained.[2]

Appetite is the mechanism by which individual living things are driven to obtain the materials necessary for their growth and preservation. Rocks do not have appetites of any kind; their existence, and their "order," if they may be said to have any, is entirely the result of external forces. In the case of plants, very simple nutritive functions are at work. They draw nutrition from the soil from which they grow, without being conscious of doing so, but nevertheless they function in such a way as to draw out of the soil and air that which they need to survive, as well as drawing on the sun's energy for the necessary transformations of the raw materials of the soil and air into sugars. Clearly, their nutrition comes from their own work on inorganic raw materials. Although plants do not have appetites, properly speaking, they do have functions that govern how much of any given nutrient is assimilated or rejected, and so on. Animals do have appetites, which prompt them to find something to feed on, and to eat that which they are equipped to digest and ignore (for the most part) that which is inedible for them. Unlike plants, animals do not take nutrition at all times that their environment makes it available, and it is appetite which prompts them to return to the task of eating after any period of rest.

The case is obviously somewhat different for human beings. Tallis notes that "observation of animal feeding makes it reasonable to suspect that human beings are the only animals who truly *relish* their food, although non-human animals may feel the brief pleasure that comes from the relief of hunger."[3] A great difference lies in the fact that, for human beings, the greater part of their time is not taken up with eating, and indeed, "Just how far human eating is from animal feeding is illustrated by the way meals are often connected with breaks in work: the time and duration of meal breaks are the result of minute and protracted negotiations. In animals, the gathering and eating of food *is* the work. Indeed, work is not a separate part of life."[4] There is a distinction between the production and the consumption of the food that assuages appetite in human beings that is simply not present

---

2. Tallis, *Hunger*, 10.

3. Ibid., 37.

4. Ibid., 22.

amongst animals. This gap, I hope to show, is the source of our distinction between the pleasant and the good, amongst other things.

> "I think," said the Major, taking his pipe from his mouth "that desire is the most wonderful thing in life. Anyone who can really feel it is a king and I envy nobody else!" He put back his pipe.
>
> "But Charles!" she cried, "Every common low man in Halifax feels nothing else!"
>
> He again took his pipe from his mouth.
>
> "That's merely appetite," he said.[5]

For Lawrence's Major, there is a difference between mere appetite and desire properly speaking. Appetite, we may assume, is common to many kinds of animals and is a biological stimulus to eat, providing the animal with sufficient nutrition to continue its existence. Human desire is not such a simple biological process. If there is anything in human life that cannot be accounted for in purely material terms, desire must surely constitute an element of it. Desire is perhaps that felt gap between the situation I am in and a situation I would like to be in, hope to be in, and will attempt, unless some condition prevents it, to attain. (Thus Lacan understood Merleau-Ponty's later notion of the "hiatus" or non-coincidence of the feeling body with the felt body, between the eye and the gaze, in terms of desire, as the structural basis of the subject.)[6]

Appetite and Desire

For Spinoza, "there is no difference between appetite and desire except that desire is usually related to men in so far as they are conscious of their appetite. Therefore it can be defined as follows: desire is 'appetite accompanied by the consciousness thereof.'"[7] Spinoza is, of course, correct about this, but he minimizes the significance of the making-conscious of appetite, so that he can say "there is no difference" except this, suggesting that the consciousness makes no real difference to the appetite. Indeed, in the definition of desire at the end of Part II of the *Ethics*, he proposes the following definition: "Desire is the very essence of man in so far as his essence is conceived as determined to any action from any given affection of itself." In the explication of this definition, he relates this to the statement that "appetite is the

5. Lawrence, *The Virgin and the Gypsy*, cited in Tallis, *Hunger*, 80.

6. See especially Lacan, *The Four Fundamental Concepts of Psycho-analysis*, 67–104.

7. Spinoza, *Ethics*, 109 (Sch. Pr. 9, III).

very essence of man in so far as his essence is determined to such actions as contribute to his preservation."[8] For Spinoza, then, desire and appetite both constitute the essence of the human; the idea of desire reflects the notion that what is desired is determined by the human being's affection. To understand Spinoza's use of the term "affect" correctly, we must understand that what is "affected" is the shape taken on by a thing, the form in which it appears; desire, then, proceeds from a human as a particular form of his or her essence, which is to be a desiring-thing. But the fact that this is the same as appetite for Spinoza shows that he does not consider the particular form desires take to be uncaused, desire does not "proceed from" a person as a result of her whim, but rather is determined by *conatus*, by her drive to preserve herself and increase her power. Claiming that appetite and desire are the same thing is consonant with Spinoza's system, which sees the appetites of human beings as essentially determined.

> Desire is the very essence, or nature, of each individual in so far as that is conceived as determined by some given state of its constitution to do something. Therefore, according as each individual is affected from external causes with various kinds of pleasure, pain, love, hate, etc., that is, according as his nature is conditioned in various ways, so must his desire be of different kinds; and the nature of one desire must differ from the nature of another to the same extent as the emotions, from which each single desire arises, differ amongst themselves.[9]

In the case of animal hunger, Spinoza's account would seem to hold true, at least in outline: the animal desires to eat, and it desires to eat that which it requires to survive and to grow: the cow and the sheep to eat grass, the calf and the lamb to drink milk, and so on. This is also partly true of the human infant. Augustine writes of himself in this state, "You granted me not to wish for more than you were giving, and to my nurses the desire to give me what you gave them."[10] But a long tradition has thought of mature human eating as somewhat different to that of animals. Jean-Anthelme Brillat-Savarin, the nineteenth-century French gastronome, begins his 1825 book *La Physiologie du Goût* with a series of aphorisms that are instructive here:

---

8. Ibid., 141 (Def.1 and Exp., III).
9. Ibid., 137 (Pr. 56, III).
10. Augustine, *Confessions*, 6 (I. v (6)).

I. The world is nothing without life, and all that lives takes nourishment.

II. Animals feed: man eats: only the man of intellect knows how to eat.

III. The fate of the nations depends on the way they eat.[11]

We must ask whether, if the human being is a natural thing, it must have a nature. For Aristotle, humanity, like everything else, has a *telos*, a goal, an end. Human beings' end is *eudaimonia*, human flourishing, which is to be rational. But this is not the rationality of modern rationalists. Rather, it is the ordering of human life that most enables human life to flourish. But then, if flourishing is acting rationally, and acting rationally is acting in such a way as to enable human flourishing, what is the content of either?

By contrast, for Sartre and modern existentialism, there is no human nature. Our existence precedes our essence; the only human fact is that we must choose how to live, and there are no pre-existing criteria for our choice.

But there is another human fact, one that transgresses the normal terms of philosophical inquiry. I am hungry. And what I really want to eat is a plate of sausages with mashed potatoes, with a thick onion gravy. That I must eat to live is an animal fact. My desire for some food is reducible to physical facts. But my desire for sausage and mash surely is more than an animal fact; it rests upon culture, geography, agriculture, and my personal tastes, as well as a certain kind of whim. Is it in my nature to desire sausage and mash? This seems unlikely since it is dependent on so many "environmental" factors. Is my hunger for sausage and mash the result of my absolute freedom? This also seems implausible, since the hunger is driven in part by my bodily need.

The human being is a natural thing, an appetitive animal, but it also shapes its nature; the human being's desire is not only to fill his or her belly, to survive, but is also hunger for *particular* things, and of course humans hunger not only for food, but for so much more: for relationship with others, for sex, for beauty, for meaning, for God. The human difference from the purely natural is embodied in the difference between appetite and desire, between a particular body and an undistinguished mass of stuff. The difference, it seems to me, is *thought*. It is human beings' nature to think,[12]

11. Brillat-Savarin, *Physiology of Taste*, 13.

12. The terminology is necessarily slippery here. If humanity somehow escapes nature, as I have suggested, what does it mean to speak of human nature? I will address this point more fully in chapter 6, having expounded and developed Merleau-Ponty's thinking on nature in light of the logic of institution in chapter 5. Here, the point is that nature exceeds itself. It is precisely because nature is resistant to thought that thought can arise within it, that thought has something to "push against." For Ted Toadvine, "Insofar as philosophy is incapable of thematizing its own emergence, insofar as it remains conditioned by a nature that escapes its reflective recuperation, nature is disclosed

but how we will think is not determined by nature; rather, how we think determines nature. The human being's patterns of thought shape his or her relationship to the world, though they are not strictly *determinative* of that relationship, which depends on features of the world as well as our own features.

Human beings' essence is to think, and in so doing to shape ourselves and all of nature, but what and how we think are not given by nature. Nevertheless, some patterns of thought (we often call them addictions) are destructive of human life and diminish our capacity to think and the efficacy of that thought in shaping nature and our relationship to it. Other thoughts add to our ability to live, enrich our relationship to nature, and stimulate further thoughts.

Both Aristotle and Sartre were right, in a sense: human beings have a nature, which we are continually making. Humanity is that part of nature that is self-shaping, which, in David Morris's terminology, is *labile*. What kind of nature, then, must human beings make for themselves? Note that the question is ambiguous, and this indicates a broadening of the philosophical question. No longer may we ask: Is there such a thing as human nature? And if so, what is it? Rather, we ask: What part of nature are human beings? And what kind of nature should we make? Humanity depends on creation, but creation also depends on human beings.

Eating amongst humans, then, differs to animal eating. Firstly, it "owes as much to culture as it does to biology."[13] The case for human appetite is more complicated than that of the lamb or the cow, for humans are omnivorous and can eat many different things; a choice of what to eat must be made, subject to the constraints of what is available, what is preferred, and what is nutritious. This element of decision, as well as the fact that human beings, as Marx and Engels said, produce the means of their own subsistence, and so must choose what and where to farm, makes Gastronomy both possible and necessary, and so forges the distinction between animal feeding and human eating.

---

indirectly as a silent resistance internal to philosophy's own movement." So "we can never be a 'part of' nature in the sense of one thing among many in an assemblage that collects them all. The nature in which we are involved and inhere is not a collection of determinate things but a horizon that we open onto from within and that we find ourselves already having emerged from." Toadvine, "Merleau-Ponty and Lifeworldly Naturalism," 372; 379. I am grateful to Dylan Trigg for his perceptive questioning on this point.

13. Pollan, *In Defence of Food*, 7.

Spinoza goes on to argue that "a passive emotion ceases to be a passive emotion as soon as we form a clear and distinct idea of it,"[14] suggesting that when purely physical appetite is transformed, in human beings, to the conscious state of desire that I will call "hunger," it does not remain unchanged. Human hunger is not a state that leads its subject to take food in any way possible; it is not simply the demand for nutrition. Rather, it lies at the core, I want to suggest, of what makes human beings *human*, and is related to the distinction between animal feeding and eating proper, which finds its highest expression in dining. Unlike the animal, for whom the specifics of eating are fixed by its nature, for human beings hunger can be satisfied in a plethora of ways. It is for this reason that we may speak of many and varied human "hungers": to be sure, any human being who is without food will hunger for food. But food is not all she hungers for, and indeed hunger is in this sense open-ended. I hunger for recognition, for the esteem of others, for experience that transcends the ordinary, and may develop hungers for all manner of things. Hunger is the gap, as it were, between what and where I am and what and where I would like to be, and so my hunger operates within the full range of human possibility. Its limit is not fixed by nature but by imagination. For the Anglican theologian Tim Gorringe "desire, in our analysis, may be defined as imaginative work on appetite, including the appetite for knowledge."[15] What Gorringe calls desire here is what I am calling hunger, and the use of "hunger" is important because it captures the thought that, although hunger is not determined by nature in the way that appetite is (it opens onto endless possibilities), it is nonetheless stimulated by a fundamental bodily need. "Desire" might be imagined to be the operation of a pure will, but hunger, while not determined, is neither completely voluntary. Gorringe goes on, "It [desire] begins, as both Plato and Aristotle did, with appetites, which accounts for the energy of desire, but it recognizes that all desire is culturally constructed, or, in my terms, is shaped by the imagination our culture makes possible."[16]

Spinoza, of course, might be thought to remain too Cartesian, accepting Descartes's division of the human being into body and soul, mind and matter, resolving this dualism into a monism by calling thought and matter two attributes of the one substance. In so doing he inverts the Cartesian picture, according to which the soul, which is the seat of reason, is thought of in terms of a pure and voluntaristic will, whose "desires" are free-floating, and must be asserted to govern animal appetites. In Spinoza there is no

---

14. Spinoza, *Ethics*, 204 (Pr. 3, V).

15. Gorringe, *The Education of Desire*, 91.

16. Ibid., 91.

(or minimal) difference between the two. The Cartesian picture is, for the most part, consonant with that given by Plato, in which the rational soul is the essence of the human being, and the appetites simply a temporary encumbrance of bodily life.

Lisa Heldke, commenting on *The Republic*, writes: "By carving the soul into reason, spirit, and appetite, Plato separates reason from all other faculties. And in elevating reason above the others, he makes it alone the proper governor of the soul. He terms bodily appetites unreasonable, and regards them as things to be controlled by reason."[17] The confusion here over whether appetite is a function of the body or the soul is a symptom of the problems with a simple dualism, and reflects the fact that hunger is always, in the human being, a mediation between the body and thought, and so often slips between the two in dualistic accounts. Plato explicitly makes the soul isomorphic with his ideal republic, in which reason and the philosopher-kings rule over the appetites and those whose work is to satisfy the appetites. This division may be the source of the proto-Puritanism of Platonic texts such as the *Gorgias* and the *Republic*, in which the demands of the body are thought to contribute nothing to the formation of the mind, and the pleasant is thought to have nothing to do with the good.[18] This conception of the human being and of social organization depends on agriculture and the division of labor in the city; for the foraging, hunter-gatherer human no such distinction between the pleasant and the good could hold. Plato, of course, also defines desire in places as a lack of the desired object.[19] In the *Philebus* he makes this argument on the basis of the examples of thirst and hunger, which are clearly expressions of a lack of something (food and drink). But this is not all they are, and indeed the difference between the two may help to demonstrate this. Extreme thirst always prompts us most urgently to drink water, which is always what thirst lacks. There is

17. Heldke, "Foodmaking as a Thoughtful Practice," 211.

18. This, of course, is not the final word on desire in Plato. In the *Symposium* bodily desire is affirmed as a route towards the pursuit of the good, even if it looks as though the ladder will ultimately have to be kicked away. The hierarchical ordering of desire is emphasized less in the *Phaedrus*, for which love guides us to contemplation of the eternal truths of the forms. This is the source of the positive account of desire with which Augustine begins his *Confessions*, and the notion that what we truly desire is God. But the ambiguity about the place of desire, of course, remains, as Tim Gorringe, for example, has suggested (*The Education of Desire*, 133.) I am grateful to Simon Ravenscroft for helping to clarify my thinking on this point.

19. It is crucial to the understanding of *eros* presented in the *Symposium* that desire, though motivated by lack, is not simply constituted by lack. As a state of searching between lack and posession, desire is also productive. Cf. Sheffield, *Plato's Symposium*, 77; 200.

not usually a strong imperative to choose what to drink. If I choose to drink other drinks, either it is not mainly to assuage thirst, or it is to deliver the needed substance, water, along with some other substances (sugars, salts, etc.). But the case with hunger is not the same. There is no basic food that hunger demands in the same way that thirst is for lack of water. I must eat a variety of things to achieve the best possible nutrition, and though hunger may drive me to certain kinds of foods (salty or sweet or fatty ones, most commonly), it also creates the conditions under which I may eat not to meet a specific lack, but rather according to my imagination and fancies. What I have called appetite is, of course, a lack. And there is no hunger without appetite. But hunger itself is, in everyday experience, not only felt as lack, but as possibility; I can eat a whole range of things, and indeed hunger prompts me to do so. I eat not only what I lack, but also what I like, and the huge amount of human ingenuity that is invested in food preparation is not only to meet the lack expressed by appetite but to meet our hungers for food that stimulates, nourishes, and entertains.

For Leon Kass, in *The Hungry Soul,*

> Lack, experienced as desire, is the spur to all aspiration, to action and awareness, to having a life at all. Bodies as incorruptible as diamonds, or bodies lacking in nothing beyond themselves, would have no impulse or orientation toward the world beyond their borders. Waste makes need, and need makes for everything higher than need. Here, in the germ of hunger, is the origin of all the appetites of the hungry soul.[20]

Timothy Gorringe cites Sebastian Moore, commenting on Aquinas's synthesis of the accounts of desire given by Aristotle, Augustine, and the Neoplatonists:

> Sebastian Moore puts this tradition into contemporary terms in defining desire as "what I really want and have always wanted[;] . . . to be more and more myself in the mystery in which I am . . . . Desire is love trying to happen. . . . It draws into its fulfilling meaning all the appetites of our physical being." Agreeing with Aquinas that true desire always issues in union, he argues that its real opposite is egoism. "It is because we do not understand desire but equate it with egoism, that we see the cross of Jesus as opposed to it. Real desire is what the cross empowers, bringing us to the death that its liberation entails. The death is the death

---

20. Kass, *The Hungry Soul*, 27.

of our present ego, whose perpetuation is the work of egoism posing as desire."[21]

This egoism is fundamental to Spinoza's account, and it is the fact that there is no possibility for overcoming the individual *conatus* that prevents him from allowing for an account of desire that moves beyond the realm of the quantitative, which always seeks an increase of power, to the qualitative, which opens on the realm of imaginative possibility rather than determined need. Such would require us to pass through death (figuratively speaking), to relinquish our desire for an increase in power, which Spinoza will not countenance. This opening onto imaginative possibility, which I have argued is a part of human hunger properly understood, makes human life a part of nature that is not purely determined *by* nature, but is determinative *of* nature. We develop cultures of eating and farming, which allow the conscious shaping of hungers to be sedimented in unconscious structures of habit in ways that can be both positive and negative. The core of this conscious shaping, which is determinative of unconscious life, can be observed in a common (though not everyday) experience of human eating: taste can be educated, so that we may eat and come to enjoy things that cannot be enjoyed on first bite; we can have "acquired tastes." In her *Making Sense of Taste*, Carolyn Korsmeyer argues

> The ability to educate one's palate is an almost uniquely human trait. [She cites Brillat-Savarin's dictum that animals feed, but only man eats, and can dine.] Humans are distinctive in their cultivation of taste sensations that on first experience are unpleasant or irritating, such as those delivered by chili peppers.[22]

Clearly such eating habits cannot be acquired as the result of a simple lack; nor is the appetite that drives me to eat chillies for the first time a simple desire for pleasure. Rather, this hunger is a hunger for a different, more sophisticated hunger, a hunger for participation in a food culture and a gastronomic experience that can only be achieved by the education of my tastes. For Gorringe,

> All high cultures recognize that the non-divine imagination needs training and exercise. This work is called education, and this introduces *the normative dimension of desire* which Plato sets out in the *Symposium*, and Augustine in the *Confessions*. God, or the true, good and beautiful, is what desire strains

21. Gorringe, *The Education of Desire*, 89, citing Sebastian Moore, *Jesus the Liberator of Desire* (New York: Crossroad, 1989), 93.

22. Korsmeyer, *Making Sense of Taste*, 93.

towards. Education is the recognition that the imagination only flourishes when it is trained, pruned, disciplined, and that it requires goals. *All human cultures rest on an education of desire in this sense.* Jesus speaks of it as discipleship. He calls people to be disciples, which is to say to learn discipline. He is engaged in an education of desire.[23]

Our conscious or imaginative relationship to our appetites moves us on from the appetite that leads us to fill our bellies to the general structures of desire that constitute our human world. For Tallis,

> It is because we are self-conscious that we live in, and in relation to, a *world*—a human and natural world had in common—and have a sense of our life course. Here our hungers breed and multiply and proliferate and give rise to the dreams and longings that consume us. Our hungers, then, are rooted in mystery. Hunger is the paramount expression of the mysterious burden (or gift) of consciousness and the even more mysterious burden (or gift) of human consciousness.[24]

He argues in this book that the satiety of basic human appetites opens us to hunger in a broader sense. But this desire remains hunger since it is driven, at some level, by human needs, worked and shaped by conscious life. Tallis speaks of the "second hunger," the hunger that drives hedonism, as derived from a "hunger for hunger," which arises when primary hungers, what I have called appetites, are met. This, it seems, is a specifically human phenomenon. To have enough to meet my need is somehow not enough. We cultivate new hungers to drive us, "wants" that far exceed our needs. This hunger for enjoyment, for diversion, is a result of the interplay of appetite and imagination in human beings, a result of our being thinking and bodily things. This, of course, demands that we attend not only to our desires but also to their effects: Are the things we hunger for giving us the things we *really* hunger for, and what is the difference? How can we tell? In a brief attempt to justify his project, Tallis writes: "Making human hunger less obvious than it seems and following its metamorphoses in those who live above subsistence level seems justified if it promotes the kind of reflection that could slow the bonfire of consumption that occupies us for most of our waking hours."[25] And it would seem that ultimately philosophy

23. Gorringe, *The Education of Desire*, 91.

24. Tallis, *Hunger*, 137.

25. Ibid., 6.

may constitute an extension of our "imaginative work on appetite," asking whether what we seem to hunger for is what we really hunger for.

Hungers, we have said, are "imaginative work on appetites." It seems, though, that we can reflect on our hungers and find that we have hungered for the *wrong* things; that what we hunger for does not ultimately satisfy. The conscious development of appetite constituted by hunger, though it frees us from the purely determined patterns of eating characteristic of animals, remains tethered to a biological and ecological reality, and this despite the fact that our investigation of hunger has suggested that there is no simple "right" object of hunger.

If we understand hunger as an intentional state, then we must say that when we receive what we hunger for, that hunger is satisfied. But perhaps the underlying appetite is not satisfied. This is not to suggest that human hungers are superfluous, and the important thing is to meet human appetites, to provide as many people as possible with the means to subsistence. Rather, it is to say that the expression of the essentially human lies in the cultivation and satisfaction of hungers that go beyond the essential—the development of art, love, politics, culture, philosophy, and so on. But for these hungers to be satisfied for anything more than a brief moment, their satisfaction must be compatible with the satisfaction of our fundamental appetites. So we must allow that the "imaginative work on appetite" that constitutes true hunger *can* operate in such a way that the hunger is no longer truly in accord with the appetite it develops; where our "rational" appetites lead us to eat, for the most part, what is good for us, in the context of a food culture that is breaking down, our choices are driven by a culture that is orientated towards the hunger not only of some individuals for profit, but also the pathological hunger built into the economic system, the system that we have developed for the meeting of hungers, for the pure increase of profit, rather than my own appetite for nutrition, in such a way that I end up hungering for (and eating) food that does not nutrify me, that makes me unwell.

The human situation, in which appetites are imaginatively developed into hungers, leads to a further appetitive dysfunction: unlike the animals, whose appetites are simple and strongly related to a set of environmental sources of their fulfillment, the human being is not tightly integrated into a natural situation that provides the means for his desires to be met; as we have said, following Marx and Engels, humanity produces the means of its own subsistence, and can hunger for all kinds of possibilities that are not easily actualized. Very commonly, one human being's various hungers are disparate and conflicting, and he or she is neither able to satisfy them all nor to resolve them. Augustine identifies this in writing of his situation as an adolescent: "You gathered me together from the state of disintegration in which I had been fruitlessly divided. I turned from unity in you to be lost in multiplicity."[26] For Augustine, of course, the true object of our desires is God, so he writes later of his time as a student "My hunger was internal, deprived of inward food, that is of you yourself, my God. But that was not the kind of hunger I felt. I was without any desire for incorruptible nourishment, not because I was replete with it, but the emptier I was, the more unappetizing such food became. So my soul was in rotten health."[27]

Augustine's thought highlights a problem with the thought that there is a difference between what we think we hunger for and what we *truly* hunger for: How should we tell? How can we know the difference between what we want and what is truly good for us, the true object of our distorted hungers? Can this come only after a kind of religious conversion, or from the perspective an individual has on their life in their old age?

We turn, then, to an investigation of the matter of taste and human knowledge, before we go on to probe further the question of whether there is a "human nature" and finally to ask whether the idea of food that is good for us might tell us anything about what is good in a more general sense.

Taste, Vision, and Perception

As we come to the question of taste, we must note that, despite there being a dearth of philosophical material dealing with the sense of taste properly speaking, philosophical aesthetics has long made use of the word "taste" to refer to something rather different—a sensibility with regards to aesthetic experiences that cannot reasonably be called into question on philosophical grounds. It is on the basis of this metaphorical use of the word "taste" that it is said that *de gustibus non disputandam est.*

Taste, for Hume, is the aesthetic variant of opinion, which arises from sentiment. So he writes, in his essay "Of the Standard of Taste,"

> Beauty is no quality in things themselves: It exists merely in the mind which contemplates them; and each mind perceives a different beauty. One person may even perceive deformity, where another is sensible of beauty; and every individual ought to acquiesce in his own sentiment, without pretending to regulate those of others. To seek the real beauty, or real deformity, is as

26. Augustine, *Confessions*, 24 (II. i(i)).
27. Ibid., 35 (III. i(i)).

fruitless an enquiry, as to pretend to ascertain the real sweet or
real bitter. According to the disposition of the organs, the same
object may be both sweet and bitter; and the proverb has justly
determined it to be fruitless to dispute concerning tastes.[28]

For Hume, then, taste is a matter of sentiment, in regards to aesthetic
objects just as much as to food. It is clear that there *is* much agreement on
what is sweet and what is bitter, and that we would normally think that
sugar really is sweet and quinine really is bitter, though our preferences for
them may vary. Hume goes on to acknowledge that many matters of "taste"
do not really allow of disagreement. Nevertheless, he maintains that since
there is no accessible standard or measure against which tastes are to be
compared, they are a matter of sentiment alone, and he holds that the same
is true for morality. Any broad agreement is down to uniformity of sentiment, not to the existence of an external standard.

Hume's use of the term comes within the context of the emergence
of aesthetics as a distinct philosophical discipline in eighteenth-century
Europe, in which this source of judgments about beauty is not always considered to be purely sentimental. Taste is "conceived as a sensitivity to fine
distinctions and an ability to discern beauty"[29] and as such "good taste"
could, for some thinkers, be the ability to see real beauty.

This difference over whether or not matters of taste can be measured
by some standard will have some bearing on our discussion of tastes properly speaking: nevertheless, the discussion here referred to is *not* about the
sense of taste, but about taste in a metaphorical sense: "The literal sense
of taste has rarely caught the attention of philosophers except insofar as it
provides the metaphor for aesthetic sensitivity."[30]

One of the reasons I wish to focus on taste is that it may help us to
get past the Cartesian notion of perception located in a mental theatre
of representation. For Descartes's consideration of perception—which
makes visual perception, and especially optical illusion, paradigmatic
—the question is whether I can be sure that what I think I see is what I really
do see; this is a question of the correspondence between an internal mental
object and an external one. The problem with any such account is that it
fails to properly think of the subject. It defers the question of subjectivity by
asking whether the "internal" picture matches the "external" one. Merleau-
Ponty's account of perception is an attempt to get beyond this, to do away
with the Cartesian conception of the mind as a theatre of representation.

28. Hume, "Of the Standard of Taste," 230.

29. Korsmeyer, *Making Sense of Taste*, 40.

30. Ibid., 1.

In vision, we tend to think that my seeing occurs "in my head"—somewhere behind my eyes, where two optical images are combined into one "sense." This is based on a reliable scientific account of the physiology of seeing: light is reflected by objects, and some of that light reaches our eyes, where it is projected onto our retinas and there transformed into electrical signals conducted by the optic nerve to the brain. So my perception of an object and the object itself are divorced from one another in space.

A similar physiological account might be given of touch or taste. But where do these senses reside? Physiologically, of course, they become "electrical activity" only in the nervous system and the brain. But this does not necessarily close the philosophical question—*where* is my sense of touch? It is clear that an everyday account would locate touch in the part of the body that touches, pain in the part that is damaged, and taste in the mouth and on the tongue. There is no sensation of touch without a touched object, nor any taste without some *thing* to be tasted. Though I may see a mirage, I cannot drink from one. The proof of the pudding is in the eating, as it were.

This is the significance of the question about whether taste can be illusory: while the distance between perceiver and perceived allows for visual and auditory hallucination, it seems as though tastes cannot be hallucinated. We may dream of visions and sounds, perhaps even faintly of smells, but no one, I submit, dreams the full experience of eating, tasting, satisfying hunger and feeling full. One might dream a taste-experience in a comparable way that one might imagine a taste-experience, but this is always discernibly different to the actual experience of eating food.

This is not to argue that taste experiences are self-verifying, as some might argue in the case, for example, of religious experiences. This idea of self-verification again presupposes that the epistemological question is about whether what is inside my head matches what is really going on out there in the world. The reason taste experiences cannot be illusory is not that they have some quality that could only have come from an outside object which grounds the taste perception. It is rather that taste opens up the question of subjectivity. I can taste something because I am part of a world that is *in principle* tastable, because I am eating something. The end of the taste experience comes in the waning of hunger and the feeling of having eaten, or being full.

That hunger, which is both a biological and a conscious state in the embodied human being, is assuaged in the act of eating, and this intertwining of psychic and physical states grounds us in a world that must be the source of our sustenance; though imagination plays its part in the genesis of hunger, and is a crucial driver of the activity that we engage in to meet our hungers, they cannot be fulfilled by imagination alone.

Touch and taste, as such, are located not at a distance from their object, but rather in direct contact with their object. Things touched and tasted are not elements in a mental theatre of representation, but rather objects in contact with me their subject, grounded in a world that cannot be an illusion, because I am in it.

To exclude the possibility of gustatory illusion is not to discount the possibility that tastes may be dependent on subjective conditions, and not just on the properties of the sensed object. I have already mentioned that the way things taste (particularly whether or not they are appetizing, whether or not they taste good) can depend on my desires, physical conditions, and beliefs. Furthermore, evidence reveals that pregnant women often report extreme (sometimes debilitating) intensification of the sense of taste. This acuity of taste can make possible taste experiences that are usually impossible; nevertheless there is no illusion involved; what is tasted is not in the imagination, but in the foodstuff.

This line of thinking begins to show how taste differs from visual (and other kinds of) perception, in that it does not proffer concepts to consciousness so readily. I can fit taste experiences to concepts (say, I taste carrot in a soup and recognize it as such), but I need not do so. Indeed, much of the work of developing one's ability to taste involves learning the concepts that allow one to identify features of a food (or wine) that would otherwise go unrecognized.

The paradigmatic example of vision, in which Descartes looks at an inanimate object on his desk (the piece of wax) or out of his window (the tower), fails to properly account for visual perception at all. It isolates a moment of visual perception, abstracts it from time, movement, and bodily action, and as such cannot even really account for perspective (which depends on movement and our understanding of ourselves as embodied perceivers located in a relationship to what we see) or depth. I do not wish to argue that vision is a bad paradigm or exemplar for understanding human perception. That is not at all the case. Rather, the problem with Descartes's philosophical investigation of perception, a problem that has persisted in philosophy at least since Plato's allegory of the cave, is that it fails to make sense of sight. We have made provisional arguments that sight itself is reversible; that the one who sees must also be potentially see-able. Descartes's example flattens vision out, abstracts it from human movement, from time and change, putting a theoretical pane of glass between seer and seen. It thus fixes the object and the subject of vision in separate realms, disallowing the possibility that the subject might also be the object of some other perception, and that the seen object is also a subject.

So our investigation of the nature of taste is not an attempt to correct the philosophical bias towards vision by means of a counter-emphasis. Rather, I hope to show that prevailing accounts of perception are based on a misunderstanding of vision. It may be the case that these misunderstandings bring about examples of visual perception forced into the mold they make for it; that the popular reception of this errant account of perception has lead to the attempt to reduce perception to something that matches this account in embodied life. The ubiquity of television, the rapid growth of the internet, the whole cultural edifice which Guy Debord denounced as the "Society of the Spectacle," may in fact be an attempt to produce a kind of life that corresponds to the theory played out on a grand scale, to install the (sometimes literal) pane of glass into the perceptive situation that philosophy anticipated.

Vision, as Merleau-Ponty showed us, depends on the bodily subject who sees. Illusion is recognized as such by the continued investigation of perception; when we are unsure of what we see, we look again, we continue looking, we move in relation to our object, and so on. We do not aggregate a series of perceptual scenes any more than we do a variety of discrete "sensations"—rather, visual perception *is* bound to the human body, the passage of time and movement. Comparison with the example of taste-perception makes this explicit. Taste is patently not completely separate from the other senses. We know that if a taster puts a peg over his nose, or has a cold, his ability to taste, and so *the way things taste*, is affected, sometimes quite dramatically. We know that the smell of freshly-baked bread, or the sight of a beautifully ripe apple, can arouse hunger, which itself transforms the experience of taste. Further, we know that our sense of taste demands that we touch some object to offer any experience at all, that we must eat to taste.

Eating obviously brings about a certain kind of relationship between the perceived object and myself—I cannot eat an object without removing it from the world, without destroying it. Not only do I destroy it, I also admit it to become part of me, to be broken down, partly assimilated, and partly rejected during its short sojourn within the confines of my body. The subject/object relationship can only be established here at the moment it is also undermined. In eating something I at once admit my independence from it (I am free to eat it or not, it exists outside of me) while establishing my dependence on it (once I ingest it, it starts to become material nourishment for my body).

For Descartes, thinking from his paradigmatic optical illusion, perception is taken to accurately represent the world in a limited way, under certain conditions. When perception leads us to form clear and distinct ideas, he argues, it must be that those ideas correspond to some outer reality.

If we were to replace the optical illusion with an example from the sensorial world of eating, the results would be different. I cannot be deceived by my sense of taste insofar as it does not offer "representations" of the world to consciousness; rather taste sensations always seem to me a result of my interactions with the world. Taste sensations are less likely to lead me to confuse the world as it appears to me with the world as it really is. As Descartes saw, the world as it appears to me is not the same as the world as it is. But the confusion that arises with the example of visual illusion is that some part of my perception (that which is clear and distinct) represents the world to me accurately, gives me access to the world as it really is. The other parts of perception, those elements that are clouded by subjectivity, are to be mistrusted, and avoided altogether for philosophical purposes.

Descartes failed to see that the world always appears under an *aspect*. No perception could represent the world as it is without including the fact of the perceiver; the world always appears as *the world as it appears to me*. It is not the case that some part of my perception represents the world accurately, but rather that my perception accurately represents some part of the world, which is always grounded in that part of the world that I am, my body. Martin Jay draws out Levinas's understanding of Merleau-Ponty on this point:

> "As Merleau-Ponty has shown," Levinas wrote, "the I that constitutes the world comes up against a sphere in which it is by its very flesh implicated; it is implicated in what it otherwise would have constituted and so is implicated in the world."[31]

Levinas's observation of Merleau-Ponty's thought here is the same insight that eating offers, and that we continually repeat in our daily lives, if unconsciously. I constitute the world—that is to say, it is in my seeing that bare stuff is made into "things," it is in human reason that what there is becomes nature, a nature that is always to some degree the recipient of grace since it only is what it is because of the working of reason. That there is a world for me depends on my being able to perceive a world; in this sense I constitute a world that depends on me. The same is true, and explicitly so, when we think about taste. This leaf of rosemary only, in a sense, tastes of rosemary because I eat it. Of course, left uneaten, it remains the kind of thing that will taste of rosemary if eaten, but there would seem to be little sense in saying that that which is untasted nevertheless has a taste. But all this is subject to an inversion: for the "I" that constitutes things, the tongue that tastes the rosemary taste, is located amongst those things, is nourished

31. Jay, *Downcast Eyes*, 507.

by the rosemary already eaten. The I that constitutes the world is already part of that world, so there can be no absolute priority of the subject. If the world is in a sense mind-dependent (as the taste of rosemary depends on my experience of the taste), nevertheless the mind is world-dependent (as the nourishment eating gives me is a precondition for further nourishment, further taste experiences, and all of my continued conscious bodily life, which intertwines mind and world, intelligibility and materiality.)

This tension is not resolved, and in the end the problem lies with Levinas's dependence on the notion of constitution. In the final chapter I will develop a logic of institution that will help us to move beyond this problem; for now, the tension remains.

Eating and Ontology

For the Plato of the *Gorgias*, the true good of the soul's ascent from the body must be sharply distinguished from the false "good" of bodily pleasure. But this already precludes taking a position that understands the human being as an integrated whole, that understands the soul, as Aristotle does, as the form of the animal, that is intrinsically related to matter, that brings life through a certain kind of organization, and that understands that life depends on the maintenance of this order, which occurs in nutrition.

The reified and pure subject of much philosophy fails to understand subjectivity because it extracts it from relation, and subjectivity must always be *to be the subject of something*, some object, just as objectivity must be to be the object for some subject, and not purely a mute thing. This reification of the subject (as *res extensa* or the immortal soul) allows for the ossification of the lived world of objects into the inert and "objective" universe of scientism, which must always fail to account for the human subject at its center.

> We have largely adopted the view of nature associated with modern natural science. The nature we think we know through modern science is not the nature we know through ordinary experience—or at least not through experience that was ordinary before it was overwhelmed by the technological transformation of the world.[32]

But this is not to reverse an inert realism into idealism. For Levinas,

> Eating, for example, is to be sure not reducible to the chemistry of alimentation. But eating also does not reduce itself to

32. Kass, *The Hungry Soul*, 3–4.

the set of gustative, olfactory, kinesthetic, and other sensations that would constitute the consciousness of eating. This sinking of one's teeth into the things which the act of eating involves above all measures the surplus of the reality of the aliment over every represented reality, a surplus that is not quantitative, but is the way the I, the absolute commencement, is suspended on the non-I. [. . .] To be sure, in the satisfaction of need the alienness of the world that founds me loses its alterity: in satiety the real I sank my teeth into is assimilated, the forces that were in the other become my forces, become me (and every satisfaction of need is in some respect nourishment).[33]

This point may be developed with an example. Michael Shaffer asks whether there is any objective difference in tasting ability between gastronomic "experts" and those of us who defer to their apparently superior opinions. To do so he distinguishes between two kinds of taste: "direct taste" and "reflective taste." He makes the distinction by referring to a description of a cheese in a reputable tasting guide. Such words in the description as "sour," "sweet," and "salty" are considered examples of "direct taste." The apparently more descriptive elements such as "distinctive [. . .] wine-like aroma with a touch of the farmyard" and "Lemons and leaf mold remain in the lingering flavor" are taken to be examples of reflective tasting, in which the gastronome applies what Shaffer concludes is her real expertise of articulating sensate experiences. This distinction, it is quite clear, does not correspond to any real distinction, but depends on drawing an arbitrary line between various levels of conceptualization in *the language that describes taste*. Shaffer identifies as the "direct" and, he will claim, "objective" aspects of tasting those for which it is claimed the tongue has receptors (sweet, sour, salty) and excludes as subjective all the aspects of description whose language demonstrates that they depend on a degree of conceptualization.[34]

Shaffer is drawing here, perhaps, on Brillat-Savarin, who divides direct taste sensations from complete perceptions:

I consider it certain that taste gives rise to sensations of three distinct orders, namely, direct sensation, complete sensation, and considered sensation.

The direct sensation is the first impression arising out of the immediate action of the organs of the mouth, while the substance to be tasted is still resting on the front part of the tongue.

---

33. Levinas, *Totality and Infinity*, 129.
34. Shaffer, "Taste, Gastronomic Expertise, and Objectivity," 73–77.

The complete sensation is composed of the first impression, and the impression which follows when the food leaves its initial position and passes to the back of the mouth, assailing the whole organ with its taste and perfume. Lastly, the considered sensation is the judgement passed by the brain on the impressions transmitted to it by the organ.[35]

But Shaffer solidifies the divide between sensation and perception by reducing the three stages to two. Brillat-Savarin's "direct sensation" is *not* the atomistic notion of which Shaffer makes use, and which Merleau-Ponty opposes as meaningless. The taste sensation in its totality has, for Brillat-Savarin, a temporal aspect; it takes *time* to taste things, as we commonly acknowledge when we speak of a "burnt aftertaste" or of a wine's "finish." Brillat-Savarin's three stages present a developmental account of taste sensation, rather than a bifurcation of tastes into simple physical and complex mental elements. Shaffer labors under an illusion that there is a strict divide between those aspects of perception that may be understood in causal terms, which correspond to what Merleau-Ponty calls sensation, and those that are more psychic, calling that which can be causally explained "objective" and that which cannot "subjective."

The need to make the distinction between subjective and objective aspects of taste is derived from a short passage in Hume's essay "Of the Standard of Taste," cited earlier. For Shaffer, the claimed expertise of the gastronome must be suspected, since there is no reason to believe that he has any exceptional ability to taste things in physiological terms. The gastronome's taste-experience, he seems to suggest, is no different to that of the ordinary person; their position as an "expert" is maintained by a confidence trick. We could objectively determine whether something is sweet or sour, but in the case of a disagreement over whether it tastes "farmyard-y" or has a hint of pineapple or lemon, there is no way to resolve the dispute. *De gustibus non disputandum est.*

Unfortunately, Shaffer has not seen fit to cite Hume further on in the aforementioned essay, in which he acknowledges that though he can find no "objective" basis for taste, "Whoever would assert an equality of genius and elegance between an Ogilby and Milton, or Bunyan and Addison, would be thought to defend no less an extravagance, than if he had maintained a mole-hill to be as high as Teneriffe, or a pond as extensive as the ocean."[36] By insisting on "objective" aspects of taste, Shaffer removes the "real sweet" and "real bitter" from the domain of human experience, and reduces them to

35. Brillat-Savarin, *Physiology of Taste*, 42.
36. Hume, "Of The Standard of Taste," 230–31.

certain chemical processes occurring on the tongue. But this precisely fails to account for how there can be any such thing as gastronomic expertise, and why it would be any use. As any person who has taken a wine tasting course, or even spent time attending to tastes (for example, while learning to cook), knows people can learn to taste better. As Merleau-Ponty has shown us, perception depends on the intentional perceiver's engagement with the world; what I taste depends not on a physiological transaction but on my engagement with the world.

In a sense Shaffer's reduction to physiological elements, though it looks like the exact opposite of idealism, amounts to the same thing—everyday human experience is denied in favor of an abstraction that is only accessible to the few. Fundamental reality is located at the atomic level rather than in the world of the forms, but the effect is the same. That perception can tell us what the world is really like is denied.

Though we do not seek to invert the hierarchy of the senses, or to overthrow it, we must ask what effect the division of the senses from one another has had on the accounts philosophy has given of perception. What would be the case, we have asked, if Descartes had meditated on his piece of wax a little longer, asking not only what it would tell him about substance and properties, but also what it would tell him about objectivity and subjectivity? What if he had located his epistemological foundation not in thinking but in eating? Of course, when we are dealing with visual perception skepticism has great power, since anyone can experience visual illusion, or misjudgment. But what about when we eat? Is there any such thing as a gustatory illusion?

We have argued that taste, though in some ways rightly located towards the bottom of a "hierarchy of the senses," is deeply important in forming our understanding of the nature of the world and our relation to it. Importantly, the senses are only artificially divided from one another, and usually operate in a kind of unity in human life and experience.

The eighteenth- to nineteenth-century French vitalist philosopher Maine de Biran, in his discussion of the influence of habit on thought, remarks that

> The organs of touch and sight are essentially connected with each other through natural relations of motility and it is on this that the perfect coincidence and reciprocal transformation of their impressions especially depend. From the primary and uninterrupted co-operation of the two perceptions, visual and tactile, results a third which contains both, but which is neither

one nor the other by itself. For certainly (whatever idea one can have in other respects of the characteristic functions of sight) we do not see as if we were not accustomed to touch and we do not touch as if we had never seen.[37]

The fact that "common sense" relates all the senses to one another makes the operation of taste as a sense highly important in our self-understanding, because sensual objects, which can be seen and heard, can also be not only touched, but tasted, eaten. This analysis opens up to us something of the truth of human life, that it is intertwined with and part of a natural world without which it cannot subsist, but that it has the power to organize and manipulate.

Against the scientistic consensus, we are seeking to understand human subjectivity in its relationship to the world of nature, and to understand nature in the light of what it is to be human. For Aristotle, the human is the "rational animal"; but that is not to say that he is just an animal with rationality added. Indeed, this phrase may be better translated as the "speaking animal." What is distinctively human is not the operation of an autonomous will, but rather the imaginative development that is at work on his or her appetite. Humans' desire is articulated, and, in the process, transformed. For Kass, "it is the multiple activities of the mouth—speaking, ingesting, tasting—that are truly emblematic of the peculiarly human; the conjunction of the functions of articulate reasoning and nourishing in one organ is a sign of their possible interaction, as well as a reminder that the rational remains precariously animal."[38]

If the human is the speaking animal, it is also the hungry animal; and hunger, the subjective articulation of appetite, is connected to speech by more than just the organ with which both are associated. Both demand that we understand the freedom of the human being. The notion of freedom is complex, and I introduce it here on the understanding that it is not yet fully understood. Kass explains that

> Freedom (and the human difference) is demonstrable in diet. Whereas instinct guides the senses of animals generally to "choose"—which is to say, to take—foods that are salutary and to "reject"—which is to say, to leave—foods that are not, the human imagination presents to the will as attractive foods (and quantities of food) neither naturally (that is, instinctively) desired nor healthy.[39]

37. Biran, *The Influence of Habit*, 109–10.
38. Kass, *The Hungry Soul*, 80.
39. Ibid., 84.

Later in the book, Kass quotes Kant at length in a footnote. Kant discusses the meaning of Genesis 3 in his "Conjectural Beginning of Human History":

> So long as inexperienced man obeyed this call of nature all was well with him. But soon reason began to stir. A sense different from that to which instinct was tied—the sense, say, of sight—presented other food than that normally consumed as similar to it; and reason, instituting a comparison, sought to enlarge its knowledge of foodstuffs beyond the bounds of instinctual knowledge (3:6). This experiment might, with good luck, have ended well, even though instinct did not advise it, as long as it was at least not contrary to instinct. But reason has this peculiarity that, aided by the imagination, it can create artificial desires which are not only unsupported by natural instinct but actually contrary to it. These desires, in the beginning called concupiscence, gradually generate a whole host of unnecessary and indeed unnatural inclinations called luxuriousness. The original occasion for deserting natural instinct may have been trifling. But this was man's first attempt to become conscious of his reason as a power which can extend itself beyond the limits to which all animals are confined. As such its effect was very important and indeed decisive for his future way of life. Thus the occasion may have been merely the external appearance of a fruit which tempted because of its similarity to tasty fruits of which man had already partaken. In addition there may have been the example of an animal which consumed it because, for it, it was naturally fit for consumption, while on the contrary, being harmful for man, it was consequently resisted by man's instinct. Even so, this was a sufficient occasion for reason to do violence to the voice of nature (3:1) and, its protest notwithstanding, to make the first attempt at a free choice; an attempt which, being the first, probably did not have the expected result. But however insignificant the damage done, it sufficed to open man's eyes (3:7). He discovered in himself a power of choosing for himself a way of life, of not being bound without alternative to a single way, like the animals. Perhaps the discovery of this advantage created a moment of delight. But of necessity, anxiety and alarm as to how he was to deal with this newly discovered power quickly followed; for man was a being who did not know either the secret properties or the remote effects of anything. He stood, as it were, at the brink of an abyss. Until that moment

instinct had directed him toward specific objects of desire. But from these there now opened up an infinity of such objects, and he did not yet know how to choose between them. On the other hand, it was impossible for him to return to the state of servitude (i.e., to subjection to instinct) from the state of freedom, once he had tasted the latter.[40]

Kant's story here, which understands the narrative of the fall in Genesis 3 as about humanity's movement from being governed by instinct to its full freedom, is a brilliant reading of the text, which makes sense of the notion that prehistoric humanity could bring on itself, by the alteration of its habitual action, a freedom to which its descendants would be permanently bound, in so doing bringing about a deep alteration in the life of the species. But he makes a mistake, and it is a strange mistake to make in a discussion of eating. Kant sees that the human being becomes free, even that he or she becomes somehow inevitably free, but he makes this freedom absolute, without observing that man remains bound by his physical nature, by the hunger that is so implicated in his coming to freedom, and to the facticity of his condition, of which freedom becomes an inevitable part.

Freedom must always be understood in relation to the bodily necessity that makes it possible, which grounds it and guides it. This is not an absolute freedom, a Kantian autonomy. Again Levinas expresses something of this understanding:—

> Through labor and possession the alterity of nutriments enters into the same. [. . .] The body is a permanent contestation of the prerogative attributed to consciousness of "giving meaning" to each thing; it lives as this contestation. The world I live in is not simply the counterpart or the contemporary of thought and its constitutive freedom, but a conditioning and an antecedence. The world I constitute nourishes me and bathes me. It is aliment and "medium" ["milieu"]. The intentionality aiming at the exterior [. . .] somehow comes from the point to which it goes, recognizing itself past in its future, lives from what it thinks.[41]

This freedom within limits, the necessity of eating, and the freedom to choose what one eats, makes the hungry animal necessarily an ethical animal.

---

40. Immanuel Kant, "Conjectural Beginning of Human History," trans. Emil Fackenheim, in *Kant On History*, ed. Lewis White Beck (Indianapolis: Bobbs-Merrill, 1963), 55–56, cited in Kass, *The Hungry Soul*, 210.

41. Levinas, *Totality and Infinity*, 129.

Eating and Human Nature

We return, then, to Aristotle. Aristotle's philosophical anthropology is grounded in his metaphysics of form and material, and in the *De Anima* (which forms, for him, the introduction to a course of biological study), he gives an account of the soul that is both non-dualistic and non-reductive; for Aristotle the soul is the principle of life in the animal, that which animates; it is not a substance in the sense that the *res cogitans* is a substance, rather it is a kind of organization that is theoretically separable from the matter it actually organizes while depending on that matter.

Perhaps somewhat counter-intuitively, Aristotle calls matter potentiality, and form actuality.[42] That is, it is not the case that the form of a thing, its idea or essence, is a potential reality that must be actualized by attaching itself or being attached to a specific piece of matter. Rather, *matter* is potentiality, the site of true potency, which is to be actualized by attaining to organization, to more sophisticated levels of organization. Although Aristotle thinks that "it is of the actuality that they [that is, unity and being] are most properly said,"[43] clearly his metaphysics shows that this formal actuality is deeply intertwined with the matter that gives it potency: "so just as pupil and sight *are* the eye, so, in our case, soul and body *are* the animal. It is quite clear then that the soul is not separable from the body, or that some parts of it are not, if it is in its nature to have parts."[44]

What Aristotle takes to be essential to the soul and definitive of it is presented in various ways as the argument of the *De Anima* progresses, although Aristotle always thinks of it in terms of faculties, that is, of properties of an animal that differentiate it from things without an animal soul, and without life in general. In the second chapter of the first book he says "that which is ensouled is held to be different from that which is unsouled above all in two ways, in producing movement and in perceiving. These two are pretty much the things that we have received from earlier thinkers as main characteristics of the soul."[45]

Just a few pages later, these two things have been expanded to three—"the soul seems to be universally defined by three features, so to speak, the production of movement, perception, and incorporeality."[46] By the end of the first book, the list has been expanded into a more complex arrange-

---

42. Aristotle, *De Anima*, 156 (412a).

43. Ibid., 157 (412b).

44. Aristotle, *De Anima*, 158 (413a).

45. Ibid., 132 (403b).

46. Ibid., 136 (405b).

ment with six faculties arranged in two groups: "now the soul comprises cognition, perception, and belief-states. It also comprises appetite, wishing, and the desire-states in general. It is the source of locomotion for animals, as also of growth, flourishing, and decay."[47] I take the final sentence here to be an exposition of the first two, that is, I read Aristotle as saying that the soul has two classes of faculties: the inward-directed faculties of thinking, perceiving, and knowledge, and the outward-directed faculties of simple appetite, imaginative desire (*wishing*) and *desire states in general* (which might leave room for some other kind of outward-directed states), and that these two groups of states, roughly thinking and desire, together are productive of movement and change.

At this point Aristotle has dropped the earlier specification that the soul is "incorporeal," which was mentioned in his discussion of previous accounts of the soul, and drawn directly from them, presumably because it does not tell us very much. Soon after, in book 2, Aristotle enumerates the list of the faculties again differently—"the soul is the principle of these things that we have mentioned and is defined by these things, the nutritive, perceptive and intellective faculties and movement."[48] Here he recognizes (and he soon after goes on to develop the point) that anything that lives must have the capability to nutrify itself, which is to say to bring foreign matter under the influence of its organizing principle, so that the soul and the body that it makes possible persist while their essential matter changes. Only a few lines later Aristotle claims that "where there is perception there is also pleasure and pain, and where there are these, of necessity also appetite."[49] And soon after, Aristotle makes the four faculties five:

> The faculties we spoke of were the nutritive, perceptive, desider-ative, locomotive, and intellective, plants having only the nutri-tive, other living things both this and the perceptive. But if they have the perceptive faculty they have also that of desire.[50]

The way in which Aristotle enumerates the faculties continues to de-velop, and we shall not follow it any further, for we can see, at this point, why this is so. The faculties, though they name different aspects of the liv-ing being, are complexly related to one another. Aristotle claims that there can be no perception without that perception also engendering desire; one might object to this by citing examples where there would seem to be a kind

47. Ibid., 152–53 (411a).
48. Ibid., 160 (413b).
49. Ibid., 160 (413b).
50. Ibid., 162 (414a–b).

of perception without desire, such as those of *sensitive* plants like the venus fly-trap or of simple light-sensitive organisms, but it would seem rather that *perception* names a kind of sensitivity that carries within it a kind of judgment, and that therefore is necessarily marked by pleasure and pain, and so appetite might plausibly be a corollary of perception properly speaking, which would mark the difference between it and simple sensation. (This is not to suggest that there is clear distinction between things with and without the power of appetite, any more than there is between things with the power only of sensation and those that properly perceive, in certain boundary cases.)

The faculties are enumerated in a fluid way by Aristotle because there are "fuzzy" boundaries between them; appetite (of the kind I have called *hunger*) is a form of desire that has nutrition amongst its goals (although nutrition may well not be the only or even the primary goal), that depends on locomotion for the ability to find and take food, that itself depends on perception and intellection, and so on, and some forms of appetite might serve the goal of nutrition in such an automatic and plant-like way as to be almost totally indistinguishable from it. Since nutrition is the one faculty common to all living things, including the plants, it might be seen to be the end of all the other faculties: nutrition is served by appetite and locomotion (to desire and get the needed food), which are themselves informed by perception, intellection, and in the long term aided by imagination, which allows people to find new ways of feeding themselves. But at the same time, the need for nutrition is itself a means to the end of the exercise of all the other faculties, which only together make us what we are.

So, to re-introduce the term "hunger," as we understood it earlier, hunger might be seen to be essential to the human being insofar as it involves and depends on all that is fundamental to her existence, whether unique to the human animal or shared with the other animals. The goal of such hunger is *life*, in the sense of the preservation of meaningful organizations of matter in biological individuals, but also extending to the sense of the full expression of the essentially human through the exercise of the faculties. In this sense, then, we may think of the human being as the *hungry* animal:— humankind is always concerned with biological necessity; we must eat to live. But, more than that, I eat not only as one who affects the world around me by being more or less successful at surviving, reproducing, hunting, and so on. As we have said, following Marx and Engels, human beings produce the means of their own subsistence. As human beings, we *make* our food, in so doing transforming the world.

Where natural systems, which rarely attain to the ecological ideal of balance, are in near-constant flux, such change is governed not by a creative will but by the success or otherwise of the various species that comprise it at doing whatever it is that they do, guided by instinct. Men must also succeed in surviving, but what it is that they do is not given to them in so clear a way; they must decide what and how to eat, and their means of feeding themselves inevitably bear on the whole of the natural system of which they are a part. As the hungry animal, humanity is given responsibility not only for itself, but, in a sense, for all of nature, at least in so far as it is able to transform it, and in fact does so.

MIDDLE PART

The Crossing

3

The Old Ontology

> Our goal is to understand the relations of consciousness and
> nature: organic, psychological or even social. By nature we un-
> derstand here a multiplicity of events external to each other and
> bound together by relations of causality.[1]

IN PART ONE OF this book, I developed an embodied account
of perception on the basis of Merleau-Ponty's thought in the
Phenomenology of Perception, deepened through an investigation of
eating as a mode of perception, situating an embodied understanding
of perception in the history of philosophy with reference to eating as a
hidden theme of philosophical reflection. In Part Two, we will seek to
bring the non-dualistic ontology that this account of perception implies
to clearer expression. The present chapter forms a crossing-point between
the two parts, in which we interrogate the old, Cartesian ontology and
its problems, seeking to clarify the questions on which an alternative
ontology must be brought to bear.

When Merleau-Ponty died unexpectedly in 1961, he left on his desk a
copy of Descartes's *Optics*, a text to which he often returned. He had written notes on it in September and November 1959,[2] and had dealt with it at
length in *Eye and Mind*, his last writing published during his lifetime. Here
he condemns it for the effects it has had on contemporary thought, saying
"it is the breviary of a thought that wants no longer to abide in the visible
and so decides to construct the visible according to a model-in-thought.

---

1. Merleau-Ponty, *The Structure of Behaviour*, 3.

2. Merleau-Ponty, *The Visible and the Invisible*, 210; 217.

It is worthwhile to remember this attempt and its failure."[3] As the intellectual historian Martin Jay suggests,[4] Descartes is often considered to be the founding father of the visual paradigm of modern philosophy: precisely because he was no longer willing to "abide in the visual," as Merleau-Ponty puts it, he must establish contact between the mind and the visual world by making the visual abide in him; that is to say, he develops a notion of representation which attempts to cross the dualist chasm. This is not to say that the Cartesian ontology, of the separation of mental substance from extended substance, which bequeaths to modern philosophy all the problems of finding a bridge between the two (in the problems of epistemology, of knowledge and illusion, of representation, of freedom and determination, of mechanism and vitalism) is totally new; rather, it makes concrete a new form of visual dominance that goes back to Homer and the Stoics, was present in Augustine, that began to turn in a new direction in the Middle Ages as the early medieval imbrication of the senses gave way to an externalized account of vision, that found a crucial visual formation in the Renaissance invention of perspective, and that reached its philosophical zenith some time later in Descartes's formulation. For Rodolphe Gasché,

> Although it is true that the Augustinian notion of *reditus in se ipsum*—a return upon and into oneself constituting the medium of philosophy—prefigures the modern concept of reflection, the philosophy of reflection is generally considered to have begun with Descartes's *prima philosophia*. There are good reasons for this assumption, for in Descartes the scholastic idea of the *reditus* undergoes an epoch-making transformation, whereby reflection, instead of being merely the medium of metaphysics, becomes its very foundation. With Cartesian thought, the self-certainty of the thinking subject—a certainty apodictically found in the *cogito me cogitare*—becomes the unshakeable ground of philosophy itself.[5]

The theologian Catherine Pickstock writes that Descartes's "departure from the pre-Scotist notion of being as something with unknowable and unanalyzable depth, inaugurates the 'object' as a phenomenon."[6] In this reduction of the thickness of experience to the pure surface of a geometrical conception of the world, because it must locate within that world the reality of a human perceiver and their subjective experience, a reality that is

3. Merleau-Ponty, "Eye and Mind," 169.
4. Jay, *Downcast Eyes*, 70.
5. Gasché, *The Tain of the Mirror*, 17.
6. Pickstock, *After Writing*, 63.

fundamentally inimical to geometrical description, "there arises [. . .] an epistemological circuit whereby knowledge is based entirely on objects, whose 'being' does not exceed the extent to which they are known. Representation is now prior to ontology."[7]

For Descartes, this geometrization of external nature is established as an implication of the discovery of and progress in "the inventions which serve to augment" the power of sight, which are "among the most useful that there can be."[8] The discovery that light could be manipulated by lenses, that this could aid sight and correct it in its deficiencies, and that these lenses were discovered to be amenable to geometrical description and governed by geometrical laws made it seem clear that the operations of light are reducible to mathematics. Descartes makes an analogy through another form of a perception, with a blind man holding a stick.[9] And though this analogy could possibly have been used to re-install vision in the circuit of the body and of action, to build a sense of "visual palpation," the opposite was in fact the case. In fact, the man with the stick, the body, the eye, and the whole of nature (which thus required to have all psychic reality excised from it) were in this moment reduced to geometry. This finally confirmed Galileo's claim that "this grand book the universe . . . is written in the language of mathematics, and its characters are triangles, circles, and other geometric figures without which it is humanly impossible to understand a single word of it; without these, one wanders about in a dark labyrinth,"[10] and received mutual confirmation from it. As we see in the epigraph at the head of this chapter, Merleau-Ponty assumed the same conception of nature at the beginning of his first major work, *The Structure of Behaviour*. Nature is understood as an extended multiplicity of events, *partes extra partes*, in the phrase that Merleau-Ponty later came to use. The big question of Merleau-Ponty's philosophy, then—that of the relations of consciousness and nature—is determined in terms of a pre-existing understanding of nature as essentially geometrical. This thought of nature, of course, though it gained dominance in modern philosophy, was not really new even with Galileo; as David Abram notices, it goes back at least as far as Euclid.[11]

This Euclidean geometry, though, was soon to be called into question by Merleau-Ponty, in particular as he came under the influence of the thought of Husserl and took seriously Husserl's conception of the crisis of

---

7. Ibid., 63.
8. Descartes, *Optics*, 65.
9. Ibid., 66–68.
10. Galileo Galilei, cited in Abram, *The Spell of the Sensuous*, 32.
11. Abram, *The Spell of the Sensuous*, 198.

the sciences. For Husserl, particularly in his text *On the Origin of Geometry* (to which we will return), the Galilean revolution, which began the reduction of nature to geometrical space and its simple contents, had forgotten that geometry was grounded in an ideal abstraction from nature, produced by the human mind, and came to be held up as what was true in itself. As Albert Rabil (a commentator on Merleau-Ponty's thought) puts it,

> Galileo completed this revolutionary change by mathematizing all of nature, relegating the *Lebenswelt* so completely to the status of subjective appearance that the relation of knowledge of nature understood mathematically to men who live in the *Lebenswelt* became a problem. In short, the world was so objectified that subjectivity was completely lost. Galileo set the stage for the attempt, first made by Spinoza, to construct an ontology on the basis of geometry.[12]

Descartes simply carried this analysis to its logical next step by realizing the necessary separation of the psychical and the physical, because the construction of mathematical nature depends on an abstraction from the lived consciousness of things that are performed inside consciousness, and even when the abstraction of geometry is forgotten, there must be some geometer before whose mind the geometrical world is held. For Rabil, "Descartes' *epoché* was not radical enough: he suspended the physical world but not the psychical soul. The result was that the soul was placed in the body as a reality distinct from it, but just as abstract."[13] This dualism failed, as it inevitably must, to bridge the infinite chasm between the two realities, and philosophy turned to the strategy of eliminating one of the two by reducing it to the other; this lead to the empiricism and intellectualism which Merleau-Ponty opposes from the first. The dominance of scientific naturalism, which, for Husserl, occasioned the recognition of a crisis in science and in philosophy, had led to what one commentator calls "a nihilistic conception of reason,"[14] unable to approach questions of value, and, we would add, unable to think questions of situation, of freedom, and of relation: this is because the mathematization of nature, by its insistence that one point in space is homogeneous with but absolutely external to another, thinks that one point of observation is identical to another, that the observer always looks on dispassionately from an absolute distance, unable to form a notion of the mind among things because it is always governed by the contradictions of thinking of geometrical things as held in the mind as well

12. Rabil, *Merleau-Ponty*, 56.

13. Ibid.

14. Brown, "The Real and the Good," 7.

as existing in the pure space of physics, outside of every inside, and holding this together with the two realities considered as parallel but separate.

> Exterior nature is then reduced, according to Descartes, to extension. Extension possesses two characteristics: it is indefinitely visible, and to the extent that we can speak of points of extension, we must consider them as non-substitutable for one another; that is, each has its own locality. Each part is nothing other than its alterity in relation to the others. Hence, the result is that each part is a plenitude of being. In effect, each point being nothing other than its alterity, extension is the same in all of its points, with neither heavens nor reliefs. Extension is everywhere equally full, because it is equally empty. It is only what it is. That is why the exterior world will be wholly actual: there is no place for a difference between actual beings and possible beings, nor for a reshaping of the past or an anticipation of the future. There is neither more nor less in its simultaneous parts, any more than in its unfolding across time. By being placed in the point of view, we understand that conservation is implied in creation. The laws according to which the World is conserved are inscribed in its structure: as soon as it is created, extension is necessary.[15]

This Cartesian conception of nature as extension not only reinforces a visual understanding of nature, but also develops into a geometrical understanding of vision. This extensive, geometrical understanding tends towards a conception of sight as passive and surveying, precisely because it does not know how the mind is installed in the world; it has made of this question an insoluble problem by defining nature in terms that already exclude the mind. Despite Descartes's insistence on the intimate connection of mind and world,[16] the subject, in the Cartesian conception of vision, always ends up looking on from a distance.

The Dominance of Linear Perspective

The mathematized conception of nature fed back into and reinforced the particular kind of *visual* understanding of nature that had brought it to birth, making the human being's place in the world paradigmatically that

15. Merleau-Ponty, *Nature*, 126.

16. "Nature also teaches me, by these sensations of pain, hunger, thirst and so on, that I am not merely present in my body as a sailor is present in his ship, but that I am very closely joined and, as it were, intermingled with it, so that I and the body form a unit." Descartes, *Meditations*, 56 (Meditation 6, 81).

of a visual perceiver. We can see this happening quite clearly in Descartes's *Optics*, which (as the very word "optics" suggests) explains vision in terms of a set of geometrical operations on light, that are ultimately "perceived" by an eye that is modeled on the camera. As Hwa Yol Jung has it, "This reductive abstraction is a Cartesian trap in which everything is streamlined to edify the epistemological Panopticon of the *cogito* which, by being mesmerized by the eye, is turned into a scopic regime and ocularcentric machine."[17] The Cartesian "scopic regime" has roots that go beyond Galileo's mathematization of nature, though; the dominance of linear perspective had begun in the Middle Ages. Suzannah Biernoff, in her work *Sight and Embodiment in the Middle Ages*, notes that

> It would not be an exaggeration to say that geometrical "perspective"—from *perspicere*, to survey or scrutinise, to investigate thoroughly, to "see through"—became the metadiscourse of the later Middle Ages. As David Lindberg observes, because "optics could reveal the essential nature of material reality, of cognition, and indeed of God himself, its pursuit became not only legitimate, but obligatory." More than just an *object* of study, *perspectiva* was a way of seeing—and knowing—with certainty (*perspicue* means "with clarity of perception").[18]

This optics, crucially, was *not* an attempt to understand sight in its relation to bodies as they move around the world, to take seriously the importance of the location of the viewer in the formulation of perspective. Rather, it pretended to understand the nature not only of material reality but of God; that is to say, that perspective gives us an ideal of knowledge in which everything is in its place, viewed by a neutral and absolute observer. As Biernoff tells us, for observers such as Umberto Eco the development of the scopic regime was overwhelmingly positive; it is a move away from a fundamentally neurotic conception of the world. For Eco, what is missing in the pre-Renaissance understanding "was any conception, however slight, that nature had a structure of itself and was intelligible in itself."[19] Perspectivism constituted a move away from a symbolism that was the rejection of concrete reality, and of the attempt to understand nature in its own terms, preferring to understand it in terms of "a *super*natural world of order and

---

17. Jung, "Merleau-Ponty's Transversal Geophilosophy," 243.

18. Biernoff, *Sight and Embodiment*, 68, citing David C. Lindberg, *Theories of Vision from Al-Kindi to Kepler* (Chicago: University of Chicago Press, 1976), 99.

19. Umerto Eco, *The Aesthetics of Thomas Aquinas*, trans. H. Bredin (Cambridge: Harvard University Press, 1988), 141, cited in Biernoff, *Sight and Embodiment in the Middle Ages*, 9.

unity."[20] This claim is in the last instance a historical one that is not of primary concern here. But it seems problematic, in that the use of the idea of "the supernatural" is anachronistic and perhaps already begs the question: by excluding the dimensions of depth and meaning from a picture of nature, Eco relegates them to the "supernatural." But before the advent of a mathematized ontology, which called "nature" only that which could be understood on a geometrical model, there was no "supernatural" in this sense: there were hidden and poorly-understood aspects of reality, whose connections to the observed world we cannot fathom, as there still are. The notion of the supernatural that Eco rejects depends on a geometrical conception of nature, and so is unlikely to make sense of the medieval understanding.

My work here will be to present a case against Eco's claim. I will not expend great energy in an attempt to establish that a geometrical-perspectival account of nature is incomplete, although it should become obvious as we progress that such is the case. Rather, I will focus our attention on establishing that a different, non-geometrical account of nature is more plausible. I have nothing at stake in defending the worldview of the Middle Ages; but this worldview may to some degree agree with the ontology I will develop as an account of nature. Suzannah Biernoff seems to think so, claiming that

> Of modern theorists, Maurice Merleau-Ponty's insistence on the mind's incarnation (in a generalized "flesh" that exceeds individual bodies), and his metaphor of perceptual intertwining perhaps brings us closest to the reciprocal, corporeal flux of medieval vision.[21]

And this, for Merleau-Ponty, does not mean a return to the obfuscatory "theology" that renders the medieval thought of nature inaccessible to most.

> We could believe that the universe of facticity appeared at the moment theology was excluded from science. Yet this is not at all the case. There are theological perspectives that include facticity, and there are non-theological thought [sic] that do not have the feeling for it: "I do not need the hypothesis of God to explain the universe," Laplace will say, but this is in no way decisive. The very concept of Nature, such as it is often allowed by scientists, belongs to a conception that is entirely theological in its infrastructure.[22]

20. Biernoff, *Sight and Embodiment in the Middle Ages*, 9.

21. Ibid., 5.

22. Merleau-Ponty, *Nature*, 88.

Indeed, in these 1956–57 lectures on nature, Merleau-Ponty makes the striking claim, of Laplace's idea of nature (and in particular his *causalism*) that "at bottom, this conception is a theological affirmation, the affirmation of a view of totality capable of subtending all evolution of the world."[23] This is Laplace who, in his oft-cited reply to Napoleon's question about what place God held in his system, claimed "I have no need of that hypothesis." Laplace proposed a thoroughgoing causalism, such that if one knew the position and motion of every atom at a given point in time, one would know the whole history and future of the world. But this conception is essentially the ultimate formulation of a certain kind of dogma, and it is not a dogma that is able to stand any longer. "The determinist conception of intraworldy necessity is synonymous with Cartesian ontology, condemned by modern science."[24]

Science and the Observer

For Merleau-Ponty,

> To suppose Nature as being one sole truth is to posit a spectator for which this unique truth exists. Evidently, for Laplace, it is a matter of the mind of the scientist. But in making this argument, he defines thereby the ideal of knowing more than the mind of the knower. In fact, by positing such a natural being, such a thought posits a nature as *kosmotheoros*.[25]

The separation of the lived world from an idealized, mathematized nature transforms the scope of knowledge. Where knowledge had been based on what could be observed of the in-principle finite world in which we live, as knowledge became assimilated to mathematics it became possible to think of "grand theories" whose applicability is inexhaustible; everything became subsumed to the universal knowledge of geometry, and rather than knowledge of things being predicated on what *is*, being became predicated on what could be known: *possibility* came to be understood not as determined in terms of the limits of the world in which we live, but as logical possibility, as conceivability and calculability, and reinforced a promethean science to which it was linked. For Carolyn Merchant,

> The Baconian–Cartesian–Newtonian project is premised on the power of technology to subdue and dominate nature, on

23. Ibid., 89.
24. Ibid.
25. Merleau-Ponty, *Nature*, 135.

the certainty of mathematical law, and on the unification of natural laws into a single framework of explanation. Just as the alchemists had tried to speed up nature's labour through human intervention in the transformation of base metals into gold, so science and technology as the way to control nature and hence recover the right to the garden given to the first parents. "Man by the fall, fell at the same time from his state of innocency and from his dominion over creation. Both of these losses can in this life be in some part repaired; the former by religion and faith; the latter by arts and science." Humans, he asserted, could "recover that right over nature which belongs to it by divine bequest," and should endeavour "to establish and extend the power and dominion of the human race itself over the [entire] universe."[26]

There is no doubt that a mathematized conception of nature enabled great progress to be made in the sciences. Taking measurable extension as basic to the real made solving the problems of measurable extension possible in a new way: so it is that Galileo was able, by abstracting himself from his earthly position, to show that earth is revolving, in orbit around the sun, and orbited by its moon, and so on for the other known planets. The importance of this discovery and the scientific development in which it plays its part is not to be underestimated. But the success of this way of looking at the world has led to an unhinged commitment to it that can get in the way of human engagement with the world. Max Picard complains that

> in science today there is no real meeting between man and the object of his investigation. [...] Formerly the encounter between man and the object was an event: it was like a dialogue between man and the object under investigation. The object was given into man's care and keeping, and through the personal meeting with man the object became *more* and man became *more* because through the meeting he had helped the object to become more than it was before the meeting.[27]

This encounter, which Picard sees as desirable, in fact gets in the way of modern science since it undermines the division between neutral, mathematizable nature and the meaningfulness of human life. Fundamentally, it undermines the Cartesian distinction. As we will discuss later, Einsteinian relativity tried to think the relationship between the observer and the observed, and of course modern physics depends on thinking this relation. But, as Merleau-Ponty claims, Einstein does not go the whole way, he does

26. Merchant, "Reinventing Eden," 136, citing Bacon, *Novum Organum*.
27. Picard, *The World of Silence*, 76.

not yet reinstall the thinker as a body in the lived world; even after Einstein, science still tends to think of the world as present to an absolute observer who is outside it.

In Husserl's notion of the "Crisis of the European Sciences," the crisis is essentially this: that we are no longer able to think our situation, our situatedness amongst the things. Husserl's original project was that of seeking a rigorous, scientific grounding for philosophy, and his understanding of this project developed in such a way that he no longer understood the extant sciences to be a sufficient model for philosophy; for they themselves were not rigorously grounded in that phenomenal experience of our relation to the world. Whilst Merleau-Ponty was sympathetic to judgments against Descartes's philosophy, and especially those Husserl makes in the *Crisis*:

> The complexity of his position would be underestimated if he were to be classified as unequivocally critical of Descartes or as sharing Husserl's attachment to a specifically European destiny. [. . .] It is the Cartesian *legacy* that is primarily blamed here for having become a straight jacket that closed off Descartes's originally more open questioning. Descartes himself is credited with being a more complex and ambiguous thinker who was torn between radical doubt and edifying certainty.[28]

This whole notion of nature as pure externality excludes from itself notions that do not fit its requirements for clear and distinct perception and measurability. So, as we will see, mind must be totally abstracted from nature, and the connection between the two becomes *the* philosophical problem. Further, God, as Absolute Mind or as incarnate transcendence, must be excluded from the workings of the world (though a God may be postulated as its original source) except where no better explanation can be found; that is, God is pushed into the "gaps" in human knowledge; God becomes the best available hypothesis for the explanation of certain phenomena. God is also the only solution to the epistemological problem, the last and only bulwark against skepticism; in this role God really must be held apart from humanity in a kind of dogmatic deism. If this God were to surprise us, to step out of the determinations that epistemology lays down for him, a chaos of knowledge and all manner of trouble would result.

This is what Pickstock calls "ontology prised away from theology."[29] But by "theology" Pickstock means here something like "Christian Orthodoxy," and it will be crucial to understand that, though Pickstock is right that there are very deep ontological implications of the rejection of medieval theology,

28. Coole, *Merleau-Ponty and Modern Politics*, 31.

29. Pickstock, *After Writing*, 64.

the new situation does not leave ontology devoid of theology. It may, as we have suggested, derive its theology from its ontology rather than starting with theology, just as Descartes's philosophy requires a certain kind of God, to play a role that only a god can fill, that of guaranteeing his epistemology. The reality is likely that neither one nor the other is prior, but that this ontological change comes hand in hand with a theological development. What is "prised away" is the robust conception that the Middle Ages had of human beings' rich, sensual entwining in a world that exceeds them. The discovery of a geometrical conception of the world, which we have suggested comes partly through the discovery of optical technology, forces a question on us: If nature is essentially mathematical, *am I*? If nature works like a mechanism, am I also fundamentally mechanical? The medieval conception of the sensual imbrication of self, body, and world was, at least in part, linked to a theology that took seriously the doctrine of incarnation and the concept of incarnation. For Merleau-Ponty

> Descartes comes to conceive this type of extension by a method of purification, which is a step toward an essence. He undoes the unreflected communion with the World by striving to discern "objective reality" and to reduce it to what it can signify when we think it clearly and distinctly.[30]

Science (and indeed the whole of humanity) is now faced with pressing questions about the effects of human behavior on our ecosystem. The repercussions of those effects on forms of life, including our own, make the problem of the relationship between the observer and the observed world in science more urgent than ever. The objectivist conception of nature is not serving us well, and there is sudden shift in emphasis to an arena in which our science finds itself unable to maintain a neutral distance from its object, since its object (the climate, how it is changing, and how such changes affect life on earth) determines the future of humanity, and not only that, but also one's own future and that of one's children. For the environmental philosopher Ted Toadvine, "scientific naturalism is an insufficient basis for thinking the human relation with nature, as it relies on an ontology of positive beings that exist *partes extra partes*," and moves towards systems theory do not do away with that assumption. "The naturalistic tendencies of 'environmental' thought are therefore metaphysical in Heidegger's sense, adopting a standpoint outside the *phusis* they purport to describe, and treating nature, the human subject, and their relations in terms of presence and availability—ultimately in terms of *Bestand*, 'standing reserve.'"[31] This

30. Merleau-Ponty, *Nature*, 126.

31. Toadvine, *Merleau-Ponty's Philosophy of Nature*, 107–8.

limited understanding of environmental thought, which rests on the flattened, mathematical ontology that finds concrete formulation in Descartes's philosophy, "reveals the need for a richer, multifaceted philosophical investigation of nature, one that includes its ontological, epistemological, aesthetic, and theological dimensions, and that also appreciates the intertwining of the history of philosophical reflection on nature with the concept of nature itself."[32]

The limitations of the old, problematic conception of nature are beginning to be addressed by Husserl in the *Crisis*, but as the quote at the beginning of this section suggests, Merleau-Ponty needs more than the extant phenomenology of his time to overcome it. As David Wood sees, "Phenomenology was born out of resistance to the threat of naturalism." But to be able to think nature anew, "it must either rescue nature itself from naturalism, or work out a new relationship to what it had perceived as the danger of naturalism. Or both."[33]

For this investigation, the method of phenomenology alone will not suffice, and it is for this reason that Merleau-Ponty, as his thought progresses towards its final, ontological mode, draws on the thought of early twentieth-century intuitionist philosopher Henri Bergson, and his close contemporary, the process philosopher Alfred North Whitehead, in particular. Phenomenology's method of *epoché*, of reduction, and its commitment to intentionality are crucial, but the study of phenomena demands an understanding of its (bodily) situation, and it is here that Merleau-Ponty is influenced by Bergson's method of intuition. Bergson contrasts the analytic method of science to the intuitive method of what he calls metaphysics. In *An Introduction to Metaphysics*, he contrasts the absolute with the infinite, an analytical concept with which it has become confused. For him,

> An absolute could only be given in an *intuition*, whilst everything else falls within the province of *analysis*. By intuition is meant the kind of *intellectual sympathy* by which one places oneself within an object in order to coincide with what is unique in it and consequently inexpressible. Analysis, on the contrary, is the operation which reduces the object to elements already known, that is, to elements common both to it and other objects.[34]

This intuitive method thus takes seriously the notion that there is more to be understood than the unfolding of some pre-established way of things in time, whether according to mechanistic law or to a finalistic

32. Ibid., 6.

33. Wood, "What is Eco-Phenomenology?," 211.

34. Bergson, *An Introduction to Metaphysics*, 23–24.

pre-established harmony. As Thomas Goudge puts it, "if things are merely realizing a program previously arranged, no creativity and therefore no genuine change are occurring. In that case, 'time is useless.'"[35]

The Exclusion of Mind from Nature

The geometrical-perspectival conception of nature, we have said, made possible modern science in all its success. It now grounds the attempts of some brain science to identify the physical bases of consciousness, not solely as that which makes consciousness possible, but as that to which consciousness can, finally, be reduced. If the mind just *is* the brain then thoughts just *are* physical events, and the Cartesian enigma, the problem of how mental substance can interact with physical substance, can be dissolved. Unfortunately it is not clear that this will be possible; not because it is too difficult, but because it would seem that there is more to thought than physical events, even if it can be explained entirely in terms of them.

To describe thoughts in terms of electro-chemical interactions will be to miss what is important about them, i.e., to fail to really describe thoughts. To explain to someone how their behavior is absolutely mechanistically determined, or probabilistically determined, in virtue of its being part of a very complex determinate physical mechanism or of some kind of quantum system, will not do away with the necessity of their choosing. Whatever consciousness looks like from the "outside," it will still have an inside that cannot be captured in the same way. In an essay on Merleau-Ponty's relationship to the thought of Gilbert Ryle, Gabrielle Bennet Jackson writes,

> Gilbert Ryle is credited with identifying and opposing "the Dogma of the Ghost in the Machine." But Ryle was not just interested in exorcising the Ghost. He was also occupied in dismantling the Machine. [. . .] Ryle simply was not interested in defending the claim that all statements about the mind are translateable into statements about mechanical bodily behavior. Indeed, he rejected this claim outright. "If my argument is successful," he wrote, "the hallowed contrast between Mind and Matter will be dissipated, but dissipated not by either of the equally hallowed absorptions of Mind by Matter or of Matter by Mind, but in quite a different way."[36]

35. Goudge, "Editor's Introduction," 18.

36. Jackson, "Skill and the Critique of Descartes," 65–66. The citations are from Gilbert Ryle, *The Concept of Mind* (Chicago: University of Chicago Press, 1949) pp. 11, 15–16, and 22.

This is in part due to the fact that thought deals with structured patterns of part and whole that cannot be adequately accounted for by a three-dimensional geometry. Merleau-Ponty takes up this idea in his early work, drawing on the thought of the gestalt psychologists: As Toadvine has it, "the position established in *The Structure of Behaviour* is foundational because it aims to reconcile mind and nature" and so to move from the purely transcendental Husserlian philosophy to a philosophy that is reinstalled in the body and the lived world "by starting from the holistic and meaningful configurations already encountered in the perceptual world." Merleau-Ponty's notion of "structure" is the necessary ground for the possibility of "behavior," which cannot be determined in any simple way, but must in some sense organize itself. "*Structure* characterizes the natural world as a self-organizing system of 'gestalts'—embodied and meaningful relational configurations or structures. Physical matter, organic life, and conscious minds are increasingly complex strata of such gestalts."[37] This helps to explain the necessity, for Merleau-Ponty, of thinking the perceived world not as distinguished from the *world as it is* but as grounding any idea we might have of the world as it is: "the function, 'figure and ground,' has a meaning only in the perceived world: it is there that we learn what it is to be a figure and what it is to be a ground. The perceived would be explicable by the perceived itself, and not by psychological processes." Reducing perception to atomic physical sensations will fail to get to grips with perception as a structured phenomenon at all.

> On the basis of a word as a physical phenomenon, as an ensemble of vibrations in the air, no physiological phenomenon capable of serving as a substrate for the signification of the word could be described in the brain; for we have seen that, in audition and also in speaking, a word as an ensemble of motor or afferent excitations presupposes a word as a melodic structure and this latter presupposes a sentence as a unity of signification.[38]

The idea of a melody is often used to explain this gestalt notion. As the ecological philosopher Arne Naess puts it, "Whatever the part of the melody that is heard, the particular character of the whole influences the experience of the part." A melody is not made up of parts, just as a perception is not made up of atomic sensations. "A 'part' of a gestalt is more than a part. That is, if we listen to a part of an unknown melody the experience is different from listening to that part when the melody is known."[39]

37. Toadvine, *Merleau-Ponty's Philosophy of Nature*, 21.

38. Merleau-Ponty, *The Structure of Behaviour*, 92.

39 Naess, "Reflections on Gestalt Ontology," 119.

The melody example is helpful insofar as it introduces the dimension of time, in the sense that Bergson's thought demanded: time as felt *durée* rather than as space stretched out along a line. Euclid's geometry, of course, was not concerned to deal with time but only with space. Galileo, however, in plotting the paths of the planets around the sun had to conceive of a time that was absolute and linear, like a fourth dimension of Euclidean geometry. No longer was this notion of time tied to the time of the earth as structured by years, seasons, day and night, but rather was stretched out as an "empty container," like Euclid's space, in the unstructured time of the sun, which relativizes the structured times of the motions of the planets. This notion of time, and of the universe working as a great machine or a celestial clock, occasions the development of geometrism into mechanism.

As we moved from a picture of the world constructed and operating according to the unchanging laws of a God or gods to one based on the ability of humans to construct self-regulating systems in the form of machines, the "geometric" view of the physical world as a pure for-itself, divided from an in-itself that is totally alien to nature, develops into the "mechanistic" view, which seeks to explain the apparent appearance of the for-itself (as subjectivity, desire, freedom, intentionality, and purpose) in terms of the in-itself: what looks like something alien to the "natural world" of particles in motion is in fact just a very complicated machine that is ultimately reducible to them. In this way I understand mechanism as a development of geometrism that presents fundamentally the same problems (though they may be superficially different). David Abram, a Merleau-Pontyan environmental philosopher, argues that it was Descartes who firmly established in modern thought the notion that material reality could be spoken of in strictly mechanical terms, building on Galileo's abstraction of physicality from all subjective experience.[40] Merleau-Ponty himself says that "when we think of space, we think of an intellectual unity (cf. *Geometry*, 1637); when we see it, we find ourselves faced with juxtaposed parts. The mode of action in this real extension can only be movement; hence Cartesian mechanism."[41] Merleau-Ponty goes on to make a distinction between the mathematical and mechanical conceptions of nature whose continuity we have here been emphasizing:

> Spinoza, on the contrary, does not recognize this opposition between real extension and extension in thought. The relation between the two terms is a wholly different relation; an intrinsic relation, a correlation between the idea and its *ideatum* (*idéat*).

40. Abram, *The Spell of the Sensuous*, 32.
41. Merleau-Ponty, *Nature*, 15–16.

> The idea of intelligible space and the idea of perceived space are separated only by a difference of more or less finite ideation. Likewise, mechanism is also not found in Spinoza: mathematics envelops all. Physical actions are no longer reduced to the transports of movement, but rather to intelligible relations. The possible and the actual are equivalent.[42]

The mechanical notion of nature, it seems clear, lies behind that empiricist realism, which Merleau-Ponty rejected along with a rationalist intellectualism which would seem to derive from the mathematized notion of nature that paved the way for mechanism. Thus, though their philosophical out-workings might be different, they stem from the same root, and, as we saw in the first chapter, they share the same fundamental problems.

In *The Structure of Behaviour*, animality constitutes for Merleau-Ponty a level of being that exceeds the purely physical. This is not to say that it is non-physical; it is closer to Aristotle's understanding of the animal as possessor of an "animal soul," which is not a substance but its "principle of life." An animal, unlike the non-living, displays behavior properly speaking. To say that the animal behaves is to say that what it does is not to be understood in terms of mechanical cause and effect but rather in *vital* terms; what it does is not simply obey the laws of physics but rather obey some kind of internal law. In his first major work, Merleau-Ponty gives an extended analysis of reflex behaviors in humans and animals, showing how reflexes that seem to be explained by a theory of pre-established correlations, on a mechanistic model, between stimulus and response,[43] in fact respond to and are conditioned by global elements as well as by immediate stimuli. In this way experimental results problematize the mechanistic understanding of reflexes.

Merleau-Ponty uses gestalt theory to develop an understanding of reflex behaviors as a basic case of behavior properly speaking, which responds to its environment, its milieu, in a manner that is not mechanistic but that takes account of the animal's total situation, relating this to the notion of *Umwelt* in the proto-ecologist Jacob von Uexküll. Merleau-Ponty gives many examples, just one is that of a person whose reflex response to a jarring mis-step varies according to whether he is walking uphill or downhill: If I mis-step, for example I catch my foot on root, while walking uphill, "the flexor muscles of the foot are suddenly relaxed and the organism reacts by accentuating this relaxation, which will liberate my foot." But the reflex response is different when I am walking down a hill. "If [. . .] I miss my step

42. Ibid., 15–16.
43. Merleau-Ponty, *The Structure of Behaviour*, 8.

while coming down a mountain and my heel strikes the ground sharply before the sole of the foot, the flexor muscles are once again relaxed suddenly, but the organism reacts instantly by a contraction."[44]

The variation in response is conditioned by what psychologist Kurt Goldstein calls "the holistic utilization of stimuli,"[45] and the response is conditioned by the meaning of the situation to the organism. Merleau-Ponty deals with manifold examples, many of them quite complex, in the first two sections of *Structure*, on "Reflex Behaviour" and "Higher Forms of Behaviour," which demonstrate animal behavior of this kind: what Merleau-Ponty calls behavior is precisely this kind of action that responds to a total situation understood as a structured relation between the animal and his environment. In his late lectures on *Nature*, Merleau-Ponty's thought is still determined by this structured behavior; there he writes, "The body belongs to a dynamic of behaviour. Behaviour is sunk into corporeity. The organism does not exist as a thing endowed with absolute properties, as fragments of Cartesian space."[46] This understanding of behavior must totally escape the geometrical conception of nature.

Merleau-Ponty's use of the word "behavior" is a response to the behaviorism that held sway amongst many psychologists in his time, and continues to do so. According to Albert Rabil, "If the adequacy of a scientific theory depends on its ability to account for the phenomena, then behaviorism fails,"[47] because, as Merleau-Ponty has shown, it cannot account for the changing reactions according to global, structural conditions at the level of the organism and because the notion of "stimulus" itself cannot be adequately defined without reference to the organism's structured relation to its *Umwelt*. In the philosopher Mary Midgley's striking phrase, the division between behaviorism and introspectionism in psychology has reduced that field "to the state in which the study of teapots would be if one half of the people engaged in it were sworn as a matter of professional pride never to mention the inside of a teapot, while the other half were just as unwilling ever to mention the outside."[48]

And as Rabil is keen to make clear, this dispute is not simply a methodological one. It is a philosophical matter, with roots that go back at least as

---

44. Ibid., 45.

45. Goldstein, *The Organism*, 166, cited in Merleau-Ponty, *The Structure of Behaviour*, 45.

46. Merleau-Ponty, *Nature*, 183.

47. Rabil, *Merleau-Ponty*, 6.

48. Midgley, *Beast and Man*, 108–9.

far as Plato, that seeks to isolate a simply-defined domain of the "real" that escapes the complexity and ambiguity of our primary intuitions.

> The problem is to give a philosophical explanation of the structure of behavior which will not be subject to the criticisms that can be brought against idealism and materialism. What is necessary for this task is an "enlarged reason" which can deal with the lived world without reducing it to mind or matter, without bifurcating it, and without declaring it unintelligible.[49]

Merleau-Ponty uses the notion of *Umwelt* (deriving from von Uexküll, via Husserl) as the correlate of the notion of behavior. His project in *The Structure of Behaviour* involves showing that reflex actions are not purely mechanistically determined. They can no longer be thought to belong purely to the order of the in-itself. But neither are they of the order of the for-itself: they are not the result of acts of will nor of freedom on any normal understanding of that word; neither are they compelled or determined. They belong to the order of the living being acting in response to its world; not its *bloße Sachen* physical surroundings but its *Umwelt*, its environment.

So behavior is *not* a result of consciousness or of thinking, of the cognitive order, but of the vital order of animality. This order will ground the mental and bind it to the physical order, but behavior, as contemporary Merleau-Pontyan philosophers William Hamrick and Jan van der Veken observe, does not depend on consciousness.[50]

Gestalt Ontology and Human Exceptionalism

Arne Naess, in his short article "Reflections on Gestalt Ontology," notes that "thinking in terms of gestalt ontology implies rejection of at least one central part of Gestalt Psychology, but certainly not all."[51] He notes that Husserl almost entirely rejected gestalt psychology, and certainly Merleau-Ponty criticizes its adherents for, in the words of Forrest Williams, "failing to live up to their own findings [. . .] he in effect accused them [in *The Structure of Behaviour*] of running with the hares of gestalt theory while hunting with the hounds of Cartesian dualism."[52] That is to say, they were willing to investigate the operations of the mind in gestalt terms, but not to apply these

---

49. Rabil, *Merleau-Ponty*, 9–10.

50. Hamrick and Van der Veken, *Nature and Logos*, 169.

51. Naess, "Reflections on Gestalt Ontology," 126.

52. Williams, "Appendix 1: Merleau-Ponty's Early Project Concerning Perception," 147.

terms to their understanding of the "real world": they confine structure to the mind and expel it from nature.

> The "gestalt ontology" proposed in *Structure* anticipates later systems-theoretical descriptions of nature by treating physical, vital, and mental structures as nested sets of holistic relations. Yet gestalts in Merleau-Ponty's sense are irreducible to systems in the realist's sense of this term, no matter how holistic or relational, because the gestalts of which reality is composed are essentially perceptual. Nature at its most fundamental level is meaningful and experiential; its structures manifest the kind of unity and coherence that characterizes perceptual wholes.[53]

This claim, made by Ted Toadvine, might initially seem confusing: on the one hand, gestalts are not systems in the realist's sense, they are structures of perception. Yet nature itself is fundamentally characterized by these structures. We would normally think that perception belongs in the mind, and not in the extended reality of nature. But this helps us to see that we are still too Cartesian. For Merleau-Ponty, the perceived world is basic, the fundament from which extended nature must be abstracted. And the perceived world is always already structured. Toadvine goes on,

> According to Merleau-Ponty's analysis, vital form is more than simply a complex physical system because it introduces original and irreducible properties inexplicable at the physical level. [. . .] Consequently, the organism is oriented toward a "milieu" or "environment" distinct from the world described by physics.[54]

Toadvine goes on to spell out that just as the vital order cannot be reduced to the physical order, so for Merleau-Ponty in *The Structure of Behaviour*, the human order cannot be reduced to the vital.

> On the one hand, the description of the vital level allows us to reconceive the emergence of human consciousness from a level of perceptual involvement within which it remains oriented toward the physiognomies and sensible configurations of the world, rather than the "true" objects of the scientific realist. But the specifically human dialectic transcends this "lived consciousness."[55]

53. Toadvine, *Merleau-Ponty's Philosophy of Nature*, 21.

54. Ibid., 82.

55. Ibid., 82–83.

In the previous chapter we proposed that we might consider the human being as "the hungry animal." Do we need to look for *the* difference between human beings and other animals, and other forms of life? In part, as Teilhard de Chardin suggests, we do need to understand humanity in its difference from other animals, because we are human. And on the face of things, humans seem to play a different role on the life of the planet than do most other animals.

But does Merleau-Ponty's distinction between the "vital" and the "human" in *The Structure of Behaviour* betray his anti-dualistic motivation and constitute a problematic exceptionalism? It is a good start, at least, to acknowledge that humans are animals and that their humanity is not divorced from their animality, as Merleau-Ponty does. And we may think that his use of the term "human" to name the highest order of being is incidental; it is an order that we encounter in other human beings, and there is nothing in principle that would prevent us from acknowledging it in other beings if we were to find it in them. Further, as Merleau-Ponty's philosophy develops he ceases to use the term "human" to describe the order of thought, as his complex reflections on animality in the lectures on nature show. Nevertheless, there remains a structural difference between some human behavior and common animal behavior, of which we may sensibly try to give an account. Midgley suggests that "instead of a single distinguishing mark for man, we look rather for a knot of general structural properties."[56] Indeed, to think about nature is to demand that we be able to give an account of our difference from it. As the contemporary philosopher Kate Soper puts it

> all ecological injunctions—whether to sacrifice our own interests to those of nature, or to preserve nature in the interests of our future well being, to keep our hands off it, or to harness it in sustainable ways, to appreciate the threat we pose to nature or to recognize our kinship with it—are clearly rooted in the idea of human distinctiveness. For insofar as the appeal is to humanity to alter its ways, it presupposes our possession of capacities by which we are singled out from other living creatures and inorganic matter.[57]

For animals, their engagement with the world is determined by a relatively fixed orientation to their environment that is for the most part given by the demands of their species. These demands may be labile at an evolutionary level; indeed, they must be so if one species is to emerge from another. But this lability belongs to the animal in its lived dialectic with its

56. Midgley, *Beast and Man*, 243.

57. Soper, *What is Nature?*, 40.

Umwelt and to the interaction of animal and world in a way that is very different from human lability. Animals are not, for the most part, labile at the lived level. This need not be a matter of absolutes, and indeed later, as the implications of Merleau-Ponty's thought on this matter are being worked out more fully in the notes for the lectures on *Nature*, Merleau-Ponty will take the view that animality does attain this lived lability, precisely where we see what is properly human prefigured in animality. He writes of "strange anticipations or caricatures of the human in the animal," as the human body emerges "as different from the animal, not by the addition of reason, but [. . .] in the *Ineinander* with the animal [. . .] just as higher life appeared as singular points of physical Nature."[58] So "we must say: Animality and human being are given only together, within a whole of Being that would have been visible ahead of time in the first animal had there been someone to read it."[59]

On Hamrick and Van der Veken's understanding, Merleau-Ponty needs, if he is to establish a new ontology, to achieve a "double overcoming," doing away with the philosophy of consciousness that is still suggested by his earlier thought, and overthrowing "the Galilean-Cartesian concept of Nature that, as he stated in his first nature course, 'still overhangs contemporary ideas about Nature,'"[60] and that we all too often fail to notice in their privileged position, still highly determinative of our thought. Merleau-Ponty addresses both these problems in the terms of his continued development of a new understanding of perception, one that continues to privilege vision but that does so in order to overturn the Cartesian scopic regime. We will turn, in the following chapter, to interrogate and to develop a Merleau-Pontyan understanding of vision, as a route towards this "double overcoming." This will lay the ground for the positive development of the ontology of flesh, which is brought to expression in the human orientation to the virtual: "humans have the capacity to vary their points of view and adopt an orientation toward the virtual as such, toward the 'structure of structure' itself,"[61] writes Toadvine, and this orientation to the virtual, which arises from and is prefigured in perception, reorientates life towards a single, "true" world of inter-corporeality, reconfiguring the physical through expression and desire. For Merleau-Ponty, in the notes for his *Nature* lectures, "the human body is symbolism—not in the superficial sense, i.e., where a representative

---

58. Merleau-Ponty, *Nature*, 214.

59. Ibid., 271.

60. Hamrick and Van der Veken, *Nature and Logos*, 2. The citation is from Merleau-Ponty, *Themes from the Lectures*, 67.

61. Toadvine, *Merleau-Ponty's Philosophy of Nature*, 83.

term takes the place of another,—but in the fundamental sense of: expressive of another. Perception and movement symbolize."[62] But this symbolism leads us not into a world of thought determined by symbols, not into intertextuality, but into history. My own body in its historicity rejoins nature, and sediments there its operations of expression and desire, to find itself necessarily involved in the world of praxis and of politics, as Merleau-Ponty had already anticipated in 1947:

> What accounts for there being a human history is that man is a being who externalizes himself, who needs others and nature to fulfill himself, who individualizes himself by appropriating certain goods and thereby enters into conflict with other men.[63]

62. Merleau-Ponty, *Nature*, 219.

63 Merleau-Ponty, *Humanism and Terror*, 102.

PART TWO

Ontology

4

"Restoring Sight to the Blind": Towards a Renewed Understanding of Visual Perception

> We see the things themselves, the world is what we see: formulae of this kind express a faith common to the natural man and the philosopher—the moment he opens his eyes; they refer to a deep-seated set of mute "opinions" implicated in our lives. But what is strange about this faith is that if we seek to articulate it into theses or statements, if we ask ourselves what is this *we*, what *seeing* is, and what *thing* or *world* is, we enter into a labyrinth of difficulties and contradictions.[1]

THE MODERN ONTOLOGY (WHICH is characteristic of the "objective thought" against which Merleau-Ponty argues in *The Phenomenology of Perception*) tends to think of nature as "pure externality" that stands in contrast to the pure internality of subjectivity. This contrast is expressed in the dominance of linear perspective in image-making. This *perspectiva artificialis* in turn reinforces an understanding of seeing as something like looking through a window; as static, passive, distanced, and separated from the other senses. We have seen, in the first chapter, how Merleau-Ponty challenges the objectivist notion of perception through the notion of reversibility, which extends from its conspicuous role in the sense of touch to a subtler but equally important place in the sense of sight. I have spoken of the perceptual faith, which is necessary for perception to serve

1. Merleau-Ponty, *The Visible and the Invisible*, 3.

as a ground of knowledge. We have then thought through the notion of perception on the basis of the sense of taste and eating more generally, rather than the sense of sight, which philosophy has traditionally made paradigmatic for perception. I questioned there the notion of the hierarchy of the senses and suggested briefly that the senses might be best understood in their relation to one another, referring to Merleau-Ponty's thought that the separated senses are abstractions from a primary synaesthesia. In this chapter I will attempt to synthesize a new model of vision that will help us to develop an ontology of flesh on the basis of Merleau-Ponty's thought, and in the next I will develop this ontology in terms of Merleau-Ponty's notion of *institution* and the logic of incarnation implied in this ontology.

Sight in the Cave

Martin Jay observes that our ordinary language is deeply marked by metaphors of vision, and that our cultural understanding of vision is entwined with a philosophical construction, which thus affects human history in its unfolding. Religious understandings, from primitive sun-worship to sophisticated metaphors of light in developed theologies, are closely related to our thinking about sight.[2] Manichaean Gnosticism and Zoroastrian dualism strongly divide the light of the sacred from the corrupt and sometimes evil heaviness of the material world; the popular quasi-Christian eschatology of contemporary capitalism views heaven as a bright, weightless world of pure light opposed to the darkness and suffering of bodily life.[3] The spiritual truth-seeker is sometimes viewed as the bearer of a third sight, the seeing of the "eye of the soul," and this can be contrasted to the frailty of bodily sight, or (as, for example, in Augustine) be seen as higher than but continuous with bodily sight,[4] or, more strongly (as in St. John of Damascus's *On the Divine Images*) as the completion and fulfillment of bodily sight, which is not conceived as lower than but as a necessary precursor to spiritual sight.[5]

2. Jay, *Downcast Eyes*, 12–14.

3. For example, see Maria Schriver, *What's Heaven?* (New York: St. Martin's Press, 1999), quoted (disapprovingly) by the former bishop of Durham, Tom Wright, in *Surprised by Hope*, 24: Heaven "is somewhere you believe in. [. . .] [I]t's a beautiful place where you can sit on soft clouds and talk to other people who are there. At night you can sit next to the stars, which are the brightest of anywhere in the universe."

4. For Augustine, "corporeal vision is ordered to the spiritual, and the spiritual to the intellectual." *The Literal Meaning of Genesis (De Genesi ad Litteram)*, trans. J. H Taylor (New York, 1982), book 12, ch. 8.20, cited in Soskice, "Sight and Vision," 34.

5. "We are led to the understanding of divine and immaterial things by using material images" John of Damascus, *On the Divine Images*, 35.

Nevertheless, suspicions of terrestrial sight have often dominated religious movements, as in the Islamic rejection of figural representation, amongst the Byzantine iconoclasts with whom John of Damascus argues, and motivating the *Beeldenstorm* of the Reformation.

For theologian Janet Soskice, Jay's implicit claim that the Christian tradition is for the most part anti-ocular or anti-oculocentric is hard to resolve with the beauty of medieval cathedrals, whose architecture so powerfully leads the eye, as well as with Byzantine icons, early Renaissance painting, and so on.[6] There has been great variety in attitudes to vision within Christianity and in religious traditions more generally, and no "monolithic" position can be taken for granted, although it is clear that orthodoxy affirms the place of vision as at the very least instrumental for knowledge of God and knowledge of the world. Soskice rightly claims that we can certainly say that patristic and medieval aesthetics were driven by theological concerns and in this regard are very different from modern understandings of vision, in crucial ways. The overlapping concerns of humanist science, Protestant iconoclasm, and Puritan nonconformism, in Britain especially, were bound up with the rise of deism, which conceived of God as distant from the world, as the one who views the world from a pure outside, rather than being incarnated in it, and of human rationality as belonging to a Cartesian soul whose relation to the world is contingent, rather than to an essentially corporeal, sensual human body. Soskice observes, "not surprisingly, man was soon to discover that he could dispense with the divine hypothesis and do his 'God's-eye-viewing' for himself. This doctrine is perhaps the early modern theological background of the gaze."[7] To this topic of the gaze as the normative model for vision, and its alternative, the glance, we shall return later.

Jay is also uncompromising in his insistence on the importance of understanding the metaphor of sight for philosophy in general. "The development of Western philosophy cannot be understood," for him, "without attending to its habitual dependence on visual metaphors of one sort or another."[8] The shadows in Plato's cave, Augustine's divine light, Descartes's need for ideas that are clear and distinct before a steadfast mental gaze, and indeed the very notion of enlightenment, depend on a privileging of the eye above the other organs of sense. "Whether in terms of speculation, observation, or revelatory illumination, Western philosophy has tended to accept without question the traditional sensual hierarchy."[9]

6. Soskice, "Sight and Vision," 36.
7. Ibid., 37.
8. Jay, *Downcast Eyes*, 186–87.
9. Ibid., 187.

The twentieth-century phenomenologist Hans Jonas emphasizes, with Merleau-Ponty and so many other recent thinkers on vision, the importance of movement for sight:

> What is obvious in the case of touch, seems at first inapplicable to the case of sight: that its cognitive feat should depend on movement. For was not the point of our essay precisely that sight is the sense of the passive observer par excellence? That to look at things, at the world at large, is compatible with a state of complete rest, which even seems the optimal condition for visual attention and contemplation? Was not even the whole opposition of "theory versus practice," and hence of the *vita contemplativa* versus the *vita activa*, derived from this very aspect of vision? This still stands. Yet we should not be able to "see" if we had not previously moved. We should, e.g., not see the world arranged in depth, stretching away from us indefinitely, if we were not more than seeing creatures: if we were not creatures that also can move into space and have done so in the past.[10]

This begins to show us the problem with one of the oldest metaphors in philosophy, that of Plato's Cave, from *The Republic*. This allegory comes at the end of a trio of examples Plato gives to demonstrate how the ideal "Good" relates to the government of his republic. The first example is the Simile of the Sun, which already conceives sight under a certain passive conception and understands knowledge of the good under an analogy with it. In the visible world, the sun is the source of light and of growth, making sensible objects visible and thus making possible visual perception, the exercise of the faculty of sight. Similarly, in the world of the Platonic Forms, the Good is the source of reality and truth, making the objects of thought intelligible and thus making possible knowledge, the exercise of the faculty of knowing.[11]

Plato follows this with the analogy of the Divided Line, in which reality is divided again into the two orders of visibility and intelligibility. The visible order is subdivided into two further orders: the order of illusions, reflections, and shadows, and that of physical objects. Plato's extreme rationalism is highlighted by his ascription of the world of physical objects (and, in the later *Timaeus*, the physical sciences)[12] to the domain of belief (*pistis*), as opposed to the (uncritical) reasoning of mathematical knowledge (*dianoia*) and the full knowledge of the Forms (*noesis*), which, though attained

10. Jonas, *The Phenomenon of Life*, 154.

11. Plato, *Republic*, 245 (507a).

12. Plato, *Timaeus*, 40 (§3, 28a).

by the use of assumptions, does not depend on them and is able to revise all true knowledge (of the forms) by derivation from knowledge of the highest principle, the Good.

After these two preparatory examples we get to the famous allegory of the Cave, in which prisoners have been secured immobile since childhood, able only to see a wall onto which are cast the shadows of puppets moved around by persons behind them, by the light of a fire they are unable to see. These shadows and their accompanying noises would seem fully real to these prisoners who knew nothing else. And if one of the prisoners were released, he would shrink from the light of the fire and of the outside sun, and, if he were forced nevertheless to continue, the things he saw would at first seem fantastical to him. Eventually "he would come to the conclusion that it is the sun that produces the changing seasons and years and controls everything in the visible world, and is in a sense responsible for everything that he and his fellow-prisoners used to see."[13] If he were to return to the cave he would find himself unable to see, and the other prisoners would think that his visit to the upper regions had ruined his sight, and would resist if anyone tried to make them go up there.

The elegance of this allegory has led to its becoming one of the best known in the history of philosophy, and it has acquired a force greater than that given to many arguments, though it is not an argument, but a story; and its force is limited by some basic problems. As we hope to make clear, the "sight" of those bound in the cave has become the model on which philosophers understand sight, that of a passive viewer unable to move, looking at a depthless image and somehow having to reconstruct from this a whole world. But the inhabitants of Plato's cave cannot truly be living beings; they do not eat, and were they to eat they would not think of the world of shadows as a greater reality than the world of tastes. If there were no further contrivance to prevent them from seeing their food in the dim light of the fire, then they would know the difference between the tangible world to which their food belonged and the specular world of the shadows. And as contemporary philosopher Slavoj Žižek notes in *The Parallax View*

> There is a deeper problem here [. . .] which could be best put in Hegel's terms. We can, of course, start with the naive notion of people perceiving true reality from a limited/distorted perspective, and thus constructing in their imagination false idols which they mistake for the real thing; the problem with this naive notion is that it reserves for us the external position of a neutral observer who can, from his safe place, compare true

13. Plato, *Republic*, 258 (516b).

> reality with its distorted mis(perception). What gets lost here
> is that all of us *are* these people in the cave—so how can we,
> immersed in the cave's spectacle, step onto our own shoulder, as
> it were, and gain insight into true reality?[14]

The bifurcations of the dividing line are based on a model of things that can only be presumptuously conceived. The analogy of the light we see, and its source in the sun, is needed to get there, only to be discarded as the "belief" of inferior knowledge of physical things compared to the true knowledge of the contemplation of the forms. And this model of sight as the purely passive reception of the sun's light is problematic.

In *The Sense of Space*, David Morris describes *Atlan*, a work of art by James Turrell seen in 1986 in the Musée d'art contemporain de Montréal. In a darkened room, the viewer sees a rectangle of blue light on the wall, which looks like that light cast by a projector without any input, as if there is some technical problem or a projected video has ended. He wonders what he is really supposed to be seeing.

> The whole experience is obscure, ambiguous, and vague. So you
> wander around. You discover there is no projector playing the
> beam. As you move, you perceive that the rectangle doesn't sit
> right; there is something strange, disturbing about it. I would
> put it this way: your movement provokes a queasy question as
> to the being of the rectangle, it directly provokes ontological
> unease. Eventually, you discover there is neither a flat rectangle
> nor a wall behind it: there is a rectangular hole in the wall, and
> behind it a ganzfeld, a uniformly lit room (in this case lit with
> ultraviolet light). Where you perceived a flat rectangle, there is
> nothing.[15]

For Morris, this example shows us how in normal perception, we have a sense of the inexhaustibility of things, the fact that they transcend any perspective we have on them, and its connection with the inexhaustibility of the places in which we have our perceptions of things, that they constantly change as we move about in relation to them through the available space.

By contrast, we could say that the Platonic prisoners in the cave do not have an experience of sight at all; there is no "place" available to them but only the confusion of a pure and passive reception of sense-data based on light entering the eyes.

---

14. Žižek, *The Parallax View*, 162.
15. Morris, *The Sense of Space*, 109.

Sight as Representation

Visual perception has been understood, at least since Plato's cave, on the model of representation. The shadows on the cave wall of the analogy are soon redoubled as the inner representation of outer things. The information carried by light enters the eyes, but must be reconstructed in some way, by the soul, the mind, or the brain, into something inside that is knowable. On this model, the inner reconstruction of something outer is the *very meaning of perception*. What would it be to deny this? If perception is not inner representation, what can it be?

Although this issue is not directly addressed in the *Phenomenology of Perception*, the critique that Merleau-Ponty gives there of the intellectualist and empiricist accounts of perception does imply a challenge to representationalism. As we saw in our first chapter, Merleau-Ponty argued that perception cannot be an aggregation of sense-data, because if those sense-data are reconstructed according to a model given by the perceptual object, then it is that model and not the sense-data that is the basis of the perception. And if they are not reconstructed according to a pattern given by the object but rather according to a pattern conceived in the perceiver's mind, then it is hard to see that what is happening is truly perception rather than imaginative reconstruction. This confusion between perception and imagination, which Todes saw in Kant, is what must be picked apart.

Sight is strictly bound up, for Merleau-Ponty, with the existential dimension: "I have only to see something to know how to reach it and deal with it, even if I do not know how this happens in the nervous machine."[16] My seeing is intertwined with action in such a way that "my mobile body makes a difference in the visible world, being a part of it; that is why I can steer through the visible." But by the same token, vision is attached to movement and determined by action; it is not a purely passive process. "We see only what we look at. What would vision be without eye movement?" But if it is correct to say that it is not purely passive, how does the active element in perception contribute to it? Does it not falsify what is seen, introducing distortion into sight? Merleau-Ponty asks "how could the movement of the eyes bring things together if the movement were blind? If it were only reflex? If it did not have its antennae, its clairvoyance? If vision were not prefigured in it?"[17] What can it mean, then, for vision to be prefigured in sight?

16. Merleau-Ponty, "Eye and Mind," 162.

17. Ibid., 162.

For Merleau-Ponty in "Eye and Mind," it is still the case that "the enigma is that my body simultaneously sees and is seen."[18] The self who sees is not transparent, like the self who thinks or who imagines. Indeed, this difference between perception and imagining is crucial for Todes's account of what is wrong with the Kantian model of perception, in which conceptual categories must be applied to the data of sense; he calls this Kant's "imaginizing" of perception. The imagination itself does not wander around among the imagination's contents; the faculty of the imagination is the world to which imagined objects belong. But this is not so for perceived things; they do not belong to perception but to a perceived world in which the perceiver and his faculty of perception are implicated and themselves appear.

> Visible and mobile, my body is a thing among things; it is caught in the fabric of the world, and its cohesion is that of a thing. But because it moves itself and sees, it holds things in a circle around itself. Things are an annex or prolongation of itself; they are incrusted into its flesh, they are part of its full definition; the world is made of the same stuff as the body.[19]

We have imagined vision as if it were the operation of a mechanical device, as if the eye were an analogue of the camera. But the camera only transforms light from one mode into another; to understand the mechanics of seeing, and of light, as Descartes so lucidly does in his *Optics*, is by no means to account for seeing. This is not so for painting, and Merleau-Ponty makes a case for this in "Eye and Mind." The painter "is obliged to admit that objects before him pass into him"; painting presupposes having seen and made sense of the world (although in no sense having an "explanation" of the world or an answer to its questions). The world that the painter paints is a purely visible world, in which, nevertheless, the invisible appears: that is to say, the painter makes an image, but the image is not just paint or light but also meaning. "Painting awakens and carries to its highest pitch a delirium which is vision itself, for to see is to *have at a distance*,"[20] and while photography and the optical model of seeing it is built on can reveal the mechanics of light (and so explain how the lens gathers the light from a distance into a single plane, collapsing the distance) it can do nothing to explain what it means to *have* the object of sight. The seer grasps the world in its relation to himself, drinks in that world, but affects it, moves around in it, shapes it, and changes it. The operation of seeing is much closer to that of painting than to that of a camera. This is not to disparage photography,

18. Ibid., 164.
19. Ibid., 163.
20. Ibid., 166.

for the photographer is more than a camera, and often shapes his image in an art similar to the painter's; as the casual photographer knows, the hardest photograph to take can be the one in which things are made to appear *as they really look*, in spite of the camera.

So it is that, like a ghostly photograph, vision admits essence and existence, imaginary and real, visible and invisible, mixed up and sometimes dream-like. Descartes's *Optics/Dioptric* (the name of the text has been translated in both ways) is an attempt to un-mix them, to meet Descartes's epistemological requirement of "clear and distinct" vision. As we have mentioned, this book was found open on Merleau-Ponty's desk after he died unexpectedly in 1961. In his essay published a year earlier, he had written "it is worthwhile to remember this attempt and its failure." Of course, to call the *Optics* a failure is not uncontentious; it is the earliest full statement of the theory of refraction, and as such was important in the early days of the construction of microscopes, telescopes, and corrective lenses. What Merleau-Ponty means is that while it may help us to find technical solutions to optical problems, it fails to help us understand what it is to *see*. Descartes's theories of reflection and refraction as explained in the *Optics* are explained in terms of the imagined action of a small ball thrown at a hard surface or puncturing through a thin cloth. This makes light an "action by contact" and dispels "the whole problem of vision" by doing away with "action at a distance."[21] So, Merleau-Ponty says, a "Cartesian does not see *himself* in the mirror; he sees a dummy, an 'outside,' which, he has every reason to believe, other people see in the very same way but which, no more for himself than for others, is not a body in the flesh."[22] The last lens in the optics of sight is there, the retina, the mechanical subject of vision, but no seer can appear since there is no real sight. It is clear that understanding the mechanics of sight will not and cannot lead us to make sense of what it is to see.

With regard to representation, it is to Descartes's credit that, though he has no theory of how mechanical vision in the domain of *res extensa* becomes psychological sight in the domain of *res cogitans*, he denies that the action of light produces an inner mental representation of what is seen. Where Kepler and Leonardo knew that the workings of the eye as understood would produce an inverted image on the back of the retina, they assumed that there must be some mechanism by which the image was reinverted, since we see things the "right way up." Kepler also assumed that there must be some mechanism by which the two retinal images are combined, in the brain, into a single mental image. Descartes recognized the

21. Ibid., 170.
22. Ibid., 170.

problem with this view, writing "It is necessary to beware of assuming that in order to sense, the mind needs to perceive certain images transmitted by the objects to the brain, as our philosophers commonly suppose," which images, we philosophers assume, must resemble the objects that they stand for, though we cannot understand how such resemblances would persist through the change from object in the world to object in the brain.

> And they have had no other reason for positing them except that, observing that a picture can easily stimulate our minds to conceive the object painted there, it seemed to them that in the same way, the mind should be stimulated by little pictures which form in our head to conceive of those objects that touch our senses; instead, we should consider that there are many other things besides pictures which can stimulate our thought, such as, for example, signs and words, which do not in any way resemble the things which they signify.[23]

And it would seem that, whilst Merleau-Ponty uses Descartes's geometrism as a foil, and finds problems in his account of vision that ultimately stem from his metaphysics, we see here the brilliant Cartesian insights that kept driving Merleau-Ponty back to him: while there is no composite inner mental picture that the soul sees, "rather, [. . .] it is the movements of which the picture is composed which, acting immediately on our mind inasmuch as it is united to our body, are so established by nature as to make it have such perceptions."[24] Descartes sees the problem with the homunculus theory, which just repeats the problem of perception "inside the mind." For him the inverted retinal image is not a problem, since we do not "see" the retinal image, it is just a link in the mechanical-causal chain that transmits visual sense from world to mind. As regards the problem of the synthesis of the two retinal "images," Descartes recognizes this also as a false problem deriving from the mistake of thinking that the retinal "images" are pictures that we see; we do not think it a problem if I touch something on my right with my right hand and something on my left with my left hand (or vice versa), nor indeed do we normally think that we need an explanation of why I do not seem to perceive two different objects if I touch the same thing with both hands.

---

23. Descartes, *Optics*, 89.

24. Ibid., 101. This recognition of the great advance that Descartes made over Kepler, and over many more ancient theorists of vision, I owe to Noë, *Action in Perception*, 44.

Later on Merleau-Ponty explains: "my act of perception, in its unsophisticated form, does not bring about this synthesis." That is, the synthesis that perceptual experience presupposes,

> benefits from work already completed, from a general synthesis constituted once and for all. This is what I express by saying that I perceive with my body or with my senses, my body and my senses being precisely this habitual knowledge of the world, this implicit or sedimented science.[25]

This is easier to grasp with regards to tactile perception because we do not there have to deal with the complication of our tendency to think of perception as forming an "inner image," as we do with visual perception. There is no mechanism by which the two retinal images are combined into a single mental image; rather, my lived body is the incarnate principle of their joint and several access to the world.

The denial of an inner visual representation seems to require a reformulation of certain visual problems. The philosopher Alva Noë, in *Action in Perception*, takes up the example of perspective deformations, for example, in the case that we see a plate from the side as elliptical, but we immediately interpret it as round. The image of the circular plate seen as comparable to a two-dimensional ellipsis he calls the *perspectival shape* of the plate, in contrast to its actual shape, and, under normal circumstances, its perceived shape. For Noë, we perceive the plate as round because we understand the transformations the perspectival shape undergoes as we move around the object. We have an implicit grasp of the "sensorimotor profile" of the plate.[26] So seeing the plate as round depends on the tacit knowledge that, looked at from a certain perspective, it is round. But this would seem to leave us with a problem, since all elliptical things will look circular from two perspectives, just as all rectangular things will look square from two perspectives; but some things look circular and some things look elliptical but not circular. Why? There must be some kind normative perspective that determines them, but where could such norms derive from? Not simply from our moving around an object but from our use of it. A plate is circular not just from the perspective of being directly above it when it is on the table, but also from the "perspective" of eating from it.

The reason we have to learn to see things as appearing deformed, and the reason the formulation of linear perspective was such a momentous turning point in the history of art, is because things *do not* appear to us as

---

25. Merleau-Ponty, *Phenomenology of Perception*, 247.

26. Noë, *Action in Perception*, 78–79.

deformed, but as a certain shape; as circular, in the case of the plate. We can, under poor conditions for seeing things, mis-recognize their shapes; more often we see them indistinctly and either they are ignored or are perceived in a questioning way as a thing about which we are unsure. We only know that an illusion has occurred when we see a thing in a new light, from a perspective that gives the object a new shape because we can identify a new norm for its shape. The perspective deformations of linear perspective are an abstraction from this prior form of perception. The *look* of things, which Noë is happy to attribute to perspective, is not inexhaustibly variable but rather stable, and so is related (as we will see, and as etymology would suggest) to the Aristotelian notion of visible *species*.

Noë uses the twentieth-century psychologist of visual perception J. J. Gibson's notion of perceptual invariants to explain the difference between the perceived thing and its perspectival "look":

> As you move around a rectangular table, you perceive its vary-
> ing trapezoidal perspectival shape. The perspectival shape var-
> ies as your spatial relation to the table varies. In this pattern of
> variation, however, there is invariance. Mathematically what
> is invariant is the relationship between the four angles and the
> four sides and their proportions. This invariance corresponds to
> the actual shape of the table. Active exploration of the occlusion
> structure presents you with the actual shape of the table. The
> invariant structure of reality unfolds in the active exploration
> of appearances.

For Noë, this position helps us to see that whilst phenomenalism is wrong, it gets a certain amount right about sense perception—that there is a difference between the "data" our senses receive and what we perceive. It seems that Noë is reluctant to accept the consequences to which his "enac-tive" view of perception seems to lead; he must allow for some objective account of the "look" of things because his thought is still committed to a certain kind of objectivism, a naturalism that preserves the remnants of Cartesian dualism. The natural consequence of the fact that we see *things* and not *images*, that perception offers not atomic sense data but a world that is independent of any judgment or synthesis of the contents of perception, would challenge this naturalism by suggesting that the meaningful contents of perception are really there in the world and not simply produced in my head. He struggles to hold together the claim that what he calls "looks," perspectival appropriations of objects, are "objective, environmental prop-erties," though dependent on the relations of light, object, and perceiving body, with the claim that "what is encountered in perception is not sensational qualities or sense data, but rather the world."[27]

This claim seems problematic. First, as I have already argued, a given "shape"—understood as an invariant structure that is perceived as a certain set of sensorimotor possibilities, insofar as its perspectival shape (or P-shape) will vary in certain understood ways as we move around it—is not experienced as a set of perspectives, but simply as a shape. What is it about the circular plate that makes its shape normatively understood as specifically circular rather than as broadly elliptical and subject to a certain set of perspectival deformations? It would seem that the plate's circularity is something to do with its being functionally or existentially circular; that is, that when eating from it, it takes up a circular part of the space of the table with which you are reckoning in using motor skills to get food from the table into your mouth. But how is the knowledge that the flattened, "round" P-shape of the plate is normative related to our sensorimotor knowledge that links that P-shape with the other possible, elliptical P-shapes? Perhaps by the knowledge that if it does not look round, I am not close enough to it to eat from it. The normativity of "circular" as the shape of the plate depends on more than the variation of the P-shape; from Noë's perspective the shape that is taken as normative would seem to be conventional or arbitrary. But I want to argue that the plate *really is* round, and this is a property not of the way we usually use it but of the plate itself. For this to be the case, there must be something more than an invariance to the plate, there is an invariance that is specified in some way, that has a *sens* in the full set of implications of that French word; it has a kind of material meaning, an orientation. The set of perspectival shapes that can present the plate in thought are not primary; indeed, I want to argue, they do not present the plate at all, but *it presents them*. We see the plate as a circular thing without difficulty; seeing it as elliptical must be learnt.

Sartre's *Look*

The historian of culture and aesthetics Peter de Bolla, in an article on visuality in Lacan, shows how Lacan's account of the gaze is directly influenced by that of Sartre. For him, "[t]he gaze, as conceived by Sartre, is the gaze by which I am surprised—surprised in so far as it changes all the perspectives, the lines of force, of my world, orders it, from the point of nothingness where I am."[28] But Lacan rejects this phenomenological analysis. For

27. Noë, *Action in Perception*, 85.

28. Lacan, *Four Fundamental Concepts*, 84, cited in Bolla, "The Visibility of

Sartre, subjectivity is thought of in terms of a single point of "nothingness" in which is contained our absolute freedom, and this "for-itself" is installed in the midst of the "in-itself" world of things as an alien in a foreign land. This makes the encounter with the "look" of another strange, since "through the look I experience the Other concretely as a free, conscious subject who causes there to be a world by temporalizing himself toward his own possibilities."[29] She and I both are absolute nothingnesses in a world of positivity, but Sartre's conception of subjectivity is strangely solipsistic, so that I cannot recognize the Other as a subject who mirrors my own subjectivity. The Other appears as a limit, so that when I feel myself looked at, as the object of another's gaze, I feel myself objectified, as identified, for the looker, with an object, my body, which, in Sartre's philosophy, has very little to do with the real self of subjectivity. As objectified in this way I feel *shame*, for Sartre; recognizing the Other as subject reduces me to an object before their subjectivity.[30]

Lacan uses three diagrams, which de Bolla cites and which I reproduce here.[31]

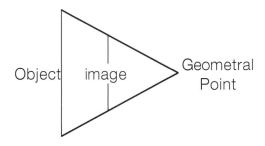

This first image is a model of the relationship constituted by the objectifying gaze, and it is in many ways familiar; it corresponds to the basis of Leon Battista Alberti's formulation of linear perspective, in which the image reproduces at one remove the pattern of light as it would converge on a single geometrical point. Lacan notes that, on this understanding of vision as the operation of a monocular gaze, the subject is "vanished away,"[32] and this would seem cognate with Sartre's Cartesian reduction of the subject to a singular point of nothingness.

Visuality," 66.

29. Sartre, *Being and Nothingness*, 247.

30. Ibid., 247–78.

31. The original images appear in Lacan, *Four Fundamental Concepts*, 91; 106.

32. Bolla, "The Visibility of Visuality," 68.

The art historian Stephen Melville argues that this Sartrean conception of vision is the same as that which Frederic Jameson condemns as *"essentially* pornographic,"[33] which is to say that, as in Sartre's example of the voyeur looking through the keyhole, the looker is understood as absolutely outside the scene he looks at on this model. Although the sexual dimension of perception should not be given priority here, we want to say that in contrast to Sartre's pornographic or onanistic voyeurism, Merleau-Ponty's idea of vision will be more full-bloodedly *sexy*. The one I look at is a "thick" subject, desirable precisely because she escapes me, because she is not reducible to an object, but constitutes a second person. This Thou, in the best case, in mutual recognition confirms my bodily existence as an expressive realization of an "I," though there is not full coincidence between our subjectivities, because expression is not transparent. In sexuality I relate to the other as another subject-object or body-subject; but this does "not mean that the body is the transparent envelope of Spirit [*l'Esprit*]."[34] So it is that

> We must recognize, without any doubt, that modesty, desire, and love in general have a metaphysical signification. That is, they are incomprehensible if we treat man as a machine governed by natural laws or even as a "bundle of instincts," and that they concern man as consciousness and as freedom.[35]

Sartre's "obsessive hostility to vision"[36] makes a positive metaphysics of intersubjectivity absolutely impossible; his narcissistic account of "the look" excludes the possibility of love in favor of a solipsistic kind of desire, making for a "problematic epistemology" which is bound up, as we are seeing, with "the hegemony of space over time" and with the domination of nature, as Jay has it, producing "profoundly disturbing intersubjective relations and the construction of a dangerously inauthentic version of the self."[37]

---

33. Jameson, *Signatures of the Visible*, 1, cited in Melville, "Division of the Gaze," 103.

34. Merleau-Ponty, *Phenomenology of Perception*, 163.

35. Ibid., 169–70, translation modified. (*Phénoménologie de la perception*, 194).

36. Jay, *Downcast Eyes*, 276.

37. Ibid., 276.

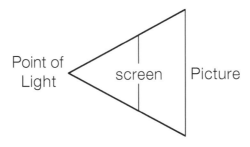

The second Lacanian image is the inverse of the first, and represents the Sartrean shameful subject, the object of the gaze observed from a single point in space to which his fullness feels reduced, not to an intention or to an awareness but to a simple "point of light." It will be noted here that this Sartrean *agon* of the gaze is a transformation into visual terms of the Hegelian narrative of Master and Slave. It is Hegel who calls the "disparity [. . .] between the 'I' and the substance which is its object"[38] the *negative*, providing the basis for Sartre's understanding of subjectivity as nothingness. For Hegel's dialectic, the synthesis of *recognition*, which must be the ground of self-consciousness, begins with the conflict that occurs when

> self-consciousness is faced by another self-consciousness; it has *come out of itself*. This has a twofold significance: first, it has lost itself, for it finds itself as an *other* being; secondly, in doing so it has superseded the other, for it does not see the other as an essential being, but in the other sees its own self.[39]

If the first image portrays the perspectival reduction of the world to a geometry characteristic of idealism, the second portrays the same reduction as it occurs in empiricism, in which seeing is reduced to operations on rays of light brought to a point. The "screen," Lacan insists, is the only way the subject can appear as a picture, and this structurally mirrors the empiricists' mistake of thinking that the world's appearance on a screen of some kind (the painting, the retina, the "inner representation") helps us to understand what it is to see.

---

38 Hegel, *Phenomenology of Spirit*, 21.

39. Ibid., 111.

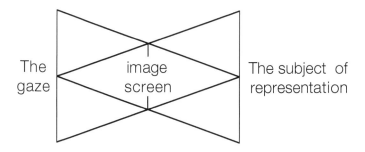

Lacan's third image combines these two and displays a thicker conception of subjectivity, no longer oscillating between two unstable states but combining the two as seer–seen, subject–object. This conception is better, but it does not do away with the logic of nothingness that Sartre inherited from Hegel: the self is now seen as filling a space between the nothingness of freedom and the pure positivity of the object, but still the conception of sight as a reduction to a single point remains. The spreading-out of sight, between the two eyes, across time, in a moving body, engaged with its objects in a bodily relation that exceeds visual apprehension, is still missing.

The links between a geometrical ontology and the optical understanding of sight are becoming more obvious. Sartre's account of the look also begins to reveal to us the location of these difficult conceptions of things in relation to a theological notion, an understanding of God that similarly removes all thickness and dissolves an incarnational understanding into total transcendence. For Sartre, shame depends on the encounter with the Other as objectifying subject, but this subject can appear as a "they," and if I posit an eternal "they" "I thereby posit the eternity of my being-as-object and so perpetuate my shame. This is shame before God; that is, the recognition of my being-an-object before a subject which can never become an object."[40] Sartre's theology locates God as the absolute observer before whom the believer is an object with regards to the absolute. "I posit my being-an-object-for-God as more real than my For-itself; I exist alienated and I cause myself to learn from outside what I must be. This is the origin of fear before God."[41] Indeed, Sartre calls the existence of the Other "my original fall,"[42] as if it were just this other with whom my freedom must contend that stops me from being a God.

Melville, too points up the implicit theology of Sartre's position, in which the big-"O" Other is the only true "first person," is "he who sees

40. Sartre, *Being and Nothingness*, 266.

41. Ibid., 266.

42. Ibid., 239.

without being seen" and before whom "all others are merely others with a small 'o.'"[43] Every second-person relation is denied, there is only subject and object of the gaze, no intersubjectivity, and the God in whom Sartre disbelieves is conceived as ultimate voyeur, looking through a keyhole into a dirty world, but not susceptible to being discovered as are those upon whom he looks. As the art critic John Berger has it, the invention of (artificial) perspective centers the world around the single, immovable eye and so "The visible world is arranged for the spectator as the universe was once thought to be arranged for God."[44] For Martin Jay,

> If the beholder was now the privileged center of perspectival vision, it is important to underline that his view*point* was just that: a monocular, unblinking fixed eye (or, more precisely, abstract point), rather than the two active, stereoscopic eyes of embodied actual vision, which give us the experience of depth perception. This assumption led to a visual practice in which the living bodies of both the painter and the viewer were bracketed, at least tendentially, in favor of an eternalized eye above temporal duration.[45]

The conception of sight has, in many different ways, sought to bridge the gap between the mind and the world by collapsing light into an absolute, geometrical point that crosses between the worlds of mind and nature. As is possible in Lacan's diagram, this point's unintelligibility it resolved by thinking it as an illusory mirror image: the mind is brought to a point on the surface of the mirror; and the "nature" that seems to appear on the other side is in fact just a reflection of the mind, for idealism, and vice versa for empiricism. The dualism is collapsed into a monism in which it is claimed that only one side of the mirror image (whichever side I think of as the side I am on, depending whether I think of my experience of the world or the world I experience as primary) is "really there." It is this confusion that a conception of vision drawing on the philosophy of Merleau-Ponty seeks to escape.

On Jay's account, Merleau-Ponty's philosophy, like Sartre's, is preoccupied with vision. But unlike Sartre's, rather than accepting an account of emasculated vision that condemns man to imprisonment in his individuality, Merleau-Ponty's philosophy suggests and to some degree develops avenues for understanding vision that escape the Cartesian scopic regime.

43. Melville, "Division of the Gaze," 104.

44. John Berger, *Ways of Seeing* (London: Penguin, 1972), 16, cited in Jay, *Downcast Eyes*, 54.

45. Jay, *Downcast Eyes*, 54–55.

In Jay's critique of anti-oculocentrism in twentieth-century French thought, Merleau-Ponty is the sole figure who provides a way forward from this wholesale rejection of the importance of vision. Merleau-Ponty's version of phenomenology may "plausibly be called a heroic attempt to reaffirm the nobility of vision on new and firmer grounds than those provided by the discredited Cartesian perspectivalist tradition."[46]

Descartes and the *Optics*

Descartes's assessment of pictures in the *Optics* is based on consideration of copper plate etchings, which by their nature can only present geometrical line, without color, texture, or shade. Merleau-Ponty criticizes him for understanding etchings on the model of language. For Descartes, though an etching may represent things, it does not resemble them. "It is only a bit of ink put down here and there on the paper."[47] Perspective deformations preserve the differences from the scene itself which make an engraving a representative image and not a resemblance. Merleau-Ponty tells us this because

> What interests us in these famous analyses is that they make us aware of the fact that any theory of painting is a metaphysics. Descartes does not say much about painting, and one might think it unfair on our part to make an issue out of a few pages on copper engravings. And yet even if he speaks of them only in passing, that in itself is significant. Painting for him is not a central operation contributing to the definition of our access to Being; it is a mode or a variant of thinking, where thinking is canonically defined according to intellectual possession and evidence. It is this option that is expressed within the little he does say, and a closer study of painting would lead to another philosophy.[48]

How, exactly, is a theory of painting a metaphysics? Merleau-Ponty explicates this point in dialogue with Descartes's views on depth. Descartes deals with copper engravings, which involve no color, but only line, the outline or envelope of things, and this implies already an ontology like that of modern scientism, for which color is not a real property of things but only a feature of our perception of them. The only primary properties are those

---

46. Ibid., 298.

47. Merleau-Ponty, "Eye and Mind," 170. Cf. Descartes, *Optics*, 90.

48. Ibid., 171.

of extension: ultimately, of line. "If he had examined that other, deeper, opening upon things given us by secondary qualities, especially color, then [. . .] he would have found himself faced with the problem of a conceptless universality and a conceptless opening upon things." For Descartes, the perspective offered by this outline is the essence of the image: it makes us see a space where there is none. But without any understanding of lived space, this can only be a mathematical space, an arrangement of points in pure emptiness. The image effaces itself, dematerializes itself in order to construct a "rational" space that enforces a depthless and emasculated notion of reason. In the twentieth-century German art historian Erwin Panofsky's essay on linear perspective (which reached its full development in the Renaissance) he writes

> In order to guarantee a fully rational—that is, infinite, unchanging and homogeneous—space, this "central perspective" makes two tacit but essential assumptions: first, that we see with a single and immobile eye, and second, that the planar cross section of the visual pyramid can pass for an adequate reproduction of our optical image. In fact these two premises are rather bold abstractions from reality, if by "reality" we mean the actual subjective optical impression.[49]

We must notice that when Merleau-Ponty speaks of a theory of painting, he is not speaking of an aesthetics in the straightforward sense of an analysis or exegesis of paintings or of images generally. He is talking about a theory of the act of painting, an understanding of what it is that the painter does. This, crucially, introduces the expressive element of the painter's art to our thinking. Noë clarifies this for us in chapter 5 of *Action in Perception* when he comments that Ruskin's understanding of the act of painting as a recovery of the "*innocence of the eye*" is mistaken if it is taken to mean that painting means reproducing a childish vision: representing things in their innocence, as we have said in commenting on Noë's position, is indeed a difficult art to learn, is "to view it with great sophistication, stepping back from the way we naturally view it when we take our experience at face value."[50] For Noë, the aim of phenomenology is to "catch experience in the act of making the world available,"[51] and this is close to what Merleau-Ponty seeks to do in his later work. This means showing the world as it *appears*, in contrast to the child's picture, which simply displays the world as it seems to the child. But because Noë so reifies *appearance* (particularly in the form

---

49. Panofsky, *Perspective as Symbolic Form*, 30.

50. Noë, *Action in Perception*, 172.

51. Ibid.

of his "perspectival properties") his account of the success of Cubism seems awkward. By contrast, Merleau-Ponty takes the painting of Cézanne as paradigmatic.

In "Cezanne's Doubt," Merleau-Ponty argues that, having broken with the Impressionists, Cézanne wanted to "return to the object" without letting go of the Impressionist commitment "which takes nature as its model," that is, to representing *sensation* rather than *sight*. Cézanne's painting does not, though, show how our true perceptions of things emerge from perspectival sensations, as Noë would have to say. Merleau-Ponty speaks of the distortions of Cézanne's work between 1870 and 1890, saying "cups and saucers on a table seen from the side should be elliptical, but Cézanne paints the two ends of the ellipse swollen and expanded."[52] But these distortions are an inevitable product of what Cézanne is trying to do:—he paints things as they look (the plate as circular) but at the same time in a comprehensibly "visual" arrangement (unlike the child's painting or some primitive kinds of representation), and what he captures is not just sensations concrescing into an object but also the perceived object fracturing into multiple presentations, breaking down into the perspectival representations of it which are characteristic of our human mode of perception, which make it not just an object for consciousness but also a thing in a shared world. He shows primitive perception struggling to keep hold of the lived thing, in spite of an intellectualized conception of its own operation.

Merleau-Ponty criticizes Descartes's idea that the dimension of depth is derived from the other two dimensions of height and width, which are arrayed in front of us, and from whose occlusions and deformations we extract depth information. There is, for Descartes, no reality in depth understood as a structure deriving from my situation in the world; "God, who is everywhere—could penetrate [things'] 'hiding place' and see them openly deployed."[53]

Again in "Eye and Mind," the later essay in which Merleau-Ponty returns to the themes dealt with in "Cézanne's Doubt," this conception of space "without hiding places," is criticized. What I have called a geometrical conception of space Merleau-Ponty calls "identity of Being," a space that "in each of its points is only what it is," which "underlies the analysis of copper engravings."[54] On this understanding, space is an absolute in-itself, everywhere equal and measurable, "its dimensions, for example, are interchangeable." The conception of space, here, is an ontology that "builds

52. Merleau-Ponty, "Cézanne's Doubt," 13.

53. Merleau-Ponty, "Eye and Mind," 173.

54. Ibid., 174.

certain properties of beings into a structure of Being." And Merleau-Ponty applauds this Cartesian conception for what it denies: "Descartes's space is true over against a too empirical thought which dares not construct."[55] The idealized, geometrical conception of space was necessary, he says, to break with the brute conception of space in empiricism, to assert that space is ordered and not simply "there."

> This done, we were enabled eventually to find out the limits of construction, to understand that space does not have three dimensions or more or fewer, as an animal has either four or two feet, and to understand that the three dimensions are taken by different systems of measurement from a single dimensionality, a polymorphous Being, which justifies all without being fully expressed by any.[56]

The ordering according to Cartesian coordinates must then give way to an existential construction of space. "Descartes was right in setting space free," i.e., from the Aristotelian metaphysical ordering of space. "His mistake was to erect it into a positive being, outside all points of view, beyond all latency and all depth, having no true thickness."[57]

This Cartesian-perspectival denial of depth is of the essence of the metaphysics that Merleau-Ponty wants to criticize. The geometrical conception of the world leads us to a position in which we deny the reality of the dimension of *depth*. What characterizes depth as a dimension and makes it different to the dimensions of height and width? That depth must always refer to a perceiver, and cannot belong to a purely objective world; depth relates things to my body in their voluminosity and in their distance. Fundamentally, we must be able to account for depth in terms of desire, since it raises questions like "can I reach it?" in relation to a source of food, "will it hit me?" in relation to a projectile or a falling mass, and "can he see me?" in relation to a friend or foe.

Of the question of depth Merleau-Ponty writes

> The enigma consists in the fact that I see things, each one in its place, precisely because they eclipse one another, and that they are rivals before my sight precisely because each one is in its own place. Their exteriority is known in their envelopment and their mutual dependence in their autonomy. Once depth is understood in this way, we can no longer call it a third dimension. In the first place, if it were a dimension, it would be the *first* one;

55. Ibid., 174.
56. Ibid.
57. Ibid.

there are forms and definite planes only if it is stipulated how far from me their different parts are. But a *first* dimension that contains all the others is no longer a dimension, at least in the ordinary sense of a *certain relationship* according to which we make measurements. Depth thus understood is, rather, the experience of the reversibility of dimensions, of a global "locality"—everything in the same place at the same time, a locality from which height, width, and depth are abstracted, of a voluminosity we express in a word when we say that a thing is *there*.[58]

This "depth" depends on our perception of things consisting in a bodily involvement with the world, with sight being an aspect of a broader perceptive relation that relates us to things, by which we meet our needs and develop our desires. This active aspect of sight is missing in Descartes, as well as in Hume, as Todes notes: "Hume holds that we are aware of extension through sight and touch, but he never understands that we may become aware of extension through movement."[59]

Rather than resulting from an active experience, Humean "impressions" simply strike upon the mind. This is in a sense true of objects, insofar as their appearing as what they are depends not on our perception but on them as features of the world. "But it is not true of our active body, *through* which we make objects appear. In action, our body is already 'in' our consciousness as soon as we become aware that something has to be done."[60] Action begins not with us perceiving our bodies as possibilities for acting, as we would see a tool, like an umbrella on a rainy day, then make use of it. Rather, our active bodies ground the possibility of perception from the first.

It is this fact that experience does not always "strike upon" the mind that lies at the center of the contribution a bodily perspective has to make to our understanding of vision. The Humean conception of the passive, uninvolved and essentially indifferent perceiver now dominates not only our notion of vision, but also our metaphysics. Derrida could speak in terms of a critique of oculocentrism, but this does not really capture the problem, since the eye is usually employed as a moving and active component of a life lived in the world. What is more problematic is the distanced notion of vision characteristic of what Guy Debord called the "society of the spectacle," which prioritizes multiple specular virtualities over a sometimes drab reality, at the expense of active engagement (with either). The problem is not the emphasis on *seeing* in thought about perspective. It is the bias toward

58. Ibid., 180.
59. Todes, *Body and World*, 48.
60. Ibid., 43.

watching. Against Hume, and his conception of passive experience furnishing us with impressions, it must be seen that while such passive reception of data is possible, the much more fundamental human experience is the more active. Hunger stirs in the core of the human being, driving him to engage with the world around him, to seek out food. This hunger is not imposed on him from the outside—the hunger is only passively felt if we conceive the human being as a mental essence in some way subjected to his body. But the human being *is* his body; his hunger is an active part of his self-direction, towards food, towards the world on which he depends, towards *life*. The visual experience of the forager is not passive, nor disinterested, it is rather a *search*: the looker must decide where to look, combining instinct, memory, and present experience to find food. When he finds it, it fills his senses, with color, aroma, and texture. But to truly experience this object as food he must *eat* it. Perhaps he will be permitted to do so immediately. But more likely, he must prepare it, cut it up, heat it, remove certain parts. Then it may enter his mouth. Now all experience of it is brought to a head in *taste*, the experience of which includes its look and smell, the sound made and texture felt as he takes a bite, the feeling of heat or cold in the mouth that sometimes reaches up to the top of the head, the combination of sweet, sour, salty, and spicy felt on the tongue, and lasts long into the evening as that feeling of fullness, or over-fullness, or of unsatiated hunger. This fundamental engagement with the world is nothing like Hume's conception in which experience simply strikes upon us. It is through and through our active engagement with the world given in our particular situation.

> Now perhaps we have a better sense of what is meant by that little verb "to see." Vision is not a certain mode of thought or presence to self; it is the means given me for being absent from myself, for being present at the fission of Being from the inside—the fission at whose termination, and not before, I come back to myself.[61]

In depth, sight is conceived no longer as representation of things spread out in three-dimensional space but as a relation to things whose primary dimension of depth relates our bodily mass to that of what surrounds us, and which we actively explore.

> Depth has a perceptual primacy for Merleau-Ponty first because of its originality as the source of all other dimensions and the one by virtue of which "things or elements of things envelop each other." Furthermore, given its correlation with envelopment, height and width serve as measures of the ways that

61. Merleau-Ponty, "Eye and Mind," 186.

things are juxtaposed to each other. Depth therefore cannot be a dimension that stems from the others, as Descartes said in the *Dioptrics*. Rather, depth stands for a fundamental voluminosity in which we are already implicated. By contrast, the space of the *Dioptrics* is what a geometer would reconstruct as an object of a *pensée de survol*.[62]

On Morris's understanding, Merleau-Ponty is developing a new understanding of sense, or more accurately of *sens*. As I have shown, the French word already captures something of the notion of meaning as tied to the world insofar as it can mean not only "meaning," "logic," "reason," or "interpretation," but also *direction*. This meaning, like Morris's understanding of the body-schema, was easily lost in Colin Smith's older translation of *Phenomenology of Perception* since he simply translates *sens* as "meaning." So, in that translation we have, at the end of the chapter on movement and the spatiality of the body, "what we have discovered through the study of motility, is a new meaning of the word 'meaning.'"[63] But Morris offers the much better alternative, "a new sense [*sens*] of the word 'sense [*sens*],'"[64] which Donald Landes, in his new translation, also follows. When this point is made clear we can see how it ties in to Merleau-Ponty's whole project in the *Phenomenology of Perception*; idealism's strength is that it acknowledges the given meaningfulness of perception, it avoids having to form the difficult link between meaning in the world of thought and the empiricists' "fortuitously assembled contents."[65] But in so doing, it considers all meaning as "an act of thought, as the work of a pure 'I.'" Both these attempts to cross the Cartesian chasm fail. Although Merleau-Ponty thinks that "rationalism easily refuted empiricism," which cannot make sense of the meaningfulness of perceptions, it in turn fails to make sense of contingency, of the fact that not all perceptions are meaningful, of the obvious difference of the world to the mind. The shift Merleau-Ponty is trying to make is precisely that from *sens* understood as meaning, either imposed on or inherent in things, to *sens* in its more complex connotations, as intelligibility's emergence from and adherence to the sensible world.

As we have seen, the role of the moving, perceiving body in this world is central. Morris argues that *sens* is inseparable from expression, it arises in

---

62. Hamrick and Van der Veken, *Nature and Logos*, 80, citing *Phenomenology of Perception* (2002), 308 (276 in Landes's 2012 translation.)

63. Merleau-Ponty, *Phenomenology of Perception* (2002), 170. (148 in Landes's 2012 translation.)

64. Morris, *The Sense of Space*, 81–82. The additions are Morris's.

65. Merleau-Ponty, *Phenomenology of Perception*, 148.

the relations of the moving body to its world, and this is in some ways the converse of the denial of representation. Speech, for example, is not the externalization of an already-formed idea. Rather, the very thought is formed in its externalization; the act of speaking is genuinely expressive, and as such it is like perception's opposite. It is not that the outside world is somehow brought into contact with an inner world at a distance; rather, the agent and the world shape and mold each other; they are different forces at work in a common stuff. And if we return to painting, we see again that painting provides a model for sight; painting does not simply mimic what is given in the world, nor does it externalize what is in the painter's imagination. Painting brings to visibility a way of seeing that is also a way of thinking; the painting in some sense remakes the world.

This point gets to the heart of the question about depth. It should be clear by now how the geometrical conception of nature abets a "geometrical" account of perception and expression, in which everything that goes into the mind or comes out from it must pass, as a representation, through a single, unlocatable point. "Depth" is usually thought of as extending from this single point into the world as from a point of view. But when the body in all its thickness, in its motility, in its edibility, and in its dependence on and intertwining with the world, is considered as one side of depth, the world in its thickness is allowed to emerge as its correlate. As Morris has it, mental representations are supposed to help us to get over the aforementioned problem of "having the world at a distance" by duplicating the world inside the mind. The mind is somehow to the retina as the retina is to the eye and the eye is to the world. But representations are supposed to duplicate the world in a different form; the same image is converted from light into thought. "The traditional doctrine of representation endlessly [. . .] begs the question of how a brain-state becomes a representation, becomes something different and more than firings of neurons."[66] But if neither perception nor expression is a mechanical or quasi-mechanical translation between mind and world, the dualistic geometrism that it mirrors (or the physicalist or idealist monism that simply denies one or the other side, that spots the deception of the mirror-image) ceases to have such cachet. Instead, the fleshly, seeing body is intertwined with the world in depth.

Glen Mazis rightly suggests that this understanding of depth, in its relation to the active movement of my body, implicates another dimension in our perceptual experience, that of time.[67] Merleau-Ponty's focus on painting in *Eye and Mind* leads him away from discussing the notion of time, but we

---

66. Morris, *The Sense of Space*, 84.
67. Mazis, "Time at the Depth," 120.

can see that the time-bound nature of visual experience is a part of the reality from which the Cartesian optics abstracts, and helps us to understand the entwining of vision with the other senses. Our thought about vision has so often been dominated by the discussion of still images that time is easily forgotten, but temporality is clearly central to visual experience conceived as active, moving, and involving body and world in the fulfillment of needs and cultivation of desire. Depth, then, is not the primary dimension only in the sense of situating the subject in the world; in an abstracted, static conception of perception disregarding time, this would risk leading to a broken ontology that cannot account for the unity of the world, to an idealism. The world to which my body gives me access, and of which my body is a part, is dynamic and changing, and this will be fundamental to understanding vision as grounding a "fleshy" ontology.

> The spatial attributes of depth are references to the temporality of existence. This is not to say that time is derived from our sense of space, but rather that time itself is lodged within the landscape and its resounding within space is a primordial depth. The locatedness of the perceiver is to be understood by realizing that "we must understand time as the subject and the subject as time."[68]

To say that "time is the subject" would seem to contradict the claim that "time itself is lodged within the landscape." But here lies another aspect of perception that is misunderstood on the geometrical model on which we are used to thinking. As Lakoff and Johnson observe, time can be understood on the metaphor of a river rushing past me, or as forward movement through a landscape.[69] Do I, in perception, move forward through objective time as through space, or am I a passive witness to a passing time as like a stream? Neither metaphor captures the reality. I cannot stop time's movement, but neither does time go on without me. There is no absolute, neutral zero point of time or space by which to measure their movement; it is a

---

68. Ibid., 126–27. The final citation is from *Phenomenology of Perception* (2002), 490. (445 in Landes's 2012 translation.)

69. "The two metaphors [of time as a moving stream, and of time as the static landscape through which an observer moves] are, strictly speaking, inconsistent with each other: In one, times are objects that move past a stationary observer; in the other, times are locations in a landscape that an observer moves over. But these are actually minimally differing variants of one another. In short, they are figure-ground reversals of one another. In the Moving Time metaphor, the observer is the ground and the times are figures that move relative to it. In the Moving Observer metaphor, the observer is the figure and time is the ground—the times are locations that are fixed and the observer moves with respect to them." Lakoff and Johnson, *Philosophy in The Flesh*, 149.

matter of relation. We will return to the question of time, and the crucial example of the melody as a sensible idea, in the final chapter.

Ed Casey criticizes the idea that depth is revealed by the gaze, as in Descartes's clear and distinct perception, Husserl's eidetic intuition (which follows the phenomenological reduction's excision of contingency from everyday perception), and Sartre's intense interpersonal *gaze*.

> These various appeals to depth are often self-serving or at least self-supporting: just because essential structures come to us concealed thinkers consider themselves justified in employing a special philosophical method to get at them—a method prescribed by someone who is convinced that only by proposing a new procedure in philosophy or science will the truth of things become unconcealed. Moreover, it is not at all certain that gazing takes us into the depths of a given phenomenon to begin with. We do speak of "gazing into the depths"; but if this is to occur effectively, these depths must become accessible—on some surface somewhere. Let us agree that, at the least, the depths sought by philosophers and scientists—and doubtless also by the religiously minded—must find their way to some significant plane of presentation if they are to be apprehended by any human look, whether this be a gaze or a glance. "The surface," as Gibson remarks, "is where most of the action is."[70]

This antipathy to the gaze, on Casey's part, betrays a certain equivocality in the use of the notion of "depth" that must be made clear. There are three senses of "depth" at work in what we have said; first is the Cartesian depth, which is essentially the z-axis of visual perception that must be reconstructed from the putatively two-dimensional retinal image. This first sense can itself be thought through in two different ways; either the dimension of depth can be thought on the model of the other two axes of three-dimensional space, as perceived by an outside observer or *pensée de survol*, or it can be thought as the thoroughly existential dimension of the distance and separation or otherwise of the perceiver from things in his world.

The second sense of depth, which is related to the first, is that which we have called the "voluminosity" of things, which understands depth not solely in terms of naked three-dimensional measurements or of the arrangement of things around the perspectival center which is the perceiver, but rather as the holding in tension of these two notions; the "depth" of things here is constituted by their resistance to my investigation of them, what David Morris calls their *inexhaustibility*. This is to understand "depth"

---

70. Casey, *The World at a Glance*, 139. The citation is from Gibson, *The Ecological Approach*, 23.

as a dimension of my bodily involvement in a real world that exceeds me and that cannot be reduced to a picture.

The third sense of depth is in turn related to the second, and is that of the intelligibility that arises amongst things. This, we have insisted with Merleau-Ponty, is not to say that the world is entirely intelligible, that everything can be led back to essence, which would be to deny the very real contingency of things. But it is to say that in so far as meaning arises, it arises in the thick of things, *in* the world and *in* things, not attached to them from without by a judgment or an operation of the understanding.

It is in light of the second sense of depth that we must admit, with Merleau-Ponty, that immanence is never complete: even that which is most plainly open to the investigation of perception is never open *all at once* but always and only in aspects. There is in this sense no *pure* immanence. And as such we consent to call the depth of the third sense "transcendence": that is, not in the sense of an absolute outside but rather in the sense of an unknown inside. It is this union of transcendence and immanence that we call "incarnational," and it belongs not to a special domain of religious knowledge but to the everyday world of perception of things and interactions with persons. It is in virtue of our coincidence with things that they are able to transform us and it is this transforming-coincidence that is sought for in the posing of Plato's *Meno* paradox: how can I ever learn something new, if to learn something I must seek it and to seek it I must already know what it is I seek?

One of the best examples of what we mean by transforming-coincidence is that of human conversation. For Merleau-Ponty

> [a] genuine conversation gives me access to thoughts that I did not know myself capable of, that I *was* not capable of, and sometimes I feel myself *followed* in a route unknown to myself which my words, cast back by the other, are in the process of tracing out for me. To suppose here that an *intelligible world* sustains the exchange would be to take a name for a solution—and furthermore it would be to grant us what we are maintaining: that it is by borrowing from the world structure that the universe of truth and of thought is constructed for us.[71]

In good conversation, unanticipated thoughts are made available to both speaker and listener. This is not just a repetition of the structure of the world, but is rather an addition to it: the thoughts do not belong to a different world than what is thought about, but rather join it in the same world.

71. Merleau-Ponty, *The Visible and the Invisible*, 13.

A "universe of truth and of thought" is constructed that is forever joined to the physical universe and that constantly transforms it.

Glancing at the World

Ed Casey opposes the "gaze" of idealized aesthetic perception with the glance of everyday, embodied seeing. The gaze as the ideal mode of seeing, static, concentrated, and distanced from its object, is an artifact of what we have called the Cartesian scopic regime. The fact that the gaze attains to detachment from everyday, embodied seeing is not, in modern Western thought, a weakness, but a strength. "It is just because the gazer is convinced that his or her body is irrelevant—or in any case subordinate—to the enactment of gazing itself that the gaze has been so highly valorized." Because we are attached to the perspectival, Cartesian scopic regime, we think of such detached seeing as proper, as "scientific," as establishing true knowledge of the world. "The glance, in comparison, is considered by the same thinkers as a mere spontaneous gesture of the body and thus ineluctably linked to its fate: as fickle as the body's appetites, as blind as its instincts, as insatiable as its desire."[72]

On Casey's analysis, it is the glance to which vision should attain: dynamic, situated, interested, and fleeting, it takes in not a "picture" but a world, constantly being driven to develop a relation to its surrounding world by moving around in it. It is on the basis of its movement, its dynamism, that Casey attributes to the glance a real perception of the lived world of place.

> There is a close and continuing marriage between the glance and place. For the glance primarily seeks out what is happening within the boundaries of its own domain—within the "internal horizon" that place provides.[73]

Casey draws on James J. Gibson's understanding of the environment as affordances, and as composed of mediating surfaces, which seems to begin to show us how the ethical relation to the environment is specified by our glancing apperceptions, in which it is "good for" some things and not others, and where desire appears pre-cognitively.[74]

Gibson begins his seminal account of vision in *The Ecological Approach to Visual Perception* with the recognition that where vision has

---

72. Casey, *The World at a Glance*, 154.

73. Ibid., 53.

74. Casey, "Taking a Glance at the Environment."

been understood as the effect of light on the eye, connected to the brain, it has been studied by physicists, optical scientists, by anatomists, and by physiologists, and while these studies have achieved a great deal, producing interesting and important results for ophthalmology and optometry and the psychophysiology of vision, they have "no real grasp of the perplexities" when it comes to explaining vision.[75] The experimental situation of convenience has reduced vision to a "snapshot," a momentary flash in the dark presented before a subject immobilized before them in an odd re-enactment of the Platonic cave. As Merleau-Ponty observed, such experimental situations do not tell us much about perception as it occurs in the world. A new understanding of vision is required, and is what Gibson attempts to give us; an understanding of natural vision not as light interacting with eye and mind but as the function of "the eyes in the head on a body supported by the ground, the brain being only the central organ of a complete visual system."[76]

This immediately opens us onto a notion of perception that differs from the received picture. Gibson argues early on that the concept of space is irrelevant to perception, asking us to forget the Kantian maxim that "percepts without concepts are blind," and taking the perceived world, and not geometrical space, as primary.[77] On Gibson's understanding, if we perceived the entities of physics and mathematics, then we would have to impose meaning on things, for example, by bringing them under a concept in the Kantian way. But in fact we perceive "the entities of environmental science," and as such we do not impose meaning on things but discover it in them.

The central concept of Gibson's ecological optics is that of the "ambient optic array." Gibson points out that optics has tended to conceive of light as radiation, as a singular "ray" traveling from a reflecting surface (or an illuminating surface) to the eye, where it is focused into a point on the retina. In sensation-based theories of color, these points of light with intensity and wavelength detected on the retina are conducted by the optic nerve to the brain where they are translated into points of brightness and color in the mental image, which introduces the problem of the imagined homunculus (who views the mental image) that has already been mentioned. Gibson wants to divorce the notion of stimulation based on the reception of light in the eyes from perception; there can be a situation, where I am in a bright, dense, fog, a *ganzfeld*, in which there is a great deal of stimulating light coming into my eyes but I do not *see* anything because that light does

75. Gibson, *The Ecological Approach*, xviii, 1–4.

76. Ibid., 1.

77. Ibid., 3.

not carry what Gibson calls stimulus information. Stimulus information is carried not by radiating light but in light as "illumination": where optics has tended to reduce light to a "ray," the reality of our visual environment is of those "rays" reflecting off things into a manifold, so that light travels from every direction to every point, in an "omnidirectional flux."[78] When this light is different in different directions (i.e., is not a *ganzfeld*), then it carries some structure, which is the basis of stimulus information. This structured field of light is what Gibson calls the "ambient optic array" of any point in the environment that could be occupied by an observer. Gibson specifies the structure in terms of what he calls "invariants"; that is, as the optic array changes over time, or as an observer moves around, there is change in the differentiated field of light, but this change preserves certain things, a "variation of structure that serves to reveal the nonvariation of structure."[79] That is, relationships between angles, gradients, colors, and so on persist though the superficial appearances of them change. This, for example, is why the plate appears as circular; what is perceived is not the flux of elliptical appearances but the invariant shape (the circle) that grounds them. Such invariants are, generally speaking, the stable visible surfaces of solid substances, and when a solid thing changes state so that it melts, or burns up, for example, we say that the substance is destroyed: in terms of Gibson's ecological psychology, something has genuinely changed, an invariant structure has ceased to subsist, where in physical terms nothing has gone out of or come into existence, there is only a change of state.[80]

Such ecological events are, for Gibson, a primary reality. Where Newtonian thought assumed time to be an empty container that is "filled" with such events, for Gibson "this habitual way of thinking puts the cart before the horse. We should begin thinking of events as the primary realities and of time as an abstraction from them—a concept derived mainly from regular repeating events, such as the ticking of clocks."[81] He applies a similar analysis to space; space is also not an empty container that needs to be filled, in the way that the geometrical conception of nature assumes. It is first of all the spreading-out of surfaces, which neutral space abstracts from and measures. Both events and environments can constitute, for the animal, what Gibson calls *affordances*; that is, they can "demand or invite appropriate behaviors."[82] Such behaviors are not given by the animal itself or by

78. Ibid., 51.
79. Ibid., 73.
80. Ibid., 13.
81. Ibid., 100.
82. Ibid., 102.

the layout of surfaces *per se*, but by the situation, by the relationship of the animal to its environment, by the animal-environment *gestalt*. So Gibson emphasizes that in perception egoreception (perceiving oneself) and exteroception (perceiving the world) are inseparable, and it would seem that it is this inseparability that constitutes the "I," that is, that no-one else can look at the world from the position of my body as I can.

The notion of perceptual affordances also implies that "meanings" and even "values" arise in our perception of our environment. The most basic affordance, it would seem, is that of a relatively flat and relatively smooth surface that affords support for the animal and thus constitutes its ground. Various other surfaces, then, afford themselves as sit-on-able or climbable or bump-into-able and so on. This helps us to make sense of the relationship between perception and skill, so that we can see how a free-runner might see the various surfaces of a cityscape as run-up-able, jumpable, and as affording opportunities to get to otherwise unreachable places, where such surfaces would not offer any such affordances to most pedestrians. The skill of free-running is, in part, the skill of seeing surfaces as usable in certain ways. In this sense imagination is clearly a part of perception. Similarly, an excellent tennis player might see a difficult ball as reachable, and a golfer might see a long shot as putt-able, and just as the skill depends on seeing in this way, the seeing reciprocally depends on the skill, on being able to exercise the ability to reach or putt the ball. Affordances, which as we have said belong neither to the observer nor to the world but to their relation, make value a function of the relationships between things. This depends on Gibson's hypothesis that there is *information* in the optical visual array and that such information can carry not just facts but meanings.

With regards to the problem of depth, Gibson points out that while Berkeley's formulation of visual distance as of a line going from the eye to the object presents the problem of accounting for how we can see an invisible distance, if we account for distance in terms of a line extending along the ground rather than through the air, then distance is not an invisible dimension, but one closely tied to our environment. There is a perspective gradient in environmental features that makes sense of depth as an aspect of our co-habitation with things, our sharing a common ground with them.

Gibson develops an understanding of vision as "ecological," and this ecological optics makes use of what we will call a logic of incarnation, a logic that overcomes dualisms by understanding the relation between things (perceiver and object) in terms of their co-location, their co-inherence in a world that they constitute together. He calls into question the primacy of the frontal plane in the analysis of depth perception, which is understood to be the flat plane that is most similar to the curved retinal image.[83] Rather than being derived from calculations of size and visual angle, the perception of depth is based on and grounded not in artificial perspective but in the ground, whose visual texture is most coarse, and finely-detailed, directly below us and that then moves out in a gradient of increasing density to the horizon. The horizon, then, is the limiting case of our co-location with things; for Gibson "it is neither subjective nor objective; it expresses the *reciprocity* of observer and environment: it is an invariant of *ecological* optics."[84] Merleau-Ponty asks whether this perception, in which the perceiver is located as a part of his world, and in which "Being" is relegated from its position as an eternal, unchanging, intelligible reality to a reality only partly known and exhausting all attempts at interrogation, is sufficient for philosophy:

> Is this the highest point of reason, to realize that the soil beneath our feet is shifting, to pompously name "interrogation" what is only a persistent state of stupor, to call "research" or "quest" what is only trudging in a circle, to call "Being" that which never fully *is*?
>
> But this disappointment issues from that spurious fantasy which claims for itself a positivity capable of making up for its own emptiness. It is the regret of not being everything, and a rather groundless regret at that.[85]

While to accept that the human perceiver is a body is inevitably to accept that it is not everything, that its access to Being is limited by perspective, Gibson shows how it is also more than a perspective as it was understood by the Cartesian scopic regime. This "old approach to perception" centered on the problem of how depth is reconstructed from a two-dimensional and depthless retinal image, but it "never asked how one could see into the past and the future."[86] This is not an occultism: for Gibson it is clear that one's perception of one's environment is not of a momentary or instantaneous being but of an enduring reality, which is to say that "the environment seen-at-this moment does not constitute the environment that is seen."[87] Just as the plate given as elliptical is seen as round, so the environment seen from here is just a part of the environment that is seen, that is all of a piece, so the environment "seen-now" does not coincide with the environment as it is seen. This reminds us of the contemporary British artist David Hockney's

83. Ibid., 160.
84. Ibid., 164.
85. Merleau-Ponty, "Eye and Mind," 190.
86. Gibson, *The Ecological Approach*, 195.
87. Ibid., 195.

comment that "photography is all right if you don't mind looking at the world from the point of view of a paralyzed Cyclops—for a split second."[88] The "incarnational" logic that we have been arguing for is present in both Merleau-Ponty's ontology and J. J. Gibson's account of vision as "perspectival" in the sense that it takes account of the location of the perceiver in the world, it understands Being as given in limited aspects and not as a reality that could be best seen and ideally known from the perspectiveless position of an absolute observer or a purely transcendent God, or described in terms of a pure geometry. But there is a sense in which it is not "perspectival" at all: as Gibson has it, "an observer who is moving about sees the world at *no* point of observation and thus, strictly speaking, *cannot* notice the perspectives of things."[89] That is to say once again that the *perspectiva artificialis* of Renaissance art, and of photography, does not show us what it is like to see, but is an abstraction from visual perception in its imbrication with the fullness of bodily life. As Gibson suggests in his later discussion of images, there is a great and obvious difference between a picture that uses perspective and one that does not, and the difference cannot be that the first represents reality and the second does not. What then is the difference? An image that displays a scene in perspective "puts the viewer into the scene." And this is the difference between the two "perspectivisms": the perspectivism of the Renaissance, of the Cartesian scopic regime, *perspectiva artificialis*, constructs the scene according to geometrical laws and installs the perceiver as a point within the scene; it ingeniously locates the viewer in the scene she looks at by the very construction of that scene; but in doing so it must reduce the viewer to a Sartrean point of nothingness. The perspectivism we wish to affirm does just the opposite: understanding that natural perspective belongs not to the immobilized eye but to the living perceiver, it rejects the centrality of the picture in an account of vision and insists that the perceiver is installed among the things she is looking at; that what she perceives is a world, and that she knows this precisely because she sees it from a single perspective that it exceeds; this she knows because she moves around in the world, forever unhiding to herself previously unseen surfaces, and hiding others, both these acts being always reversible by reversing her path of locomotion through the world or undoing the moves made in her manipulations of things.

In *The Structure of Behaviour* Merleau-Ponty claims that "[p]erspective does not appear to me to be a subjective deformation of things but, on the

88. Cited in Peres, *Focal Encyclopedia of Photography*, 259.

89. Gibson, *The Ecological Approach*, 197.

contrary, to be one of their properties, perhaps their essential property."[90] That is, their appearing as the-same-yet-different, things' invariant structures are not hidden by the fact that I engage them from a certain perspective, but are revealed in virtue of that fact. "It is precisely because of it that the perceived possesses in itself a hidden and inexhaustible richness, that it is a 'thing.'"[91] Merleau-Ponty is clear, here, that speaking of the "perspectival character of knowledge" is equivocal. It can mean that things cannot be known in themselves, but only as they appear, as the neo-Kantianism of Brunschvicg, dominant in early twentieth-century France, against which Merleau-Ponty developed his position, would have it. But there is another sense that, with Merleau-Ponty, we affirm: "Far from introducing a coefficient of subjectivity into perception, it provides it on the contrary with the assurance of communicating with a real world. The profiles of my desk are not given to direct knowledge as appearances without value, but as 'manifestations' of the desk."[92]

For Gibson, it is crucial to realize that one's own body does appear visually, from the appearance of one's cheeks, nose, and eyebrows at the edges of the visual field to the appearance of one's hands and feet as we manipulate things and move around in the world. In this sense the body-schema is anchored to a visual appropriation of one's own body in ways that are easy to miss, and that contribute to the failure of artificial perspective: although the perspective image can include me, the viewer, and locates me with regard to itself, it cannot include my self-seeing; it seems to fracture me into a Cartesian duality, because though I am in some sense included or accounted for in the picture, my body remains resolutely outside of it.

Gibson's account of vision develops a sophisticated view of my relation to the world of things that is consonant with the Merleau-Pontyan ontology we are pursuing, but, in *The Ecological Approach to Visual Perception*, he does not get beyond the animal's relation to its environment and the objects within it. Merleau-Ponty's philosophy already attempts to locate these problems with regard to the more significant question of the relation of vision to the problem of other persons. The visual access that I have to my own body is, of course, markedly different to that I have to the body of another, so how is it that the infant is able to associate, for example, her own 'motor smile' with the seen smile of another?[93] For Merleau-Ponty, in "The Child's Relation with Others," it is because I am "a consciousness turned

90. Merleau-Ponty, *The Structure of Behaviour*, 186.

91. Ibid.

92. Ibid.

93. This example is taken from Merleau-Ponty, "The Child's Relation with Others," 116.

toward things"[94] (because I can see the actions of others as relating to my own possibilities for action) that I come to see *behaviors*, and then come to understand these behaviors in relation to the schematic bodies by which they are borne and so to see the *psyches* to whom such behaviors belong. But all this depends on a tacit recognition of my own intertwining with the world, an understanding that my body is not an "agglomeration of sensations" but a part of the body-world system that is always postured in relation to the world.[95] This body-world system develops into a self-other system, or perhaps a self-body-world-other system.

> To be aware that one has a body and that the other's body is animated by another psyche are two operations that are not simply logically symmetrical but form a real system. In both cases it is a question of becoming conscious of what might be called "incarnation."[96]

The movement among things and manipulation of things that are essential to fully embodied sight, for Gibson, are "kinds of behavior that cannot be reduced to responses."[97] He does not cite Merleau-Ponty, and Gibson does not seem to have been familiar with his philosophy, but as we have seen, this point was established in *The Structure of Behaviour*: indeed, for Merleau-Ponty, the very concept of behavior demands it. Gibson accuses his fellow psychologists and physiologists of hanging on to the Cartesian notion that animals are complex automata and so do not "behave" in this sense, but are determined by their perceptions (conceived as operations on atomic sense-data) by the mind of which the brain is the seat. If humans are somehow different, it must be because of the intervention of a soul that manipulates the nervous impulses in the human brain. For Gibson, to say that the mind is a complex computer is little better, since it still assumes that behavior is determined on a stimulus-response model. Rather, "Locomotion and manipulation are neither triggered nor commanded but *controlled*," and this control is a function not of the brain but of the "animal-environment system," that is, of the animal's relationship to its perceived world of affordances.[98] He proposes that various forms of locomotion require very different forms of classical kinaesthesis but the same form of visual kinaesthesis, and it is the visual perception of self and world that is dominant in control-

---

94. Merleau-Ponty, "The Child's Relation with Others," 117.

95. Ibid., 117.

96. Ibid., 120.

97. Gibson, *The Ecological Approach*, 225.

98. Ibid., 225.

ling locomotion. He formulates some approximations of rules that describe this kinaesthetic control, based on the outflow of texture of the ambient optic array from the point towards which one is moving, which describe the involvement of embodied visual perception in this basic mode of behavior.

All this contributes, finally, to a redefinition of perception. For Gibson, perception is not the appearance in the individual's consciousness of veridical representations of the outside world. It is rather an *achievement*, a worked-out contact with the world. Perception can be of something in the world, of something in the perceiver, or of both; it is not a mental act nor a bodily act, but a psychosomatic act, of a living, bodily perceiver.[99] It is a living contact between body and world, which Gibson describes in terms of "information pickup." Martin Jay, in his critique of the anti-oculocentrism of twentieth-century French thought, *Downcast Eyes*, takes the implication of Gibson's argument to be that vision is originarily crossed with the other senses, but is capable of an artificial separation from them, which is to some degree a cultural fact. On the basis of the Cartesian scopic regime and its failings, French anti-oculocentrism reacted against the dominance of isolated vision by denigrating sight *in toto*, but the more constructive response, which Jay proposes, is to reassert the entwinement of sight with the other senses and its fundamental embodiment.

Intelligible Structures of the World

The fundamental embodiment of sight has been developed in terms of the intertwining of perception and movement, of reversibility and the intersensoriality of an originary synaesthesia. What we see in our environment and in animal and human others is not simply information, but meaning. The perceived world is not composed of pure facts, but also of values, of opportunities and dangers, desirable things, persons, and situations, and undesirables, of needs and wants and hopes and fears, rather than simply of sensations that are to be brought under judgments. This, from the first, was the significance of Gibson's theory of affordances. Does such meaning appear in sight? It does, but not as the visible. For Merleau-Ponty,

> Meaning is *invisible*, but the invisible is not the contradictory of the visible: the visible itself has an invisible inner framework (*membrure*), and the in-visible is the secret counterpart of the visible, it appears only within it, it is the *Nichturpräsentierbar*

99. Ibid., 240.

[unpresentable] which is presented to me as such within the world.[100]

Clearly there is a paradox here: vision, according to Merleau-Ponty, gives us access to what is invisible. In the introduction to *Signs*, where Merleau-Ponty first suggests that we speak of "the visible and the invisible," as an alternative to the Sartrean "being and nothingness," Merleau-Ponty clarifies what he means by the invisible, saying that visible and invisible "are not contradictory" and suggesting that, "One says invisible as one says immobile—not in reference to something foreign to movement, but to something which stays still. The invisible is the limit or zero degree of visibility, the opening of a dimension of the visible."[101] Intelligibility no longer belongs in a Platonic heaven of the Forms nor in the application of conceptual categories to a formless reality. Meaning is at the heart of things in a way that is difficult to specify; a way in which we will have to learn to think. Meaning appears in perception not *as* what is seen, but *in* what is seen; what appears is not brute nature or the *bloße sachen,* but *things* and *persons* in all their richness, ambiguity, and inexhaustibility. While commenting on the work of Samuel Todes in *Body and World,* Hubert Dreyfus asks

> Are there two fundamentally different ways we make sense of the world, or does all understanding consist in using concepts to think about things? The philosophical tradition has generally assumed—or, in the case of Kant, argued persuasively—that there is only one kind of intelligibility, the unified understanding we have of things when we make judgments that objectify our experience by bringing it under concepts. But there have always been others—painters, writers, historians, linguists, philosophers in the romantic tradition, Wittgensteinians, and existential phenomenologists—who have felt that there is another kind of intelligibility that gets us in touch with reality besides the conceptual kind elaborated by Kant.[102]

As the contemporary phenomenologist Françoise Dastur sees, to perceive is to "organize an area of the visible," to "open oneself" to a gestalt.[103] This perceptual organization of figure against ground is not a matter of *creating* meaning in a kind of perceptual impressionism, of arranging the sensed in such a way as to determine out of it something intelligible. Rather it is to arrange the manifold meanings of a situation into a directed *sens:* to

100. Merleau-Ponty, *The Visible and the Invisible,* 215.

101. Merleau-Ponty, *Signs,* 21, translation modified.

102. Dreyfus, "Todes's Account," xv.

103. Dastur, "World, Flesh, Vision," 28.

decide upon and attend to the relevances of things by determining what, in a given situation, matters most. Gibson, in the end, calls the figure-ground structure of perception a "fallacy,"[104] but this comes in the context of the account of vision as it develops at the end of *The Ecological Approach to Visual Perception* which restricts itself to the perception of the environment, for the most part limited to landscape, in the discussion of pictures and in particular of line drawings. If we take Gibson's point to be that perception does not disregard background to focus solely on a chosen "object," then he is correct. But if the figure-ground structure of perception is understood as a dynamic sorting of the contents of perception that makes their manifold and wild intelligibilities accessible and manipulable by organizing them around a meaningful center, as we do, then he is wrong to reject it. This thought is present in Merleau-Ponty already in *The Structure of Behaviour*, where he argues that, "What is profound in the notion of 'Gestalt' from which we started is not the idea of signification but that of *structure*, the joining of an idea and an existence which are indiscernible, the contingent arrangement by which materials begin to have meaning in our presence, *intelligibility in the nascent state* [my emphasis]."[105]

Darian Meacham notes that in the working notes to *The Visible and the Invisible*, "Merleau-Ponty writes that perception is always cultural,"[106] claiming "what he means by this is that the meaning formations that structure our cultural world are not an ideal layer projected by a constituting subject over the perceptual field, but are through and through in the perceptual world itself, in the things themselves."[107]

This is not a complete picture, though; it is true (for Merleau-Ponty) that the meaning-formations from which culture is built originate in the perceived world, but the perceived world is also shaped by cultural transformations. Merleau-Ponty's key example here is that of artificial perspective. "I say that the Renaissance perspective is a cultural fact, that perception itself is polymorphic and that if it becomes Euclidean, this is because it allows

---

104. Gibson, *The Ecological Approach*, 288.

105. Merleau-Ponty, *The Structure of Behaviour*, 206–7.

106. Meacham, "Faith Is in Things Not Seen," 188. Meacham refers this claim to Merleau-Ponty's statements on p. 253 of *The Visible and the Invisible*, for example, that "the distinction between the two planes (natural and cultural) is abstract: everything is cultural in us (our Lebenswelt is "subjective") (our perception is cultural-historical) and everything is natural in us (even the cultural rests on the polymorphism of the wild Being)." There is more important material, which substantiates Meacham's claim, on p. 212, for example, "there is an informing of perception by culture which enables us to say that culture is perceived," and the claim that culture constitutes an "original layer above *nature*."

107. Meacham, "Faith Is in Things Not Seen," 188.

itself to be oriented by the system."[108] And this is about more than just paintings. In proposals for an ontology among these working notes, Merleau-Ponty proposes to "take topological space as a model of being," as Euclidean, geometrical space has been made the model for *perspectival being*" (my emphasis), and he notes that there is an "underlying appropriateness" of the notion of space that belongs to Euclidean geometry "with the classical ontology of the *Ens realissimum*, of the infinite entity."[109] The linear relations of movement and time, and presumably of volume, and of causality of the snooker-ball type beloved of some analytic philosophers, are imposed upon reality in what Merleau-Ponty calls perspectival being. A different culture, a different model of space, would result in a different framework and different perceptions. "The topological space, on the contrary, a milieu in which are circumscribed relations of proximity, of envelopment, etc., is the image of a being that, like Klee's touches of color, is at the same time older than everything and 'of the first day' (Hegel) [. . .] that is a perpetual *residue*."[110]

Merleau-Ponty is still aware, here, of how these questions arising from a geometrical conception of being necessitate some kind of theology. He argues that "the *Theodicy* of Leibniz sums up the effort of Christian theology to find a route between the necessitarian conception of Being, alone possible, and the unmotivated upsurge of brute Being, which latter is finally linked up with the first by a compromise, and, to this extent, the hidden god sacrificed to the *Ens realissimum*."[111] This is a clear rejection of the answers proffered by the theological tradition (or at least the one with which he was familiar) to the problems of understanding a world in which contingency and necessity, suffering and the good themselves seem intertwined, and there is no mention here of the promise of a theology of *incarnation*, which Merleau-Ponty in his earlier writings seems at times to have seen. Nonetheless, he maintains here some kind of appreciation that the God of the Leibnizian *Ens Realissimum* is not the only option, to hold out some kind of hope for a "hidden god" who will not be used to explain away suffering and evil. I will take up this substantive theological point in chapter 6.

We must return to the question of the presence of intelligibility in the sensible. Merleau-Ponty claims "there is no longer a problem of the concept, generality, the idea, when one has understood that the sensible itself is *invisible*, that the *yellow* is capable of setting itself up as a level or horizon."[112] This

108. Merleau-Ponty, *The Visible and the Invisible*, 212.

109. Ibid., 210.

110. Ibid., 210–11.

111. Ibid., 211.

112. Ibid., 237.

captures well the complexity of Merleau-Ponty's understanding of vision in his late work. The invisible, we must remember, is not that which is totally foreign to vision, but is to the visible as rest is to motion. But what can it mean to say that the sensible is invisible? We must approach this issue with care. Our "geometrical" way of thinking makes such a statement impossible to understand, but as he so often does, Merleau-Ponty is using this radical claim about the nature of things to provoke a different way of seeing. In what he has called a "topological" understanding, we may be given to understand that sight does not give us simple sensations, but that things appear as structures whose reverse side and normative shape is "seen" even as neither is visible. The sensible property, like the yellow of the example, is perceived not as a contingent, material singularity, nor as a necessary, ideal universal, but as a level or a horizon in the sense that there is nothing beyond yellow things that constitutes their yellowness, yet there is a participation in a field, a relation to other things, involved in the yellow that cannot be captured by the thing *partes extra partes*. Its reality, as we have said, depends on relation.

In the final fully drafted chapter of *The Visible and the Invisible* entitled "The Intertwining—The Chiasm," Merleau-Ponty writes that "no one has gone further than Proust in fixing the relations between the visible and the invisible, in describing an idea that is not the contrary of the sensible, that is its lining and its depth."[113] The appearance of the invisible idea in the visible is a matter of the internal depth of things in a way that is analogous to the appearance in sight of the unseen "depths" of things like their occluded sides and their normative shapes. How can this be the case? The occluded sides of a thing we have called visible because they can in principle be revealed to sight; if I move around the thing and find that its reverse side is empty, the whole thing "looks" different, on the basis that my sight is not the operation of a momentary instant but of a moving body interrogating the world. Sight, we have seen, is in this way bound up with temporality, embodiment and embodiment's specific form of motility. But it seems hard to see how the sensible idea can become visible in this way; although this is not spelled out, it seems likely that an "idea" is not something that affords any possibility of vision. The shape of the thing, (the roundness of the plate) we argued against Alva Noë, is not *just* the sum of our possible perspectives on it but is something more than that; there is a normative dimension to its appearance as round that prioritizes one perspective over the others in a way related to its use. Perhaps the appearance of the plate as round gives us a stronger analogy to the appearance of the sensible idea, of the invisible *in* the visible; insofar as it carries this dimension of normativity that is not

113. Ibid., 149.

visible even in theory or as a possibility. For Merleau-Ponty the question of "the bond between the flesh and the idea" is "the most difficult point"[114] of his understanding of the intertwining, but it would seem that to understand it is crucial; if in the last instance it cannot cross the chasm between sensibility and intelligibility, Merleau-Ponty's ontology has not finally escaped Cartesianism.

The Proustian example (from *À la recherche du temps perdu*) to which Merleau-Ponty gives so much weight is a musical one: the *petit phrase* of Vintueil's sonata, which expresses for M. Swann a great deal of the meaning of his relationship with Odette; which occasioned his falling in love with this girl about whom he expresses indifference up until the point that they hear the sonata together;[115] and which reminds him of her in the passage to which Merleau-Ponty refers, at which point their relationship has cooled considerably.[116] Proust says of the "little phrase," from the *andante* of Vintueil's sonata for Piano and Violin, that "Swann referred back to it as to a conception of love and happiness whose distinctive character he recognized at once as he would that of the *Princesse de Clèves* [a novel, anonymously published in the late nineteenth century and considered to be the first *roman d'analyse* or psychological novel] or of *René* [an 1802 novella by François-René de Chateaubriand, considered a founding text of early French romanticism], should either of those titles occur to him."[117] So, Merleau-Ponty surmises, with the "mysterious entity" of the "little phrase" we are not talking about a relation between the idea and the perceived reality that is particular to music, but one that is broader; that applies to other cultural items and also to ideas more generally conceived: as Proust has it,

> Even when he [Swann] was not thinking of the little phrase, it existed latent in his mind on the same footing as certain other notions without material equivalent, such as our notions of light, of sound, of perspective, of physical pleasure, the rich possessions wherewith our inner temple is diversified and adorned.[118]

The visible both "manifests" and "conceals" the "interior armature" of things which is the "idea" in its bond to the "flesh."[119] So, for Merleau-Ponty, "literature, music, the passions, but also the experience of the visible world

114. Ibid., 149.
115. Proust, *Swann's Way*, 250–61.
116. Ibid., 420–21.
117. Ibid., 421.
118. Ibid.
119. Merleau-Ponty, *The Visible and the Invisible*, 149.

are—no less than is the science of Lavoisier and Ampère—the exploration of an invisible and the disclosure of a universe of ideas."[120] The difference between these former and the ideas of science is that these "invisible" ideas do not stand on their own, "cannot be detached from the sensible appearances and be erected into a second positivity."[121] Indeed, the fact that they are not (unlike the parts of the object occluded from view at this moment) open to any possibility of appearing to visual sense *simpliciter* is what makes them the kinds of reality that they in fact are; "here [. . .] there is no vision without the screen: the ideas we are speaking of would not be better known to us if we had no body and no sensibility; it is then that they would be inaccessible to us."[122] It is in *this* sense that the analogy with some of the earlier-discussed aspects of sight comes into its own. Where the appearance of voluminousness depends on the *possibility* that the unseen sides could be seen, it also depends on the *impossibility* of seeing all the sides at once, for this perspectiveless thought would collapse all depth and neutralize the potency of my bodily engagement with the world. This would seem to clarify Merleau-Ponty's insight that the "invisible" sense of which we are speaking is not opposed to the visible; the idea's invisibility is the condition of its possibility, and is its manner of appearing in the visible, just as voluminousness depends on perspective and occlusion. In this sense the third of the three senses of depth we identified very much depends on the second.

This is a theme to which we will have to return later. But it seems worth mentioning here that it is not inconsequential that the example Merleau-Ponty takes up is one based on a melody, which from his earliest work exemplified the way in which the perceived is structured and temporal; in *The Structure of Behaviour*, discussing the level of meaning that constitutes behavior properly speaking, he writes:

> vital acts *have* a meaning; they are not defined, even in science, as a sum of processes external to each other, but as the spatial and temporal unfolding of certain ideal unities. "Every organism," said Uexküll, "is a melody which sings itself."[123]

In Merleau-Ponty's articulation of the relations of consciousness and nature as a structuration that lies at the origin of animal behavior and of human thought, the example of melody shows us how an intentional and

---

120 Ibid., 149.

121. Ibid.

122. Ibid.

123. Merleau-Ponty, *The Structure of Behaviour*, 159.

meaningful reality (a musical idea) arises from a sequence of physical events (i.e., the vibrations of strings) to which it cannot be reduced.

> Just as the painter is struck by a painting that is not there, the body is suspended in what it sings: the melody is incarnated and finds in the body a type of servant. The melody gives us a particular consciousness of time. We think naturally that the past secretes the future ahead of it. But this notion of time is refuted by the melody. At the moment when the melody begins, the last note is there, in its own manner. In a melody, a reciprocal influence between the first and the last note takes place, and we have to say that the first note is possible only because of the last, and vice versa. It is in this way that things happen in the construction of a living being.[124]

Visible Species

In the lectures on nature, Merleau-Ponty takes up again Uexküll's description of the "unfurling" of the animal *Umwelt* in terms of melody, and he himself here compares it to the idea of the melody in Proust: "When we invent a melody, the melody sings in us much more than we sing it; it goes down the throat of the singer, as Proust says."[125] As Carbone sees it, Merleau-Ponty develops "this convergence in order to conceive of the biological notion of 'species' as an essence *inseparable* from its manifestation in single individuals," that is, not as a Platonic idea or a real universal, but as a "sensible idea"[126] of the kind we have been proposing. But this provides us with a clear consonance between "species" in the biological sense and the broader sense that it contributes to a theory of sight. In her exposition and investigation of the medieval Franciscan thinker Roger Bacon's theory of vision, theorist of visual culture Suzannah Biernoff deals with the notion of species as the central principle of his understanding "of sensation, cognition and intellection," an understanding that seeks to give a *causal* account of perception to insulate perception against doubt about its veracity. The notion of species is, for Bacon, an attempt to reassert the reliability of perception and to shore up epistemology against the doubts to which perceptual mistakes, and illusions, give rise, by giving an account of the continuity of species in the world and in the mind. It may seem strange, then, that Biernoff sees

124. Merleau-Ponty, *Nature*, 174.
125. Ibid., 173–74.
126. Carbone, *The Thinking of the Sensible*, xv.

Merleau-Ponty's ontology (including his account of vision) as bearing an affinity with the medieval ideas of Bacon.

Biernoff emphasizes that though species are not objects, "they do have material existence."[127] They are incarnated or "bodied forth" in the media of air, light, water, and the humors of the eye, and in those media they have a real, physical being, just as sound, though not an object, has a material reality, for which vibration there must always be some medium. But, more than this, Biernoff expresses the Baconian understanding of intelligible species in terms strikingly similar to those of Merleau-Ponty's citation of Uexküll's analogy between melody and psychological species: "One could say that species colonise matter: the corporeal nature of a species is identical to that of its recipient because the latter is merely a 'host,' transformed into the likeness of its coloniser. Or, to use an analogy more in keeping with Bacon's visual orientation, the agent (species) 'impresses' its form on the recipient."[128]

For Aristotle (who is the source of the theory of sight as "intelligible species"),[129] the reception of species is a passive process that is attributed to the passive element of reason and whose possibility depends on its being taken up into a process of active reason. This division of reason into active and passive, taken too absolutely, and consigning perception to the passive side, lies at the source of a dualism that is the fundament of both empiricism and intellectualism, which divides intellectual functions and thus the relations of nature and consciousness into separate passive and active moments. If we are to make use of the notion of intelligible species, it must overcome the passive-active duality and attain to an understanding that better describes the phenomenology of perceiving, since we do not passively receive the forms of everything that enters our field of view, but, at least for the most part, only that which we look at, and which is not too big or too small, but of the kind of scale that allows us to see it as an individual thing, i.e., that which we can take as "figure" against a "ground."

Ockham rejected the Baconian theory of species because of its implication that of the senses, sight most strongly corresponds to the real structure of objects, and thus its privileging of visual sense. It seems that the notion that the species theory establishes sight as the prototypical sense may be less problematic if we take care to understand "species," in accordance with its etymology, as the "look" of things (from the Indo-European *spek*, to see), rather than as something substantial. "Species," if we are to understand

127. Biernoff, *Sight and Embodiment*, 75.

128. Ibid., 75.

129. For example, in *De Anima*, 87 (II.12) (in Lawson-Tancred's translation the notion is translated here as "form" rather than "species") cf. Aristotle's *Metaphysics*, 190 (Book Zeta, 7, 1032a)

them in this way, remain consistent despite variations of aspect, in the way that objects can retain a consistent look and appear as the same thing despite changes in lighting, perspective, position, speed, and so on. This does not establish "species" as an essence or as a subject, but as the relatively stable base on which the object's consistency as a thing-undergoing-changes is founded. Rather, intelligible species are understood here as something like Gibson's "perceptual invariants," but with the "normative" dimension we added in discussion of the plate example: the thing's intelligible "look" relates not just its invariant structure as an element of the ambient optic array but also as an element of the human world—its function, its value, its meaning understood existentially, but in relation not only to the existential concerns of the individual but also to the shared concerns of the intersubjective world. We can progress from the geometrical species of Baconian thought to a Merleau-Pontyan conception of species as the "look" that endures through changes of aspect, of meaning, and so on in this way.

While this understanding of intelligible species is not faithful to the Franciscan understanding, it may be that here (as elsewhere) Merleau-Ponty's thought recovers something of the rich medieval synthesis that was overturned by the challenge to analogical thought presented by Duns Scotus' doctrine of the univocity of being.[130] Adrian Pabst shows how Thomas Aquinas's account of perception as the joint action of soul and body preserves the active-passive synthesis of perception from fragmentation into a dualism. For Aquinas "[a] thing's likeness, received in the senses, represents that thing as singular. A likeness received in intellect represents that thing as the defining character of a universal nature."[131] But sensible species "cannot be either mere pictorial images or proper objects of intellectual knowledge. Instead, they activate the power of sense organs and in so doing mediate the form of a sensible object to the senses and the mind alike."[132] The species "is an effect of the thing communicating itself according to its formal structure,"[133] what I have called a "look." So for Pabst, "it follows for Aquinas that the senses perceive sensible reality itself—not a world of mere phenomena from which the mind must abstract in order to construct the world of noumena, as Kant would later assert."[134]

130. For a summary, see Pickstock, "Duns Scotus: His Historical and Contemporary Significance."

131. Aquinas, *Quaestio Disputata De Anima* lib. II, lec. 12, n. 5, cited in Pabst, *Metaphysics*, 222.

132. Pabst, *Metaphysics*, 223–24.

133. Spruit, *Species Intelligibilis*, vol. 1, 163, cited in Pabst, *Metaphysics*, 224.

134. Pabst, *Metaphysics*, 224.

Thus both Merleau-Ponty's and Aquinas's existentialism point us to a reading of Aristotle's notion of forms that reach the eyes as "looks," which ground the possibility of change by attempting to account for the "invariants," whether optical, ecological, or existential, that endure. So, on Biernoff's understanding of Bacon, who was writing on the eve of what the medievalist Olivier Boulnois calls "the Scotist rupture,"[135] "Species not only convey the pictorial 'form' of an object; they are vehicles of meaning."[136] This (ab)use of Baconian theory is doubly motivated: first of all, by the recognition (due to Biernoff) that his work attempts to preserve the imbrication of active and passive elements in perception, as we must; and second, that this synthesis allows it to think perception as relationship, and so to avoid the modern dichotomy of idealism and empiricism. That neither of these goals is fully attained in Bacon's work is due to the still too dualistic conception of the passive and active intellects; nevertheless his thought in certain of its aspects suggests a way beyond this dualism.[137] As Biernoff sees it,

> Bacon's synthesis could be read as an attempt to embrace (rather than resolve) these contradictory propositions of what Merleau-Ponty calls the "perceptual faith": the conviction that sight is both inside *and* exterior to us. What Bacon offers, in the final analysis, is an objective, extramental world that reproduces itself in the mind; and an equally real sphere of human agency, consciousness and curiosity.[138]

Ed Casey, whose notion of "the glance" emphasizes the active element of visual perception and its basis in moving bodily engagement with the world, investigates the Platonic theory of extramission, "a creative compromise that would resolve the dilemma into which previous Greek theories of vision had precipitated themselves: how can light originate equally within the eye *and* from the world?"[139] For Plato,

> The first organ they [the gods] fashioned were those that give us light, which they fastened there in the following way. They arranged that all fire which had not the property of burning, but gave out a gentle light, should form the body of each day's light. The pure fire within us that is akin to this they caused to flow through the eyes, making the whole eye-ball, and particularly its central part, smooth and close-textured so that it would keep

135. Boulnois, "Reading Duns Scotus," 604.

136. Biernoff, *Sight and Embodiment*, 75.

137. Ibid., 86.

138. Ibid., 87.

139. Casey, *The World at a Glance*, 196.

in anything of coarser nature, and filter through only this pure fire. So when there is daylight round the visual stream, it falls on its like and coalesces with it, forming a single uniform body in the line of sight, along which the stream from within strikes the external object.[140]

Although Plato's model of vision is usually considered extramissionist, like the species theory, it is not quite as unidirectional as it has been taken to be. Sight here occurs as a conjunction of the outward-flowing light of the eye and the ambient light, so that "subject and sun, eye and world contribute equally in the formation of the intermediary body, shaped as a cone or chain or cylindrical 'pencil' that is necessary for vision."[141] Of course, it is empirically false that the attention of the eye forms an actual light; if attention is a "ray" then it is so only metaphorically. But nevertheless, the theory captures the fact that visual perception is not a passive reception of sense-data, but rather "combines two quite different ingredients."[142]

Teresa Brennan argues that the passive, physiological account of vision and what she thinks of as the culturalist, active account (which understands sight as culturally constructed) are related in ways that are particularly difficult to specify in the gaze. Her use of this term is very different to Casey's, for example: where in his terms "gaze" specifies the disinterested mode of looking of idealized aesthetic perception, to which he contrasts the engaged and interested "glance," which roots perception in everyday life and the fulfillment of needs, Brennan is speaking of something more like the Sartrean "look" in which the Other somehow brings himself to bear on me, objectifying me, by the assertion of his own seeing subjectivity. If "I feel myself looked-at"[143] in the Sartrean example that we discussed earlier, it is because *something* comes out from the eyes of the looker; not light, we can be sure, but attention; and perhaps more importantly, a kind of orientation. The look of the Sartrean example constitutes the looker, the Other, as the *center* of the scene, and so causes the looked-at to feel displaced, de-centered.

Merleau-Ponty repeats Sartre's exact phrase in *The Visible and the Invisible*, "I feel my self looked at," but the meaning here is not that the world, or a scene, is re-centered around the looker, it is rather that "centers" are multiplied; the Sartrean solipsism is broken and the realization that thinking perceivers abound is made. And here also is made the link between the passivity of seeing and its activity, which exposes the indivision of the

---

140. Plato, *Timaeus*, 62 (§12, 45b–d).

141. Casey, *The World at a Glance*, 197.

142. Ibid., 197–98.

143. Sartre, *Being and Nothingness*, 252.

passive intellect and the active intellect. To put the phrase in its context: "As many painters have said, I feel myself looked at by the things, my activity is equally passivity." There is a sense in which, for Merleau-Ponty, it is not just the (human?) Other who brings their look to bear, but also the things. The art historian James Elkins tries to make this point more fully in his *The Object Stares Back*, and though his work there is evocative, he does not succeed in giving us a rigorous explanation of what the claim that objects "look" at us might mean. The extramissionist model of sight may help here, because although we may struggle to imagine that "the things" look at us in the sense of forming an image of us or becoming conscious of us, we may more sensibly think that many things cast around and interact with the things around them in the way that I do as an active perceiver. Elkins offer a comparison with the many "ways of seeing" in which science depends on technology— like a camera-flash, an electron microscope, or a radar device—that must emit something in order to make the object visible, measuring its reflection, as we might shine a torch or use a bicycle light when moving around in the darkness.[144]

Clearly, then, the ancient model of extramissionism is implausible as a scientific account of seeing; but we are driven to return to it as a metaphor for the active, creative aspect of seeing that the intromissionist, physiological account of vision fails to capture. In her account of Bacon's thought, Biernoff exposes a shortcoming of thinking in terms of the intromission/ extramission dilemma. For, according to Baconian intromission, sensed objects have an agency that they impose on the one who senses them; there is real potency in objects, in virtue of their sensibility. But the intromission that Merleau-Ponty has criticized, the accounts of sensation conceived on idealist or empiricist models, are in part problematic because they allow no agency to the sensed world; either the meaning of things is imposed on them by the perceiver, for the intellectualist, or, for the empiricist, there is no agency but only mechanical chains of causation that extend through the nervous system.

What is in question is not just whether sensation or perception are an inward or outward movement, but also what it is that is transmitted by this movement. Clearly, in the case of *light*, science rightly dismisses the idea that perception occurs by the emission of rays of light from the eyes; the light that comes from the eyes is reflected, rather than emitted from them, and is not decisive for perception. But the fact that sight depends on the reception of light does not make it passive in every sense. Indeed, this is in a sense the heart of Merleau-Ponty's argument in the *Phenomenology of*

144. Elkins, *The Object Stares Back*, 69.

Perception. In his critique of the "classical prejudices" of objective thought, Merleau-Ponty criticizes empiricism for accepting that perception is produced entirely by the workings of sense on sense-receptors; this reduction of perception to observation, this "impingement of stimuli entirely from without on the passive receptive apparatus of the sensorium,"[145] as Jay has it, cannot account for perception since it would suggest either a totally uncomprehending mechanical sight or a direct access to things, as we argued in the first chapter. Sight cannot be, on this model, simple passive reception of sensations. But similarly, the "intellectualist" account for which the world of things must be constituted "entirely out of the subject's own interiority"[146] fails to make sense of perception, because there is in it no real contact with the world, an ever-present threat of solipsism. Perception can be neither purely passive nor purely active, neither observation nor speculation, but must be passive-active, interrogative. The dominance of sight tends towards one or other extreme, depending on whether we emphasize the intromissionism of the physics of light or the role of the brain in supposedly forming perceptual constructions from the retinal images. The examples of the other senses, and especially of touch and, as we have seen, of the special case of touch that is taste, tend less strongly toward this polarization. But this is not because there is a problem with the dominance of sight. The problem is with the way we are conceiving it.

Perception is extramissive insofar as I choose where I look, how I listen, and what I touch, and thus act in and on the world by perceiving. I emit, if you will, rays of attention, and I do things with my glances. Where empiricist intromissionism of light can be denuded of all agency, so the Thomist and Baconian emphasis on the power of things over us depends not on intromissionism but on a certain perceptual interactionism.

If Merleau-Ponty rejects perception conceived as observation and speculation, Jay asks, "can it be said that he adopted the third alternative, that of revelatory illumination[?]"[147] Illumination seems like an odd choice as a proposal for a third alternative here, and Jay uses it because it is utilized by the Surrealists at around Merleau-Ponty's time. But Jay is right to say that "If the goal of the seer is understood to be the attainment of perfect transparency, fusion with the divine light, or clairvoyant purity, then obviously Merleau-Ponty with his celebration of the interminable ambiguities of visual experience was not of their number."[148] Merleau-Ponty's account of percep-

---

145. Jay, *Downcast Eyes*, 307.
146. Ibid., 308.
147. Ibid.
148. Ibid.

tion is not one of clairvoyance or of illumination but of interrogation. He understood the perceiver as an agent located in the thickness of the world; perception does not make sense of everything; necessity and contingency are entwined together in the reality of the fleshly world. And here theology can once again be brought back to its roots by philosophy; it is not a clear and distinct vision of the world that we are to seek but an interrogation of things that searches out understanding without demanding that everything is put in its place and all be contained in a monolithic and perspicuous metaphysics. An incarnational theology can learn from Merleau-Ponty's incarnational account of perception in this regard, embracing ambiguity and the process of questioning that it enables. Jay notices two senses in which Merleau-Ponty's philosophy appropriates certain positive aspects of what he calls "the visionary tradition"; first, that in the fleshly intertwining of the perceiver and the perceived world, in the renewed form of perspectivism that we have affirmed, there is an "ecstatic decentering of the subject, an acknowledgment that however active perception may be, it also meant a kind of surrender," which de Certeau has compared to the ideas of Meister Eckhart.[149] On the other hand, "contact with the visible world did not produce nausea in Merleau-Ponty as it did in Sartre, but a sense of wonder instead. Never fully throwing off the Catholicism of his early training, he reveled in the richness of created, incarnated Being available to the eyes."[150]

149. Ibid., 309.
150. Ibid.

5

Institution and Incarnation
in Merleau-Ponty's Ontology

THINKING THROUGH A RENEWED conception of vision, in the previous
chapter I began to develop an alternative to Cartesian perspectivism,
its geometrical ontology, and its theology of God as *penseur absolu
du monde*. I sought to recover aspects of the species and extramission
theories of vision, establishing depth as a fundamental dimension of
the perceived world, which installs transcendence at the heart of things,
emphasizing our perceptual imbrication with the world in its thickness
and our interrogative relationship to this world.

In this chapter, I situate this account of vision at the center of an ontology of flesh, paying particular attention to the importance of place rather
than of co-ordinate space-time, and drawing out its implications for an incarnational thought that is both philosophical and theological. I argue that
the transcendence of depth reveals a *logos* in things, a God "on the other
side of things," in Merleau-Ponty's terms. I argue for a conception of nature
as the "soil" that gives rise to this *logos*, developing the logic of incarnation
with reference to Merleau-Ponty's notion of *institution*. This will prepare the
way for a fuller engagement with theology in the final chapter.

Merleau-Ponty and Christianity

Merleau-Ponty's relationship to Christianity, and to the Catholic Christianity of his upbringing, is riven with tensions that were left unresolved at his
death. William Hamrick and Jan Van der Veken point out that, as "uniquely

about the Word made flesh and his death," Christianity continued to attract Merleau-Ponty and to hold some import for him long after he had left its institutions behind.[1] In the Christian notion of the incarnation, I want to suggest, lie possibilities for thinking the juncture of nature and its outside through which Merleau-Ponty's ontology may be developed in a fruitful direction; at the same time, Merleau-Ponty's thinking of a "general" incarnation may contribute to theology's thinking through of the particular incarnation of God in Jesus of Nazareth and the ongoing outworking of its consequences. Such development will suggest a critique of idolatrous pictures of God—a critique that Merleau-Ponty thought applied to Christianity, and to which traditional theology was unable to respond. On this point, I shall argue in the next chapter, Merleau-Ponty was wrong—because his understanding of traditional theology was mistaken. Nevertheless, Merleau-Ponty's critique of Christianity will prove useful, not least because his misapprehensions about traditional theology are widely held: in popular views of Christianity, within many forms of Christian thinking, and even within debates in academic theology. The god who is abandoned and replaced in some revisionist liberal theologians, is often not the God of orthodox Christianity at all.

In "Indirect Language and the Voices of Silence" Merleau-Ponty writes,

> It is a little too much to forget that Christianity is, among other things, the recognition of a mystery in the relations of man and God, which stems precisely from the fact that the Christian God wants nothing to do with a vertical relation of subordination. He is not simply a principle of which we are the consequence, a will whose instruments we are, or even a model of which human values are only the reflection. There is a sort of impotence of God without us, and Christ attests that God would not be fully God without becoming fully man. Claudel goes so far as to say that God is not above us but beneath us—meaning that we do not find Him as a suprasensible idea, but as another ourself which dwells in and authenticates our darkness. Transcendence no longer hangs over man: he becomes, strangely, its privileged bearer.[2]

This notion, even the thought that God has become impotent without us, is not an innovation in Christian theology. Indeed, as I am seeking to show, Merleau-Ponty's break with objectivist ontology recalls the Christian theologian to an understanding of incarnation that objectivism made

1. Hamrick and Van der Veken, *Nature and Logos*, 121.
2. Merleau-Ponty, "Indirect Language and the Voices of Silence," 71.

incomprehensible. We can trace this thought in Richard Hooker, for whom "since God has deified our nature, though not by turning it into himself, yet by making it his own inseparable habitation, we cannot now conceive how God should, without us, either exercise divine power or receive the glory of divine praise."[3] So "it pleases him in mercy to account himself incomplete and maimed without us."[4]

In his *A Christian Theology of Place*, the Anglican theologian John Inge argues that *place* is a critical category for theological understanding, and one to which too little attention has been paid, having been subordinated in the history of philosophy to the logic of space, and more recently that of time.[5] In citing W. D. Davies's comments on the spatial symbolism of the Gospel of John, Inge writes that "the vertical dimension is, of course, what Christians refer to as the incarnation, which is central to the New Testament Witness and the Christian faith that springs from it, and the fact that Jesus was not a disincarnate spirit has profound implications."[6]

To speak in terms of verticality would seem to return us to the logic of spatial geometry and to fail to think incarnation in terms of place. But for Inge, the abstractive discourses of space (beginning in the pre-existing space in which *Timaeus'* demiurge creates the world, and the Aristotelian notion of space as a container)[7] and of time (in Leibniz's insistence on the logical priority of time over space and in Kant's argument that time as succession "is the schematic expression of causality in the physical world order")[8] in which we are immersed bring about the devaluation of place, which, as phenomenologically and experientially prior to both time and space, ought to be more fundamental to our thinking.[9]

So we must understand Inge with reference to his own claim that, in Christian theology, the embodied logic of *place* has priority over geometrized space; that is to say, that the *verticality* of the incarnation is not oriented around the infinite height (thought in terms of Cartesian coordinates) of God understood as something like an absolute perceiver. Rather, we should seek to understand the incarnation in terms of *depth*; that the God who is at

3. Hooker, *Laws*, Book V, Ch. 54.6. Cited in Miles, *The Word Made Flesh*, 322, though it is incorrectly attributed there, with the quote which follows, to *Laws* V.56.10.

4. Ibid., Book V, Ch. 56.10. Cited by Miles, *The Word Made Flesh*, 322.

5. Inge, *A Christian Theology of Place*, 32.

6. Ibid., 51, referring to W. D. Davies, *The Gospel and the Land: Early Christianity and Jewish Territorial Doctrine* (Berkeley, CA: University of Californian Press, 1974), 335.

7. Ibid., 2–4.

8. Ibid., 8.

9. Ibid., 1–26.

the heart of things traverses their depths to be made known on their surface, in this particular human being (Jesus of Nazareth) and in that which bears witness to him. As we problematize this claim to verticality in denying the logic of God as an entity that occupies the place of the highest perspective on things,[10] we also call into question the other orientation of verticality—if we are to take seriously Claudel's view, cited by Merleau-Ponty, that God is beneath us, this is not to say that we are above, but that God is "under our skin," *interior intimo meo*, that the God who transcends nature is also at work in its depths, holding things in being.

For Leonard Lawlor, in his introduction to Merleau-Ponty's course notes on *Husserl at the Limits of Phenomenology*, "Merleau-Ponty is orienting his entire philosophy toward the depth, in the ground, the visible, and not, as he says, in the heights, in the ideas, in the invisible."[11] This claim is based on a citation from the lecture course on Husserl, which I am here paraphrasing for the sake of readability (in the original there are a huge number of insertions to clarify Merleau-Ponty's shorthand and terms untranslated from Husserl's German, which I translate):

> The theme of philosophy is the horizon of horizons. This goes deeper than Husserl's initial definitions of philosophy as a rigorous science. In particular, the initial definitions of the *Eidos*: the *Eidos* is from now on the interpretation of a horizon; eidetic variation seeks the invariant, "as the essence/nature [*wesen*] constantly implied in the flowing, vital horizon."[12] Does philosophy explain this essence/nature? Its theme is a "reason hidden in history" (Fink), a "teleological reason running throughout all history,"[13] but which can be grasped only in filigree, as a secret or hidden connection. Therefore essence/nature does not engulf the horizon. It is the formulation of its structure as [the] horizon of culture ("our present as a process of traditionalizing itself in a flowing-static vitality.")[14] But this "structural" or concrete *a priori* is neither a Kantian category nor even a Hegelian idea; it is the "universal ground of sense":[15] the sense, in the last in-

10. In several places (especially in the Psalms) Scripture speaks of God looking down from heaven (Pss 11:4; 14:2; 102:19; Heb 4:13; Job 28:24) on mankind. But this looking down is always a form of contact, always expresses God's involvement in the world, as well as his transcendence.

11. Leonard Lawlor, "Foreword—*Verflechtung*" (to Merleau-Ponty, *Husserl at the Limits*), xvii.

12. Husserl, "The Origin of Geometry," 112.

13. Ibid., 112.

14. Ibid., 108.

15. Ibid., 109.

stance, far from being an *idea*, is a *ground*. Philosophy seeks in the archaeology of ground, in the *depth* and not in the height (the ideas).[16]

To say that Merleau-Ponty's late philosophy is oriented toward depth is absolutely right; but of course to say that this excludes the "invisible" is a mistake. It rather seeks the invisible *in* the visible.[17] Lawlor has to make this mistake, and misread Merleau-Ponty here, because his guiding thesis is that "Immanence [. . .] must be made complete,"[18] drawn from Jean Hyppolite's claim in *Logique et existence* that immanence *is* complete.[19] This idea is not at all consonant with Merleau-Ponty's thought, which searches, as we are seeing, for a conception of transcendence that does not depend on a dualism.

Henri Maldiney, in discussing the sense of transcendence in Merleau-Ponty, returns to the Husserlian example of the perceived cube. Merleau-Ponty uses this example, Maldiney thinks, despite its potentially geometricized, disembodied inflections, because in it "the transcendence of the thing is shown in its naked and [. . .] pure state."[20] For Husserl, according to Maldiney, the ultimate reality of the thing lies in its transcendence, which is in some way vertical; this is perhaps the view that the being of the cube is the "highest" perspective, the sum of all perspectives on it, which makes the viewpoint of a *penseur absolu* the only one that can grasp the thing as it is. Merleau-Ponty, too, speaks of a "vertical transcendence" that does not have to be the transcendence of subordination, but is that transcendence that humankind bears.[21] As Maldiney has it, "we do not learn the real through reflection, but in the wild state," that is, I experience the cube as transcendent insofar as I find it in a world in which I myself am caught up and to which my mode of access does not make it transparent, but which is necessarily mixed-up because I am a part of it, am mixed up in it. So,

> In contrast to Husserl, one could speak of a horizontal transcendence of flesh to flesh. But my going out into the other, my

---

16. The source of this paraphrase is in Merleau-Ponty, *Husserl at the Limits of Phenomenology*, 67.

17. Cf., Merleau-Ponty, *Nature*, 271; *The Visible and the Invisible*, 215, 235, 257; Semonovitch and DeRoo, *Merleau-Ponty at the Limits*, 15; Barbaras, *The Being of the Phenomenon*, 240; Carbone, *The Thinking of the Sensible*, 35, and many more.

18. Lawlor, "The Chiasm and the Fold," 115. Lawlor repeats this idea in *The Implications of Immanence*, and takes it as a guiding idea in his *Derrida and Husserl*.

19. Cited in Lawlor, *The Implications of Immanence*, 4.

20. Maldiney, "Flesh and Verb," 63.

21. Merleau-Ponty, "Indirect Language and the Voices of Silence," 71.

emergence into the other, is of the same order as our two respective emergences. It is the self-emergence of universal flesh: so these horizontal, or transversal relations imply a unique vertical transcendence *in depth*.[22]

Verticality and Transcendence

This vertical transcendence locates thought not only in a physical world, nor a world of meaningful *logos*, but also in a world of history. In the second course from the lectures on nature, given in 1957–58, Merleau-Ponty declares that "our goal is the series φυσις—λογος—history,"[23] but the meaning of history here is not only that of human history but also of the history of a given body:—its institution, its natality, its belonging to a cultural world. History is here identified with "the human body as the root of symbolism," which is "the junction of φυσις and λογος," and indeed the third course, given in 1959–60, is entitled "Nature and Logos: The Human Body." A note, published with the working notes for *The Visible and the Invisible* and written in February 1959 suggests that there is a relation of this scheme to the "verticality" of depth in transcendence when Merleau-Ponty repeats the formula, writing that the overcoming (in fact he uses the word "destruction") of Cartesian objectivist ontology requires the "rediscovery of φυσις, then of λογος and the *vertical* history starting from our 'culture' and the *Winke* [pointers or signs] of our 'science.'"[24] History, then, does not begin just with the vagaries of human history, but with the *necessary* contingencies and contingent necessities of human situatedness, embodiment, and cultural formation. This personal history is vertical insofar as I rise out of the depths of my embodiment, an embodiment which must precede me. It is thus that Merleau-Ponty writes, in *Phenomenology of Perception*,

> Since it is not oriented "in itself," my first perception and my first taking-hold of the world must appear as the execution of an ancient pact established between *x* and the world in general; my history takes up a prehistory and its acquired results, and my personal existence must recover a prepersonal tradition. There is, then, another subject beneath me, for whom a world exists before I do and who marks out my place there. This captive or natural spirit is my body, not the momentary body which is the

22. Maldiney, "Flesh and Verb," 64.

23. Merleau-Ponty, *Nature*, 199.

24. Merleau-Ponty, *The Visible and the Invisible*, 183, emphasis added.

instrument of my personal choices and which fixes on a particular world, but the system of anonymous "functions" which envelops all my particular fixations in a general project.[25]

It would seem clear that the "ancient pact" between the x that is my body and the world is perception. There is ambiguity over the question of whether the anonymous body perceives or whether it is the necessary condition for perception; the body-subject of the *Phenomenology of Perception* is a subject of perception, but in *The Visible and the Invisible* there is an explicit denial that the body perceives,[26] as well as an insistence that perception emerges against the background of or "in the recess of" the body[27] and that it is not the case that one could perceive without a body.[28]

It seems reasonable to say that the body grounds perception, which could not occur without it, but that it is not exactly the same thing as the perceiver. Perception, I propose, "rises above" the body, grows out of it as its native soil. But, crucially, perception does not leave this soil untouched; as Merleau-Ponty had been showing since *The Structure of Behaviour*, there is an exchange between the levels; and sensitive, perceptual nature is bound up with physical nature in its dependence on movement. The regulative ideal of maximum clarity in perception that guides the perceiver to look at an object from a certain distance and perspective is the first moment of this exchange. And so as the vertical, pre-personal history we have spoken of grounds, through perception, *logos* in *phusis*, meaning in nature, so *phusis* is transformed into *logos*, not all at once, as it were, but by the sedimentation and accretion of "institutions," that is, of meaningful structures in the world in which it lives and on which it acts; as the word is made flesh, so the flesh is made word.

Bernard Flynn notes that "the dimension of Being that is beneath not only our personal life but also beneath history and symbolic institution is what Merleau-Ponty refers to as 'wild being.' In the context of his reinterpretation of Husserl, one could call this 'the Earth.'"[29] That is to say that the body is of the Earth,[30] that the *human* is truly of the *humus*. In his lectures

25. Merleau-Ponty, *Phenomenology of Perception*, 265. I have here re-translated from the French edition, *Phénoménologie de la perception*, 293–94.

26. Merleau-Ponty, *The Visible and the Invisible*, 9: "my body does not perceive, but it is as if it were built around the perception that dawns through it."

27. Ibid., 9.

28. Ibid., 27: "we do not mean that one could perceive without a body."

29. Flynn, "Merleau-Ponty and Skepticism," 126.

30. Regarding capitalization: "Earth" is being used as a proper name for the planet we live on; "earth" describes the kind of material ground implied by worldedness, so that human beings might leave the Earth but we will always have some kind of earth.

on Husserl's text entitled "Foundational Investigations of the Phenomeno-logical Origin of the Spatiality of Nature: The Originary Ark, the Earth, does not move,"[31] Merleau-Ponty speaks of the Earth "that the Copernican man forgets,"[32] an earth that is not an object, but a ground, which grounds my body as object just as my body grounds my subjectivity (I am hesitant to use this word without a precise idea of what we mean by it, but this meaning can only emerge from our work here). Although Merleau-Ponty, in his working notes for *The Visible and the Invisible*, criticizes his earlier work in *Phenomenology of Perception*, saying that "The problems posed [. . .] are insoluble because I start there from the 'consciousness'-'object' distinction,"[33] there is an anticipation there of the structuration of the gestalt in which subjectivity is not just "attached" to an object in a substantialist mode of thinking but is grounded in the triangulated structure of subject—object—ground in a structural (but not necessarily structural*ist*) mode of thinking.

Mauro Carbone points to[34] Merleau-Ponty's résumé of this course, in which he spells out that for Copernican man, "the world contains only 'bodies' (*Körper*),"[35] arguing that we must recover "a mode of being the idea of which we have lost, the being of the 'ground' (*Boden*) [or 'soil,' as Carbone translates], and that of the Earth first of all—the earth where we live, that which is this side of rest and movement, being the ground from which all rest and movement break away."[36] This idea of a mode of being is a crucial ontological concept for Merleau-Ponty, that of a "soil" that is not an object but the ground of objects. John O'Neill translates *Boden* as "ground," but Carbone uses "soil," and where Merleau-Ponty discusses this notion in his first lecture course on nature, given in 1956–57, three years before the 1959–60 course on Husserl, he uses the French word *sol*, which can mean both *soil* and *ground*, but transparently is etymologically closer to the former. In an introductory note to this course—not the résumé, which is published separately in the *Themes from the Lectures*—he says

---

The exception is in the phrase "heaven and earth," which is left uncapped, following convention.

31. Husserl, "Foundational Investigations."

32. Merleau-Ponty, *Husserl at the Limits of Phenomenology*, 69.

33. Merleau-Ponty, *Visible and the Invisible*, 200.

34. Carbone, "Flesh," 49–57.

35. Merleau-Ponty, *Themes from the Lectures*, 121; *Husserl at the Limits of Phenomenology*, 9.

36. Merleau-Ponty, *Themes from the Lectures*, 121; *Husserl at the Limits of Phenomenology*, 9.

> Nature is the primordial—that is, the nonconstructed, the non-instituted; [. . .] Nature is an enigmatic object, an object that is not an object at all; it is not really set out in front of us. It is our soil [*sol*]—not what is in front of us, facing us, but rather, that which carries us.[37]

In "The Primacy of Perception and Its Philosophical Consequences"[38] Merleau-Ponty appeals to the primacy of perception, claiming that it overcomes skepticism and pessimism, and locating his anti-atomism and anti-objectivism within a larger philosophical scheme: he argues against Pascal that one does not love only "qualities," but "on the contrary [. . .] we call what we perceive 'the world,' and what we love 'the person.'"[39] There is then, he argues, a type of doubt and a type of spite that are made impossible, and he finds a truth of love that Pascal destroys by analysis. "The absolute which he looks for beyond our experience is implied in it. Just as I grasp time through my present and by being present, I perceive others through my individual life, in the tension of an experience which transcends itself."[40] He closes by relating this to Christian theology:

> There is thus no destruction of the absolute or of rationality here, only of the absolute and the rationality separated from experience. To tell the truth, Christianity consists in replacing the separated absolute by the absolute in men. Nietzsche's idea that God is dead is already contained in the Christian idea of the death of God. God ceases to be an external object in order to mingle in human life, and this life is not simply a return to a nontemporal conclusion. God needs human history. As Malebranche said, the world is unfinished. My viewpoint differs from the Christian viewpoint to the extent that the Christian believes in another side of things where the *"renversement du pour au contre"* takes place. In my view this "reversal" takes place before our eyes. And perhaps some Christians would agree that the other side of things must already be visible in the environment in which we live. By advancing this thesis of the primacy of perception, I have less the feeling that I am proposing something completely new than the feeling of drawing out the conclusions of the work of my predecessors.[41]

---

37. Merleau-Ponty, *Nature*, 4.
38. Merleau-Ponty, "The Primacy of Perception," 12–42.
39. Ibid., 26–27.
40. Ibid., 27.
41. Ibid.

It is not obvious what exactly Merleau-Ponty is anticipating when he speaks of the "reversal" expected by the Christian. But it seems clear when he says "perhaps some Christians would agree that the other side of things must already be visible" that this is not a marginal view but a central tenet of Christianity. In the Gospels, Jesus comes announcing the kingdom (βασιλεια) of God, and saying "The time is fulfilled, and the kingdom of God has come near [or *is at hand*]";[42] in the New Testament reports of his ministry, which this announcement begins, he demonstrates the presence and character of that kingdom in miracles, in prayer, in community, in refusing violent opposition to the Roman occupation, and ultimately in accepting execution as a criminal and in bodily resurrection. Whether we read these events as historical or as mythological, whether we understand the kingdom Jesus announces as an inward power given to humans, as the breaking in to earthly reality of the "wholly other," perhaps in the sacraments, as the church, or as "heaven," it is difficult to take the line Albert Schweitzer takes in thinking of the kingdom as wholly future, as "an apocalyptic realm to be inaugurated by a supernatural act of God when history will be broken off and a new heavenly order of existence begun," as George Eldon Ladd puts it.[43] If it were so, Jesus' message would quickly have seemed implausible (if the kingdom were "at hand" in a purely temporal sense, and the expected apocalypse never comes) and lacking in force (if the kingdom was expected to be made known in and around Jesus and his followers but in fact nothing out of the ordinary happened), and regardless of its truth or falsity, history shows us that his message was neither of these things, but rather was effective in mobilizing a fast-expanding movement of people prepared to commit themselves to this cause, at risk of exclusion from their own communities, ostracization, and violent persecution in many places in the Roman world.

This is all to say that Merleau-Ponty's vision of the coming to fulfillment of the world within human history, of the showing of the truth of things not as a separated absolute in a heaven of ideas but as the absolute in the lives of persons, communities, and the places to which they belong, does not seem an innovation to the Christian, but a reminder of the truth that is summed up and brought to a head in the incarnation of Christ. There is, then, a logic of *imminence* demanded by this "incarnational" thought; that is, the "other side of things" of which Merleau-Ponty speaks, the invisible depths of the world, breaks through to the surface of things; but this is not a completed movement, and perception has not become absolute. The invisible remains

42. Mark 1:15 (NRSV).
43. Ladd, *The Gospel of the Kingdom*, 15.

the invisible, the world has not become transparent, but neither has it become opaque. Just as the "other side of things" is seen, though it is invisible, in any everyday object, it also crucially shapes our perception of place (the "inside" depends on the same "outside" that it excludes) and our search for truth. This imminence is not the relation of a transcendence of infinite height to a pure plane of immanence but is that of a transcendence already lodged within the earth, the realization of the depths of things, the coming-to-themselves of created realities. Lissa McCullough, reflecting on Simone Weil and Søren Kierkegaard's "revolutionizing" of the tasks of faith and prayer, in contrast to Augustine's "otherworldly" paradigm, suggests that

> Our task or calling in life is not to "suffer" the temporal in patience, waiting it out in our quest for the eternal at the end of time, but to inhabit it and love it as the manifest and living will of God in the flesh. We must not only be prepared for the grace that carries us into eternity, or death, but we must be prepared for the grace that delivers us—in a heartbeat—back into our very flesh, into the task of life, regaining the finite in faith, such that the "city of God" or "kingdom of God" is actively incarnate in us, here and now, in the very midst of the "city of man." This is the radically dialectical task that Kierkegaard describes as bringing eternity to bear within time.[44]

In the report of the discussion published with "The Primacy of Perception" Merleau-Ponty responds to Jean Hyppolite's reminder that he "said that God was dead" with the reply that "I said that to say God is dead, as the Nietzscheans do, or to speak of the death of God, like the Christians do, is to tie God to man, and that in this sense the Christians themselves are obliged to tie eternity to time."[45]

In a sense, to conduct this discussion only in terms of time and eternity is to make a mistake, as Inge shows us. If we take time to be the index of the particular, bodily life, as the locus of incarnation, without thinking of incarnation in a particular place, we simply stretch eternity out on a line; we perpetuate the mistake of constructing the world according to an Aristotelian, Euclidean, or perspectival geometry. If our task is to bring eternity to bear within time, it is also to bring infinity or the immeasurable to bear in place. To think in terms of *place* is to refuse to abstract space or time as dimensional realities from the whole, to think in terms of orientation rather than of measure, to prioritize the absolute in human beings rather than the externalized absolute. But this place needs some kind of *grounding*

44. McCullough, "Prayer and Incarnation," 209–16.

45. Merleau-Ponty, "The Primacy of Perception," 41.

that makes sensible our intersubjective life and explains why a place is not simply commensurate with a particular space at a particular time. For David Abram,

> Underneath the modern, scientific conception of space as a mathematically infinite and homogenous void, Husserl discloses the experienced spatiality of the *earth* itself. The encompassing earth, he suggests, provides the most immediate, bodily awareness of space, from which all later *conceptions* of space are derived.[46]

This latter space is what we are calling, following Inge, *place*. Husserl's argument in the "Foundational Investigations . . ." begins to build a conception of nature that goes beyond geometrization, by insisting that space is founded on the earth, which provides the zero-point of movement and rest, and so cannot itself be in movement or at rest. It is our soil, the ground of our possibilities.

Nature as "Soil"

In a sense, this Husserlian notion of earth as soil anticipates Merleau-Ponty's claim that the perceived world precedes and grounds the homogeneous "nature" of the sciences. Perhaps it will help us to get clearer on what this claim might mean. On the one hand, our understanding of the world in-itself can only be built on our perceptions of it. We can have no knowledge of a nature of which we are not in some sense a part. But does it not defy logic to claim that the world we experience is *more real* than the world that we understand by abstracting from our experience, by attempting to make sense of everyone's experience?

Science depends on the repeatability of experiments and on the independent verification of results because these combat individual bias in our understanding of the world. If many different observers observe that a particle travels faster than light, for example, then we can be more sure that such an outcome is not the result of wishful thinking, of deception, of mis-measurement, or of some other kind of mistake. If the experiment can be performed using different apparatus, so much the better. In what sense should the world as understood by such a process be made secondary?

Surely the world as discovered by the sciences must most closely approximate the *real world*; surely that world must be the foundation of our ontology? By abstracting from the role of any particular observer it gives

---

46. Abram, *The Spell of the Sensuous*, 42.

us an idea of what the world is like to an anonymous observer. Does it also tell us what the world is like when there is no one to observe it at all? If things behave in certain, predictable ways under all possible conditions of observation, it seems reasonable to think that they still behave in the same way when not under observation. It is on the basis of this claim that science abstracts from the observer's participation in the process and claims to tell us *what the world is like* and not just *how it seems*. The problem with this view, the source of its failure properly to understand the world in which we live, lies in its failure to account for the fact that the observer is not just an observer but also a human being. Even if an experiment can control all the observer's biases, it cannot control the fact that he does *this* experiment and not another one. Accounting for a certain situation or sum of facts as they are regardless of the status of observers crosses the established gap between appearance and reality in the scientific mind without firm foundations.

What scientific thought forgets, when it tells us what the world would be like regardless of the status of the observer, is that the world is not empty of human beings, and that these human beings are never (except in certain respects under certain experimental conditions) observers, but are real *actors within that world*. In Xavier Tilliette's account of Merleau-Ponty's lectures on "Husserl's Concept of Nature," Merleau-Ponty argues that

> The real, the true, the in-itself is the correlative of a pure specta-
> tor, an I which has decided to know the world. This conception
> extends by itself, without limits, applying itself to the *Weltall*
> [world in its totality]. In this sense it is everything. When a phi-
> losopher journeys he carries these notions with him![47]

This is based on an account of Husserl's view:

> In *Ideen II*, Husserl envisions a sphere of pure things (*blosse Sa-
> chen*), things which are nothing but things, without predicates
> of value or use. This is the Nature of the scientists, of Descartes,
> the Nature of the sciences of nature. But it has its foundation
> in the structure of human perception. [. . .] The idea of such a
> Nature, *blosse Sachlichkeit* [mere thingness], is circumscribed a
> priori when we make ourselves into pure theoretical subjects.[48]

Under normal circumstances we assume that our perceptions are perceptions of a prior world. This world is the world of nature, which imper-
fectly gives rise to our perceptions, and is the world to which we must lead
them back, using the methods of science. But, according to Husserl, this

47. Tilliette, "Husserl's Concept of Nature," 163.
48. Ibid., 163.

is a mistake. It is right to say that our perceptions are the perceptions of a prior world. But it is the perceived world that gives rise to them, and science brings us not to this world but to an abstract world, devoid of color, thought, or love. Scientism builds this confusion between two worlds, the world of perception and the world of nature, on the basis of a confusion between two selves; it mistakes the active, engaged perceiver of the lived world for the theoretical subject of the perceived world, and it is on this basis that it establishes its conception of the world of science: it is the essential correlate of its notion of the detached, neutral observer.

> Husserl seems to suggest that the earth lies at the heart of our notions of time as well as of space. He writes of the earth as our "primitive home" and our "primitive history." Every unique cultural history is but an episode in this larger story; every culturally constructed notion of time presupposes our deep history as carnal beings present to a single earth.[49]

> If the "core of reality" that is disclosed within perception is immemorial, then we can gain a new appreciation of the aloofness or inhumanity of the thing, that is, the sense in which it rejects the perceiving body. If Merleau-Ponty's descriptions are accurate, then the perceiving subject's relation with nature is always and essentially Janus-faced: on the one hand, and as a condition for its attunement with the sensible, the body is co-natural with what it perceives; but, on the other hand, and as the condition for being in-itself, nature exceeds the body and withdraws into an immemorial depth before the body's advances. Thus, our kinship with and estrangement from nature are essentially linked already at the level of perceptual dialogue. This structure of kinship and estrangement is doubled when we consider reflection's grasp of the prereflective body. This suggests that the kinship and estrangement of reflective consciousness with respect to its own embodied nature are equally essential.[50]

This claim that the perceived world is prior to and more fundamental than the world to which science attends would seem to risk idealism: if there are contents of perception that do not correspond to anything in the world of the *bloße Sachen*, these contents must be at some level contributed to the scene by the mind or the perceptual process. But reducing reality to an essentially mental thing would shipwreck Merleau-Ponty's entire project from *The Structure of Behaviour* to *The Visible and the Invisible*. If the world

49. Abram, *The Spell of the Sensuous*, 43.

50. Toadvine, *Merleau-Ponty's Philosophy of Nature*, 70.

is a mental reality, there can be no thought of an "incarnation," for how then would what is incarnated be any different to what is not incarnated? If flesh is reducible to word, then there can be no meaning in the claim that the word was made flesh. In Xavier Tilliette's notes, Merleau-Ponty goes on: "The universe of theories refers back to another universe, preceding it, primordial. It is a matter of unearthing a more original world *vor aller Thesis* [before any thesis]." This more original world is not a perceived world in the sense of a mental world. Rather, it is

> given to us *leibhaft* [bodily]. That is to say, consciousness has a very strong intuition of the insurmountable character of the perceived. It is stuck, bogged down in the perceived thing, even though the *blosse Sachen* form a thin universe. This pre-thetic universe is inscribed in the sense of the *blosse Sachen*, sediment-ed in them. The entire history of consciousness is found sedi-mented in Descartes. Pure things are idealizations, ensembles constructed upon what is solid. One must dig beneath them.[51]

There is simply *more to* the world than the "thin" universe of mere matter. So it is that "the scientific universe does not rest on itself. It presup-poses a sphere of experience which is the level upon which the other, the scientific universe, can draw." Husserl and Merleau-Ponty are both sensitive to this and it is for this that Merleau-Ponty is arguing when he makes a case for the primordiality of the perceived world. The world is not mere matter, but is structured, meaningful, beautiful or ugly, mysterious or obvious, ap-pealing or repulsive. To do away with these perceived qualities is to ignore certain aspects of the real world. "Perceptual consciousness is not a mental alchemy, it is global, total."[52]

Nature is our soil, which is to say that nature *per se* cannot be an object for us. This is not, of course, to deny the objectivity of the natural sciences; indeed Merleau-Ponty is careful in the résumé for this course to protect the status of science, saying that "it is not possible to reject science out of hand on the pretext that it works in terms of certain ontological prejudices," since if they are prejudices, "the science itself, in its wanderings through being, will certainly have occasion to reject them." So it is that "the philosopher [. . .] should not pretend to intervene in the field [. . .] or to arbitrate for science."[53]

The Earth, we have said, with the late Husserl, is the "soil" of the embod-ied perceiver. Nature is also our soil, but we do not wish to conflate nature

---

51. Tilliette, "Husserl's Concept of Nature," 164.

52. Ibid., 164.

53. Merleau-Ponty, *Themes from the Lectures*, 84.

and earth. The Husserlian earth is not a space, but the condition of place; that is, not a container nor a co-ordinate location but a unity that gives rise to a sum of horizons, an "immobile" that is the ground of all movement, that cannot itself, therefore, move; just as when I walk through the carriages of a train I am moving through the train, and if it is light and I look out of the window of the train I know I and the train together are moving through the landscape, but still it is never the case that the train is moving around me.[54] While the earth is not, in this understanding, an object among objects, it is a *particular* ground of possibilities that could conceivably be different, where nature is a general ground of possibilities: we can easily imagine a different earth, and indeed Planet Earth is always changing, but when we use the term "nature" we tend to mean that which does not change and which does not have a place: the laws of nature, and its processes, powers, and potentialities. We can conceive of a different "earth" in the same nature, but if nature were different, so would the Earth be. And indeed, Husserl is clear that if I could go between two earths as ground-bodies, and could fly from one to the other, I would thereby unite the two earths into a single ground. As Merleau-Ponty puts it, "wherever I go, I make a ground there and attach the new ground to the old where I lived. To think two Earths is to think one same Earth."[55] In Xavier Tilliette's notes on Merleau-Ponty's 1957–58 lectures he writes

> There is but one humanity and there is never anything but a single *Boden*. The order of objective thought is therefore not exhaustive. The earth is not, as it were, pinned down; it is not a place in the sense that objects in the world have a place. The earth is our stock, our *Urheimat* [primal home]. It is the root of our spatiality, our shared native land, the seat of an *Urhistorie* [primal history], an originary insertion. Husserl called this the originary *arche*. This means that it founds a pre-existence or a primordial existence. In this way, Husserl's philosophy is close to that of Heidegger.[56]

He is right that there is in this natural archeology a kind of Heideggerian appeal to the primordial ground of Being. But for Merleau-Ponty, as, I think, for Husserl, to assert the importance of the notion of *soil* as a way to escape the pervasive ontology of the object is not to assert that this ground is covered over nor that it must be uncovered; it is not to claim the ethical priority of the primordial nor that the answer to the question of the meaning

54. Husserl, "Foundational Investigations," 121.

55. Merleau-Ponty, *Nature*, 77.

56. Tilliette, "Husserl's Concept of Nature," 167.

of Being lies there, a question for which Merleau-Ponty shows little appetite (at least when posed, and answered, so directly). It is simply to help us to understand ontology as a structure, and as a structure that is not purely ideal but one that is *instituted*, that has a real historical depth. Where Descartes presented us with the opposed worlds of the mental and the physical, and Sartre (the neo-Cartesian) with the opposition of freedom and facticity, of negativity and positivity, Merleau-Ponty's ontology complexifies this picture with the centrality in his ontological picture of the historical world, which is composed of sedimented results of acts of institution.

The Logic of Institution

Merleau-Ponty developed the notion of institution in a specifically philo-sophical way in his 1954–55 lecture course entitled "Institution in Personal and Public History."[57] These lectures have gone largely undiscussed, and are key for understanding Merleau-Ponty's relation to Christianity and the institution of the church. In this section I offer an extended reading of these lectures, seeking to develop their significance for Merleau-Ponty's late ontology and its relation to theology.

What exactly does Merleau-Ponty mean by institution? In his notes for the introduction to the course, he writes

> Therefore institution [means] establishment in an experience (or in a constructed apparatus) of dimensions (in the general, Cartesian sense: system of references) in relation to which a whole series of other experiences will make sense and will make a *sequel*, a history.
>
> The sense is deposited (it is no longer merely in me as con-sciousness, it is not re-created or constituted at the time of the recovery). But not as an object left behind, as a simple remain-der or as something that survives, as a residue. [It is deposited] as something to continue, to complete without it being the case that the sequel is determined. The instituted will change but this very change is called for by its *Stiftung*. Goethe: genius [is] post-humous productivity. All institution is in this sense genius.[58]

Institution establishes the dimensions of experience, "lines of force" that make *sens* of the world. These dimensions are not simply subjective elements of experience, though: they are *deposited* in the world, not as de-tritus of experience but as the markers of meaning that carry forward their

57. Merleau-Ponty, *Institution and Passivity*.

58. Ibid., 8–9. The insertions are the editors'.

productivity. Merleau-Ponty makes clear that this notion bears on our conception of subjectivity, contrasting it to the Kantian notion of the constituting subject. There is an "instituted and instituting subject, but inseparably, and not a constituting subject; [therefore] a certain inertia—[the fact of being] exposed to . . . ."[59] Here institution marks the sedimentation of the subject in a living world that exceeds him, and thus the possibility of transcendence; in the summary of the course he clarifies this "exposed to . . ." by writing that "even if we grant that certain of the objects are 'never completely' constituted (Husserl), they are at each moment the exact reflection of the acts and powers of consciousness. There is nothing in these constituted objects that is able to throw consciousness back into other perspectives."[60] This again recalls the *Meno* paradox: "how can anything be *learned*?" That Platonic question guides us in the matter of transcendence; Plato's solution, of our recollection of Forms arising from an older familiarity with them, seems on the surface of things to affirm the priority of a disembodied, atemporal world of abstraction over the life of the incarnate world. The logic of institution indicates not only a solution to the paradox, but an explanation of how philosophy could have asked a question so totally alien to life as we live it: that the transcendence of the unknown, the unseen, is not opposed to the immanence of the familiar world but is intertwined with it; it is possible for us to learn something new *not* because we somehow already knew it but because knowledge is not a world of its own, is not subject to laws of conservation, because we *do not need to know for what we seek* in fullness, because our bodily life consists in an engagement with the world, which is not entirely perspicuous but that both reveals and conceals itself.

Merleau-Ponty criticizes the "philosophy of consciousness"—that logic of the world "constituted" in the mind, which he found in Husserl and whose classic formulation is in Kant's philosophy—because for it there can be no exchange, no movement, between the object and the constituting consciousness.[61] Because the unity of the world hangs on the constituting consciousness here, the question of personal identity, of what makes the past "I" the same as the present becomes a problem, as does the question of the existence of other minds, since they can only be conceived as "negatives" of myself.

By contrast, for a philosophy that considers the subject as an instituting body and not a constituting consciousness, "what I have begun at certain decisive moments would be neither distant, in the past, as an objective

59. Ibid., 6.
60. Ibid., 76.
61. Ibid.

memory, nor would it be actual as a memory assumed. Rather, what I have begun would be truly in the 'between,' as the field of my becoming during this period."[62] The philosophy of consciousness, and the logic of constitution, depends on the Cartesian logic of representation that we discussed in our previous chapter; for constitution, my relation to the world depends on the ongoing and continuous reality of my act of constitution; I must go on holding the world together in thought. Merleau-Ponty's philosophy drops this prejudice against the world:

> The instituted is not the immediate reflection of the activity of [the instituting subject] and can be taken up by himself or by others without a total re-creation being at issue. Thus the instituted exists between others and myself, between me and myself, like a hinge, the consequence and guarantee of our belonging to the selfsame world.[63]

In the lecture course, Merleau-Ponty develops the notion of institution with reference to four "levels" of phenomena. He characterizes the first three as dealing with "personal or intersubjective history," the fields of the institution of a feeling (particularly of love), of the institution of a work of art, and of the institution of a domain of knowledge (that is, a "science" in the broader sense; he takes mathematics as paradigmatic). The last he characterizes as dealing with public history, and is the field of culture, of politics, or of history proper. Before dealing with these four fields Merleau-Ponty deals with "Institution and Life" in the first notes after the introduction to the course.

Institution does not belong solely to the human domain, and Merleau-Ponty begins by thinking about institution in terms of biological organization. Rather than being purely innate, biological development is characterized by a degree of lability or plasticity (he uses both of these words, in their French equivalents) that is "limited by consideration of place," i.e., that is not arbitrary. The organism's destiny is *instituted* in the sense that it is not absolutely given in an innate structure, and is not independent from its environment. Merleau-Ponty then expounds the logic of institution with reference to puberty as a psychological, physiological, and social, as well as a biological, development, paying special attention to the dynamic of the Freudian Oedipus complex as the failed "question," a prior institution that human institution resumes. There is a biological anticipation of puberty which "human institution [is] the transformation which preserves [. . .] and

62. Ibid.
63. Ibid.

surpasses."[64] In the notes titled "Institution of a Feeling," Merleau-Ponty develops the notion of institution in relation to the phenomenon of love, and in particular in a detailed dialogue with the text of Proust's *À la recherché du temps perdu*, drawing a similar conclusion, that "what is surpassed is the idea of love as a convention or sum of accidents or appearances, or artifice. What is not surpassed is the alterity of the other and finitude," noting "the idea of institution is precisely the foundation of a personal history on the basis of contingency."[65]

Institution and Art

In "The Institution of a work of Art" Merleau-Ponty returns to a theme he had already developed in "The Indirect Language" (published in French in 1945)[66] and revisited in "Indirect Language and the Voices of Silence" (from 1952), where he first engages with the Husserlian notion of *Stiftung*, dealing with the notion of expression in painting.[67] There he writes

> There is a triple resumption through which [the painter] continues while going beyond, conserves while destroying, interprets through deviation, and infuses a new meaning into what nevertheless called for and anticipated it. It is not simply a metamorphosis in the fairy tale sense of a miracle or magic, violence, or aggression. It is not an absolute creation in an absolute solitude. It is also a response to what the world, the past, and previous works demanded of him, namely accomplishment and fraternity. Husserl has used the fine word *Stiftung*—foundation, institution—to designate, first, the unlimited fecundity of each present which, precisely because it is singular and passes, can never stop having been and thus being universally. Above all, he has used *Stiftung* to designate that fecundity of the products of culture which continue to have a value after their historical appearance and open a field of work beyond and the same as

64. Ibid., 23.

65. Ibid., 36.

66. Merleau-Ponty, "The Indirect Language."

67. It will be clear that the notion of expression is linked to that of institution. Merleau-Ponty deals with expression in such a way as to emphasize that speech, painting, and other forms of expression are not the externalization of a pre-existing mental object, but that what is expressed is formed by the act of expression, whereas, as we are seeing, the notion of institution is complex but carries the emphasis more that the act takes up pre-existing materials and surpasses them in part. On expression, see Merleau-Ponty, "Science and Experience of Expression," "On the Phenomenology of Language," and "Eye and Mind."

their own. It is thus that the world as soon as he has seen it, his first attempts at painting, and the whole past of painting create for the painter a *tradition, that is,* Husserl says, *the power to forget origins,* the duty to start over again and to give the past, not survival, which is the hypocritical form of forgetfulness, but the efficacy of renewal or "repetition," which is the noble form of memory.[68]

The creation of the work of art is not a production of the radically new, nor is it the outer reproduction of an inner vision or sense, but the resumption and transformation of a tradition, personal (like the individual painter's style and its development) and prepersonal (his place in the history of art). Merleau-Ponty's great example is that of the emergence of artificial perspective in the Renaissance, especially as understood by Erwin Panofsky in *Perspective as Symbolic Form,*[69] with which we dealt in the previous chapter. The problem of perspective is not resolved directly, as the result of focused investigation of and application to the problem. "The investigation stops at an impasse, other investigations seem to create a diversion, but the new impulse allows the obstacle to be overcome from another direction."[70] There is an interrogation that is taken up and pursued in the ongoing institution of works of art, but this interrogation does not obey a "manifest logic"; there is not a single truth of a system that gradually reveals itself and that exists in a non-temporal ideality, waiting to be revealed. The ancients sought to express the world in painting, using, for example, several vanishing axes in connection with a non-substantial understanding of space as the "gap" between bodies.[71] So "intermediary" space is not accurately represented in itself, but only as it is oriented to the subjects under consideration. Merleau-Ponty refers to Panofsky, for whom "when work on certain artistic problems has advanced so far that further work in the same direction [. . .] appears unlikely to bear fruit, the result is often a great recoil, or perhaps better, a reversal of direction."[72]

In the Middle Ages, Western painting stopped using these vanishing axes and turned to the flat mode of expression characteristic of the icons of Byzantine painting, in which linear depth is suppressed and the background is filled with gold or with a color. This deflection of the interrogation of

68. Merleau-Ponty, "The Indirect Language," 68.

69. Panofsky, *Perspective as Symbolic Form.*

70. Merleau-Ponty, *Institution and Passivity,* 78.

71. Ibid., 43.

72. Panofsky, *Perspective as Symbolic Form,* 47. This text is alluded to, but not directly cited, by Merleau-Ponty, in *Institution and Passivity,* 43.

painting, to more "primitive" modes of expression, is a "recoil" and "change of direction" (in Panofsky's terms), but also a "detour" (in Merleau-Ponty's) that establishes a distance from the problems and thus makes room for a new approach to a solution.[73] The "luminous unity" of the medieval style loses mobility and expressivity, but introduces a conception of space as a continuum: not in the modern, geometrical sense, but in a Christian-Neoplatonic sense. For Proclus, space is "the finest light," and as such is "transformed into a homogeneous and, so to speak, homogenizing fluid, immeasurable and indeed dimensionless."[74] Space here is unified, unlike in the ancient mode of expression, but is now oriented to the plane surface rather than to geometrical depth. The Renaissance invention of artificial perspective draws on this unified space, stretching it out again in the world. But, as Merleau-Ponty understands it, painting does not know what it is doing. It does not know that it is inventing a new conception of the picture and of space. "The consequences and the field open themselves, but we make something which has more meaning than we thought. [. . .] Cf. Proust: life gives us something other than what we were searching for, something else and the same thing."[75]

The point of all this is to show how institution is a process that is fundamentally in accord with Merleau-Ponty's embodied understanding. There is a mixture of chance and reason in the development of perspective. There is contingency and necessity, navigated by an "operative intentionality": not the mechanical outworking of a *telos* that is somehow absolutely given, but neither a meaningless flux, nor a pure negative freedom.

Institution and Science

In "The Institution of a Domain of Knowledge" Merleau-Ponty begins by saying that what was at issue in the discussion of the institution of a life, a feeling, and a work was the establishment of *sens*, of a history that is "not closed, not possessed by the mind, not signification, essence, or end,"[76] but rather is open, that establishes connections between contingent givens and that thus intertwines essence and event. But he asks whether in the realm of knowledge, of objective truth (as opposed to the subjective truth of the lover

73. Merleau-Ponty, *Institution and Passivity*, 40–42; Panofsky, *Perspective as Symbolic Form*, 47–48.

74. Panofsky, *Perspective as Symbolic Form*, 49; Merleau-Ponty, *Institution and Passivity*, 43.

75. Merleau-Ponty, *Institution and Passivity*, 44.

76. Ibid., 50.

or the painter) we must recognize the two orders of event and of essence as absolutely separate. If this were the case, the objective history of art would undermine the reflective history we have been commenting on. To contest this, Merleau-Ponty sets out to specify the difference "between knowledge, essence, and event."[77] For him "the true and the essence would be nothing without what leads to them. There is sublimation, not surpassing towards *another order*. The *lekton* is not supported by a logos which would be independent of the 'aesthetic world.'"[78] Truth is not absolutely independent of expression. Here Merleau-Ponty draws on Husserl's text "The Origin of Geometry," on which he lectured some five years later. Husserl investigates the being of the ideal objects of the sciences, archetypically geometrical objects. For Husserl, the knowledge involved in geometry does not exist as the contents of a mind, but as a sedimented tradition; even geometrical knowledge, in its self-evidence as derived from the most basic axioms, is never fully consciously known; the geometer depends on theorems he already accepts to construct new ones.

The problem with this, in Husserl's late thought, is its role in what he considered the crisis of European science, which was that it had become so dependent on a sedimented tradition that it no longer had any real idea of what it was dealing with, of what its objects really were. He realized that his project to ground phenomenology as a rigorous science was failing; the sciences have their *Boden* in lived contact with the *lebenswelt*, a contact with which they have lost sight. Thus phenomenology became the enterprise of re-establishing contact with the *lebenswelt* and took up the goal of *grounding* the sciences. In *On the Origin of Geometry* Husserl speaks of the geometer "re-activating" the tradition and the first theorems of geometry, and so grounding the science of geometry again in living contact with the world. For Husserl, then, there is an ambiguity about the *institutedness* of a domain of knowledge; it in some way separates us from the truth of things, from the world as it is lived, as is the case for Heidegger. Husserl shows how geometry as an institution depends on writing as a condition of its sedimentation, of its taking leave of living contact with the world and becoming a tradition.

This, of course, later provided a starting point for Derrida's textualism, which depends on the notion that writing is divorced from the lived world, and indeed that writing asserts its own priority and becomes a textual world of its own. Merleau-Ponty is not so pessimistic. Indeed, in the lecture notes it becomes clear that the institution of science does not cover over some originary truth grounded in the *lebenswelt*, but rather makes a certain

77. Ibid., 51.
78. Ibid., 51.

kind of truth possible. It would seem that the intersubjective world and its truths arise not purely from our lived contact with the other but also in the elaboration of that world in shared knowledge; the instituting operations of science do not simply aim at reproducing the truth of the world "inside the mind"; rather they create new, intersubjective truths that provide fresh ground for deepening investigations and for action in the world. Thus, the sciences can never be separate from what they study, and can never complete the attempt to attain a dispassionate observation. This fact must drive us to an understanding of the dynamic instability of our conception of nature. Merleau-Ponty observes that

> Just as arithmetical numbers, before [the] discovery of algebra, had properties of algebraic numbers [. . .], the trunk of the tree *had* the properties of the circle before the circle was known. This eternity depends on our conception of a *nature*. Nevertheless, this makes sense only retrospectively, and this remark does not only concern the order of invention in opposition to the order of objective dependence. There is truly a retrograde movement of the true.[79]

Merleau-Ponty uses the word *Sinngebung*, "meaning-giving," or perhaps better, "*sens*-giving," saying that what the solving of an animal problem and of an intellectual problem have in common is that a "problem-situation [brings forth] *Sinngebung* which fills the 'gap' by affecting [some] element of the field with new sense."[80] In the properly intellectual creation of truth, the insight to which the institution within a history gives birth is a change of structure called forth by the "problem-situation" but not given in it, and, as Merleau-Ponty understands it, this is the background to the emergence of the notion of essence. He says, "the tree branch was a possible stick before I think about it, i.e., there is an order of the in-itself in which the tree branch is by means of itself [a thing] whose proper use is to attain a goal. The reorganization offers itself as the discovery of a pre-existing, true, objective property."[81] And so he claims that "this is where the idea that there is an order of essences comes from, an order into which the individual somehow gains entrance. Insight [is] reminiscence."[82] The order of essences, then, for Merleau-Ponty, is a synthetic, but real, order of things, not an analytic order that belongs to extra-human nature. There is a certain kind of truth to the Platonic notion that insight into *eidos* is memory; but that memory is not the

---

79. Ibid., 52. The insertions are the editors'.
80. Ibid., editors' insertions.
81. Ibid., 53. Here the insertions are my own.
82. Ibid., 53, editors' insertions.

passive recall of representations of a given past, it is rather the fundamental making-sense that recalls the human being to herself, and transforms her world through her.

Is there a problem regarding the conception of time operative here? For Merleau-Ponty has claimed, as we have seen, that "time is the very model of institution," yet there is now a retroactive movement of institution, endorsement of Bergson's notion of the "retrograde movement of the true," and institution seems to escape time and transform it: the institutions of knowledge transform for us the whole of history. In a marginal note appended to this claim, Merleau-Ponty writes "that which is and demands to be; it has to become what it is."[83] What does this "has to" mean? Merleau-Ponty cannot be speaking of a teleological development of the thing, cannot be saying the thing must inevitably become what it is according to a pre-given pattern; this would run counter to the whole of his thinking in these lectures. Rather, he is saying that for a thing to be fully itself, it must *become* so; that when the thing is transformed from *bloße Sachen* to a properly human thing, entering into history, it becomes truly itself. Time as succession is no longer our model, and though there is not here a fully-developed new concept of time, there is a suggestion of a notion of time that, like space, can no longer be conceived as a container in which things are located along spatiotemporal Cartesian coordinates, but is more strongly bound up with the thing and its *sens*. So Merleau-Ponty writes

> Time carries itself beyond the succession of nows, a now is given as preexisting itself and in a certain way forever, but it preexists and endures eternally only as sense. [In other words], it is truly a creation which has taken place and it will be preserved only "in substance," i.e., we do not truly enter into the timeless, we enter only into a time which is no longer a simple uprooting, destruction, in which the subject does not encounter simple adversity, but change in an immanent way, change itself, and thereby even the requirement of truth which has first led to today's formulation.[84]

This suggests that a science that is not divorced from the life-world, that is not made sterile by forgetting its origins, would be a creator of truth; it does not just conceive an *adequatio* of timeless truths in the intellect, does not enter into the timeless, but can transform time from within.

---

83. Ibid., 7. The marginal note is in the endnotes, p. 80.
84. Ibid., 54.

Culture and Intersubjectivity

Before turning to the field of *Historical Institution* proper, there is a brief (four-page) excursus on "The Field of Culture." He begins by spelling out what he means by "culture" in terms that are both broad and provocative: he calls culture a "trans-phenomenal" cognitive process, which consists in openness to ideas but not to essences. The idea is not something that is possessed; it is not the case that we attain to an intelligible world by the knowledge of essences. Indeed, "there is no intelligible world; there is a culture," which, like the institutions of love, art, and science, is the opening of "an ideological field" on the basis of "apparatuses of knowledge (words, books, works)."[85]

But if this is right, then the argument of the *Origin of Geometry* will fail. If the sciences genuinely produce truths, then these truths cannot require "reactivation" in the sense of calling to mind the whole passage of their institution, of gaining a clear and distinct idea of every prerequisite of a given theorem, of making the adequation complete. Merleau-Ponty returns to the Husserlian claim, established in the *Origin of Geometry*, that tradition is forgetfulness of origins, that is, that tradition does not simply preserve a past but produces "a *step* to be taken." For Merleau-Ponty, this "forgetfulness" is not an unambiguously bad thing, but is at least the possibility of the sedimentation of truth in the world. If tradition is forgetfulness, it is also a better way of remembering; in some sense tradition remembers for us. But this is not simply about the limits of our cognitive capacities to remember, or actively to constitute and synthesize the truths of tradition all at once.[86] For him, "What is not at issue [. . .] is to abridge the past in order to leave some space in the mental field for a wholly psychological phenomenon. [Nor a] virtue of logic as a separate order, which would in fact contain the whole past."[87] Rather what is at stake in the notion of the forgetfulness of traditionality is a parallel to the arguments against sensationalism in the *Phenomenology of Perception*: truth, like perception, is not a sum of given parts. Rather, "the issue is a survey comparable to that of the perceived

---

85. Ibid., 58.

86. In the course notes for *Husserl at the Limits of Phenomenology*, 65, Merleau-Ponty calls into question the notion that sedimentation is a danger, asking "can we reactivate everything? In fact, it is impossible (the individual and even a cultural group have finite capacities of reactivation." On the next page, "There is therefore a truth which is the result of *Idealisierung* [Idealization], forgetfulness of its genesis—and there a more profound truth which consists in rediscovering the instituting movement of the universe of ideas." Merleau-Ponty, *Husserl at the Limits of Phenomenology*, 66.

87. Merleau-Ponty, *Institution and Passivity*, 58. The insertion is the editors'.

through which I know in one sole act that my arm is resting on the table, that I can go over there without articulated means."[88]

The implications of this consideration of the field of culture bear on subjectivity and on the question of Being.

> The notion of "field," of institution, of truth, requires that subjectivity not be for itself at first, but the holder = X of an experience, that the *Sinngebung* be, not the apprehension of this or that under an essence, but the lateral idealization or generalization, by means of recurrence on the basis of a model (this is the *Auffassung als . . .* as open), and consequently that the object is not only the correlate of my *acts*, but also provided with a double horizon by means of which it can become the object for others and not for me alone.[89]

Intersubjectivity is essential for truth, which is not a relation of adequation or representation but a productive operation that involves my relation to the other as well as my relation to the world. "The subject gives more than he has because [. . .] he proposes to the others enigmas that they decipher, [. . .] he makes them work, and what we receive, we give it for the same reason, for we receive only an incitement to *Nachvollzug* [comprehension/ enactment]."[90] So, for Merleau-Ponty, "Being [is not] what is in itself or for someone, but what, being for someone, is ready to be developed according to another becoming of knowledge, like a constellation whose figure would be continuously remade according to [a] project which appoints such changes as possible."[91]

Culture as instituted is not unmoored from nature and history, like Derridean textualism, much as Merleau-Ponty might at times sound like a deconstructionist. Culture, and the intersubjectivity it depends on, grows out of material bases. At the end of the section on culture Merleau-Ponty insists that we still need to specify "what is invariant, the pivot" of this historical Being, to understand how institution implies a future and how the past is integrated into that future through institution. Our problem, he says, is to understand whether it is possible to apply the truths of the history of knowledge to "other history," by which we take him to mean still more "objective" (though this word is anachronistic here) "public" history, whether we can move from personal history to "total history" and maintain the importance

88. Ibid., 58.
89. Ibid., 61.
90. Ibid.
91. Ibid.

of intersubjectivity within a "field."[92] This is, in some ways, the problem of how we might think through the total from "ground level," without pretending to a *pensée du survol* and reducing to the terms of objective thought.

With this consideration of the implications of intersubjectivity in mind, Merleau-Ponty's lecture course turns in its final section to deal with the "Public History" of the course title in a section entitled "Historical Institution: Particularity and Universality," asking whether we can find in universal history the same grounding in intersubjectivity that we found in the history of knowledge. He claims that the history of knowledge has unforeseeable outcomes; as we have suggested, it is radically creative in a way that thwarts any determinism, it "results in something other than what it wanted to make, is unforeseeable. But nevertheless algebra realizes the wishes of arithmetic, etc.—Is there this *Urstiftung-Endstiftung* [originary institution-final institution] relation anywhere else? Isn't there rather [a] comedy of history, societies which are something other than what they wanted to be and their emblems?"[93]

For knowledge in this sense, being situated is a means of knowing; a located, limited perspective is the actual condition of knowledge. "General history," though, as such, is opaque, it is what it is. There is no "elsewhere" to look to, no reverse of things, but only what Žižek calls "the flat, stupid reality of what is just there."[94] On Žižek's understanding, the fundamental lesson of Hegel is the importance of the problem of how something like appearance can emerge from this reality. For Merleau-Ponty and for the phenomenology out of which his thought emerges, this is not quite the right way to ask the question: the appearance comes first, and if experience leads me back to a brute nature, this nature always already contains the possibility of my emergence within it.

Merleau-Ponty's notes here describe a "reaction against Hegel" that "leads back to Hegel":[95] Merleau-Ponty rejects the notion of "a real synthesis, which truly accumulates everything, against the idea of a system, of an actual possession of all dispersed existence of humans." If history proceeds by way of institution, institutions give birth to new situations, but their sedimentation is at the level of the human body, not of the pure idea, nor of the purely material. Institutional situations have to be lived, to be reactivated, not in their ideal unity, but in their earthly significance. Merleau-Ponty's rejection of Hegelian absolutism is thus not a rejection of historicism.

92. Ibid.
93. Ibid., 62.
94. Žižek, *The Parallax View*, 29.
95. Merleau-Ponty, *Institution and Passivity*, 63.

He writes, thinking of both Sartre and Lévi-Strauss, "our contemporaries disavow the 'philosophy of history,' absolute knowledge. Therefore, they are for contingency, pure fact."[96] But this relativism of history repeats the *kosmotheoros* of the Hegelian knowledge of absolute history with a re-installation of the "omnipotence of the philosopher [. . .] in non-knowledge. [. . .] The absolute opacity of history, like its absolute light, is still philosophy conceived as closed knowledge. The one who observes the opacity sets himself up outside of history, becomes a universal spectator."[97]

Merleau-Ponty compares the radical relativism of Lévi-Strauss, which is dependent on an idea of absolute knowledge that is, for it, both impossible and necessary, with Einsteinian relativity, which he thinks has a similar problem. By identifying with Peter, and making the point that Paul's time is linked to Peter's, Einstein claims that time is dilated or contracted with movement. But this relativism assumes that one imposes Paul's time on Peter, "that one projects into Paul the image that Peter has of his time and that Paul does not have. [. . .] Einstein the physicist, interconnected with Peter, thinks that he is the universal spectator."[98] Which is to say that he relativizes the position of the universal spectator and creates a confusion. Paul's time is as universal for him as Peter's is for Peter, and so neither can know a non-universal time. For Merleau-Ponty, "it is necessary to be more Einsteinian than Einstein and re-establish the world of perception with its 'simultaneities'—likewise it is necessary to be more relativist than Lévi-Strauss and put knowledge back in the historical world of perception with its operation of 'understanding.'"[99]

We see here how Merleau-Ponty's investigation of the notion of Institution keeps on returning us to the logic of incarnation, of the implication of the knower, the bodily perceiver, the scientist, *within* the structure she seeks to know. Merleau-Ponty refers here to a citation of Engels's *Dialectic of Nature* in Lévi-Strauss: Engels writes, "It is, therefore, from the history of nature and human society that the laws of dialectics are abstracted. For they are nothing but the most general laws of these two aspects of historical development, as well as of thought itself." Hegel's "mistake lies in the fact that these laws are foisted on nature and history as laws of thought, and not deduced from them. [. . .] The universe, willy-nilly, is made out to be arranged in accordance with a system of thought which itself is only the

96. Ibid., 63.
97. Ibid.
98. Ibid., 70.
99. Ibid.

product of a definite stage of evolution of human thought."[100] This notion of a natural dialectic, while it escapes Hegel's absolutist idealism, reduces history to nature, and thus pulls apart the subject and nature. For Merleau-Ponty, finally, "the dialectic becomes a paradox when it is realized in this way. There is no dialectic of nature."[101] The world is reduced to a lawlike operation whose inside is inaccessible to an absolute observer, which forgets that the observer is *in* the world.

This makes of the question of universal history an existential problem, a "mystery" in Marcel's sense: we cannot establish once and for all a valid field of universal history, but we must relate ourselves to history, and it seems that we can do that in more or less faithful ways. As he writes in "The Metaphysical in Man," "to gain awareness of his task, the historian [. . . must] reject his claim to a Universal History completely unfolded before the historian as it would be before the eye of God."[102] But while there can be no universal history as *kosmotheoros*, a society must relate itself to the universal and find its place in it.

> There are at least, in a sense different from Bergson's, open societies and closed societies, societies which form the idea of a recuperation of history by means of history and other societies who do not do this [. . .], and we can call the latter *false* societies even if we do not call the first ones *true*. This does not mean that in certain relations they are not more beautiful. But these societies do not play the mysterious game which consists in putting all humans in the balance. They are not faithful to the a priori of institution or to its spirit, and they clench upon the letter of it. They do not intend the *Miteinander* or the *Füreinander*, the universal intermingling.[103]

Institution and Historicity

In "The Discovery of History," the introduction to one of the chapters of *Les Philosophes Célèbres*, the 1956 volume on the history of philosophy that Merleau-Ponty edited, he writes,

100. Engels, *Dialectic of Nature*, 26–27, cited in Lévi-Strauss, *The Elementary Structures of Kinship*, trans. James Harle Bell and John Richard von Sturmer, with Rodney Needham, ed. (Boston: Beacon, 1969), 450–51, itself cited by the editors in an endnote to Merleau-Ponty, *Institution and Passivity*, 70, n. 50, the note appearing on 111–12.

101. Merleau-Ponty, *Institution and Passivity*, 74.

102. Merleau-Ponty, "The Metaphysical in Man," 90.

103. Merleau-Ponty, *Institution and Passivity*, 75.

History, *precisely* because it is not nature, refuses to be treated as a second nature. It does not establish itself by substituting, in place of natural causality or finality, another order of causality or finality that annuls them. History slips in quietly, making the former adopt its language, artfully leading them away from themselves.[104]

The language here reminds us of a passage from Merleau-Ponty's third lecture course on nature, given a few years later, in 1959–60. The section entitled "Man and Evolution: The Human Body" begins with a quote from Teilhard de Chardin: "Man came silently into the world."[105] Merleau-Ponty asks what we might take this to mean, concluding that "there is a 'metamorphosis,' not a beginning from zero. This thought is not very compatible with the definition of the human by cephalization, cerebralization, and reflection—of which we said (here, with Teilhard de Chardin) that it would be better expressed by saying: transcendence."[106] That is, "transcendence" better characterizes the human than intellectualization does: we might understand this in terms of Aristotle's understanding of the human being as a "rational animal." We cannot understand the human being's situation in nature if we think he is an animal body with reason added. But I want to suggest that the human is an animal whose animality brings reason to bear on the world, and thus a being capable of transcending herself.

History, then, arises in nature, like human being, as a moment of nature's metamorphosis, internal transformation. It is not the junction of mind or of *logos* with nature; it is nature's production of a *logos* that exceeds it. But personal and public history both have their *soil* in nature, in what Ted Toadvine calls the "immemorial past." Toadvine has suggested that nature can be thought as an *archefactical* resistance, saying "nature in its primordial autonomy appears precisely as the resistance that the unreflective offers to reflection."[107] In his book *Merleau-Ponty's Philosophy of Nature*, Toadvine spells out this resistance in terms of the pre-thematic dimensions of space and time in Merleau-Ponty, the "immemorial" and the "level of all levels." On Toadvine's understanding, reflection is always situated, and Merleau-Ponty attempts to pursue "Radical reflection": "Radical reflection aims to take into account its own immemorial past, its prereflective life in nature,

104. Merleau-Ponty, "The Discovery of History," 127.

105. Teilhard de Chardin, *The Phenomenon of Man*, cited in Merleau-Ponty, *Nature*, 267.

106. Merleau-Ponty, *Nature*, 268.

107. Toadvine, "Maurice Merleau-Ponty and Lifeworldly Naturalism," 376.

as the fundamental condition for its operation as reflection."[108] As Merleau-Ponty puts it "reflection only fully grasps itself if it refers to the prereflective fund it presupposes, upon which it draws, and which constitutes for it, a kind of original past, a past which has never been present."[109] We are now in a position to make sense of this claim to the fundamental importance of this "past which has never been present," or immemorial past; it is not the past of prehistory in a temporal sense, but the very ground of temporality. Alia Al-Saji identifies it with the "vertical past" of which Merleau-Ponty speaks in *The Visible and the Invisible*.[110] This "vertical past" is that historicity that is the ground of institution, as factical vertical history is its result.

The "level of all levels" parallels in space the meaning of the "past which has never been present" in time, the phrase being drawn from a single occurrence in the *Phenomenology of Perception*, in which Merleau-Ponty denies that we could have access to such a level:

> Since every conceivable being relates directly or indirectly to the perceived world, and since the perceived world is only grasped by way of our orientation in it, we cannot dissociate "being" from "being oriented," and we cannot offer a "foundation" for space or ask what is the level of all levels.
>
> The primordial level is on the horizon of all our perceptions, a horizon which in principle can never be reached and thematized in an explicit perception. Each of the levels in which we live appears in turn, while we are anchored in the given "milieu."[111]

The primordial level, then, is *this specific* Earth, as vertical temporality is our factical history, and rests on "worldedness" in general as our history depends on a general historicity. This helps us to see more clearly how history and earth are distinct from and bound to nature, which grounds them through worldliness and historicity, which, though they are general structures of reality, are not structures of nature *per se* but rather structures that can only arise in the genesis of animality; the structures of worldedness and historicity are mutually dependent on the living beings through which they have their reality. Nature is the non-instituted soil of our being; animals (and most clearly human beings) as agents in the living, instituted system

---

108. Toadvine, *Merleau-Ponty's Philosophy of Nature*, 53.

109. Merleau-Ponty, *Phenomenology of Perception*, 252, translation modified.

110. Al-Saji, "The Temporality of Life," 186, citing Merleau-Ponty, *The Visible and the Invisible*, 244.

111. Merleau-Ponty, *Phenomenology of Perception*, 264. I have again re-translated from the French edition, *Phénoménologie de la perception*, 293.

of the earth are both instituted (they are born in a certain place, they live with this or that personal or public history) and agents of institution, in the sense that we discovered with our discussion of eating and the *hungry animal*; appetite is given, but is richly intertwined with hunger, which is the imaginative development of desire.

This raises the question of the relationship between what Toadvine calls this "silent" nature, the historicity of things, and the perceived world. If we call "nature" that silent, anonymous world, can we have any access to nature at all? For Toadvine, we must reconsider the truism that "we are part of nature," because we must think nature not as an observed category, not as a collection of things, but from within. To open on to nature from within must also mean to be estranged from it, and from ourselves insofar as we are natural things; there is a hiatus in things, and I have a "blind spot" with regard to my own emergence. It seems that natures multiply: behind the "visible nature" of the world of the sciences (*naturata*, perhaps) lies the "invisible nature" of the silent world (*naturans*), and betwixt the two (in some sense) there is a "nature becoming-visible" that marks the emergence of the subject and the world of perception. And this begs the further question, how can we establish that it is right to call the "silent ground of nature" also nature? Is it nature "all the way down," or is nature self-grounding? Toadvine is surely right that nature is not just a collection of things; but *what else* then is nature? Philosophy since Spinoza has thought of it as a substance, the one substance. The most obvious alternative is to think of it, with Whitehead, as a process, or a "complex of passing events."[112] But this would seem to risk conceiving humanity as *kosmotheoros*, that is, a subject of the world representing the world to himself as an object. For Merleau-Ponty

> there is not an experience of pure geometry in which we can grasp the structure of space. [. . .] There is the experience neither of pure physics nor of pure geometry. The same physico-geometrical ensemble is capable of covering both flat space and curved space. This puts in doubt the idea of a nature of itself of space. The part that amounts to the structure of space and to the physics of the milieu can be established only by a mind that knows space from the outside. But the world is not something that we can dominate. The result is thus not a *de facto* result, but a result in principle. To pose the question of the nature in itself of space is to admit a *kosmotheoros*. The question is not posed for living beings because it has no meaning for them: space is part of their situation, yet a space of situation is not in-itself.[113]

112. Whitehead, *The Concept of Nature*, 166.
113. Merleau-Ponty, *Nature*, 103.

Thinking nature from within, as Toadvine proposes, is a notion thoroughly concordant with Merleau-Ponty's project of developing an ontology that escapes objectivism. But this denies us access to fundamental nature, since we cannot "see" it, it lies behind our whole existence, and indeed this inaccessibility of nature is a corollary of the denial of objectivism. *L'essentiel est invisible pour les yeux.* The Earth with which we are intertwined can be taken up as an object in scientific theory, we can abstract out from our place in it, and construct a theoretical point of observation outside of it, for example a position relative to the sun that makes new sense of the observed paths of the planets in the night sky. But we can take no such stance with regards to nature. No conceivable point of observation lies outside of it.

> To say, then, that space is not Euclidean is not to say that space is non-Euclidean, or Riemannian, for example. Space is not something. The different geometries are metrics, and metrics are neither true nor false; and as a consequence, the results of these different metrics are not alternatives.[114]

The Anonymous Body and Incarnation

In the understanding we are developing, the animal as "instituted" thing, as a given "sedimentation," is what Merleau-Ponty called the "anonymous" body. Barbaras links this idea with Bergson's notion of the "turn" of experience, expressed in the claim that philosophy's "last enterprise [. . .] would be to seek experience at its source, or rather above that decisive *turn* where, taking a bias in the direction of our utility, it becomes properly *human* experience."[115] The "above" of the spatial metaphor is somewhat opaque, but since Bergson's point here is an opposition to empiricism and to "the impotence of an intellect enslaved to certain necessities of bodily life,"[116] it seems that the source of experience, which Bergson seeks *above* the "turn of experience," is for Merleau-Ponty more plausibly sought *below* that turn, in the body prior to "properly *human* experience." The anonymous body, then, is the body below the turn, and is thus the bodily or natural subject. This bodily subject is the subject of perception, as Flynn and Froman point

114. Ibid., 103.

115. Bergson, *Matter and Memory*, 240–41. Cited in Barbaras, "The Turn of Experience," 33.

116. Bergson, *Matter and Memory*, 241.

out,[117] and as Merleau-Ponty suggests when he writes in the *Phenomenology of Perception*:

> I cannot say that I see the blue of the sky in the sense that I say that I understand a book, or again that I decide to dedicate my life to mathematics. My perception, even seen from within, expresses a given situation: I see blue because I am *sensitive* to colors, whereas personal acts create a situation: I am a mathematician because I decided to be one. As a result, if I wanted to express perceptual experience with precision, I would have to say that *one* perceives in me, and not that I perceive.[118]

If this pre-personal "one" (*on*) of the body, this natural body that always precedes me, is the subject of my perception then, crucially, *nature* lies on both sides of perception—both perceiver and perceived are natural beings; in this sense, perception is part of my animality (and we have no doubt that animals, too, perceive). In the animal, as for myself, perception is bound up with motility. But animal perception is also intertwined in me with that "properly *human* experience," in Bergson's terms, with the decisions of which Merleau-Ponty speaks. These decisions set into motion acts of institution, which are the basis of that which exceeds or transcends nature. But their results are sedimented in the world of nature, which thus becomes a world of the instituted and its effects, just as my anonymous body, while prior to my own decision, exists as the result of the decisions (or otherwise) of my parents, in a cultural and physical world that is not of my making but that is the accreted result of the process of instituting performed by others. The passages in the *Phenomenology of Perception* that develop this idea anticipate the future direction of Merleau-Ponty's notion of flesh and of the ontology that he was still working toward when his life was cut short.

> The sensible gives back to me what I lent to it, but I received it from the sensible in the first place. Myself as the one contemplating the blue of the sky is not an acosmic subject *standing before it*, I do not possess it in thought, I do not lay out in front of it an idea of blue that would give me its secret. Rather, I abandon myself to it, I plunge into this mystery, and it "thinks itself in me."[119]

This movement of institution, the dialectic of the instituted and instituting, undermines the clear and distinct division of nature and consciousness,

117. Flynn and Froman, "Introduction," 16.
118. Merleau-Ponty, *Phenomenology of Perception*, 223.
119. Ibid., 222.

of the in-itself and the for-itself. In the summary of his lecture course on institution Merleau-Ponty begins by saying that "in the concept of institution we are seeking a solution to the difficulties found in the philosophy of consciousness." It is clear from his comments in the working notes from *The Visible and The Invisible* that he considers the adherence to such a philosophy of consciousness a failure of the *Phenomenology of Perception*, and as such I propose that this work on the notion of institution is a starting-point in his attempt to overcome such failings. As we have made obvious, there is much fruitful material in the *Phenomenology*, and we have shown that the way beyond the problem of consciousness is anticipated there in his notion of the anonymous body. Nevertheless, "consciousness" in its extant formulation is to be rejected. In the notes beginning the course on institution, he spells out this formulation:

> Personal life considered as the life of a consciousness, i.e., a presence to the whole for which the other is empty negation [and] indifferent action, or, at the least, making sense only for me, through closed signification: the past exists for this consciousness only as consciousness of the past, i.e., as a picture that is overcome; a mode of presence that is entirely spectacular; [. . .] Are we this immediate presence to everything before which the things that are possible are all equal—all the things that are impossible? This whole analysis presupposes a prior reduction of our life to the "thought of . . ." living. This is to say 1) a distinction of form and content: *hyle* and *Auffassung als* [apprehension as] . . . 2) a distinction which has the purpose only of extracting the content, of turning it into an ob-ject for the "thought of" . . . , the signifying activity, considered as the sole thing that is concrete.
>
> But, both this real form-content analysis and the position of the form as the a priori condition of the content are illusory. [. . .] When we approach an object or a recollection, there is no numerically distinct *Abschattungen* [profiles] and no *Auffassung als* . . . representation of one selfsame intelligible core, there are no instants and their ideal and signified unity, there is the consciousness of [the] thing and of its traces *on the basis of the thing*.[120]

A *kosmotheoros*, or specular, geometrical conception of the world, is here rejected in favor of an incarnational ontology that refuses to reduce life

---

120. Merleau-Ponty, *Institution and Passivity*, 5. The insertions are the editors', intended to make Merleau-Ponty's notes readable, with the exception of the translations of Husserl's German, which are my own.

to the "thought of" the living, and so, it would seem, to posit life as an irreducible fact, intertwined with the world. The Aristotelian hylomorphism is foregone in favor of a unity of sensibility and intelligibility in the concrete thing. It would seem that Merleau-Ponty here anticipates the Derridean rejection of the metaphysics of presence, although his proposed alternative, of a metaphysics of the flesh, is of course quite unlike Derrida's textualism. Indeed, Merleau-Ponty's model of institution, as he spells out in the following pages of these lecture notes, suggests a philosophical approach that does away with many false problems. The relation of the mind to the external world is not a problem when we resist an artificial scission between them: there is an "instituted and instituting subject, but inseparably, and not a constituting subject."[121] The problem of other people dissolves, as the other is "not constituting-constituted, i.e., my negation, but instituted-instituting, i.e., I project myself in the other and the other in me." There is a single "intersubjective or symbolic field, [the field] of cultural objects, which is our milieu, our hinge, our jointure—instead of the subject-object alternation."[122] The problem of time, too, is modified, because time is no longer "enveloping" (i.e., objective, on a realist model) or "enveloped" (i.e., subjective, as for idealism); rather "time is the very model of institution: passivity-activity, it continues, because it has been instituted, it fuses, it cannot stop being, it is total because it is partial, it is a field."[123]

The logic of institution is a corrective to the orientation of philosophy towards consciousness, and, I think, an effective one. It shows us how subjectivity is inscribed in a world that it always remakes, the earth. I have said that nature is the "soil" of this world, but it would seem that a philosophy of nature risks as much as a philosophy of consciousness at this point: just as there is no pure consciousness for the body-subject, there can be no pure nature. The milieu from which thought arises will not be able to form a concept of either, because thought is already a transformation of nature. We are reminded again that the first line of Merleau-Ponty's first book reads, "Our goal is to understand the relations of consciousness and nature."[124] To accommodate both is to refuse to prioritize either; Merleau-Ponty's philosophy, then, can be neither a "philosophy of consciousness" nor a "philosophy of nature," in the last instance, but must be a philosophy of thought and of the earth, a philosophy of history in its broadest sense. This philosophy of history would take seriously the verticality of history as it is instituted in the

---

121. Ibid., 6.

122 Ibid. The insertion is the editors'.

123. Ibid., 7.

124. Merleau-Ponty, *The Structure of Behaviour*, 3.

body and in the earth, realizing that just as there is no consciousness before nature, there is no nature after consciousness, but that the genesis of consciousness transforms nature by its self-transcendence. Primordial nature exists for thought as a limit and not as an object before it.

This incarnational philosophy is directly opposed to the very different philosophy that Michel Henry derived from Husserl. Henry's phenomenology of life thinks of the subject as "the absolute foundation of being," as Nick Hanlon puts it in his introduction to Henry's "Phenomenology of Life."[125] If we take the logic of institution seriously, the subject will always be grounded in something that comes before it; there is no pure ideal subject, for Merleau-Ponty, and this is why he tries so often to excise "consciousness" or the Husserlian transcendental ego from his ontology. For Henry there can be no such thing as the life-world; "*Living is not possible in the world. Living is possible only outside the world, where another Truth reigns.*"[126] The specter of Manichaeism hovers over this work: why would there be any created world, for a Christian thinker such as Henry, if it has nothing to do with the truth of things? Creation is seen here, in the phrase Merleau-Ponty borrows from Valéry, as a "flaw in the great eternal diamond," and it is hard to see how such a flaw may arise from the work of a good God. Henry rejects the idea, found in Hegel's philosophy and in Marxism, that "Christianity is a flight from reality, inasmuch as it is a flight from the world. But if reality resides in Life and only in Life, this reproach disintegrates to the point of ultimately appearing as non-sense."[127]

Henry fails to heed the warning he most needs to hear, and buries his Christianity in a bizarre solipsistic idealism of the kind for which, Merleau-Ponty says, "there is, strictly speaking, nothing to do. 'My kingdom is not of this world.'"[128] This is what Merleau-Ponty condemns as explicative theology, which would explain away the world and its resistance to consciousness, would make impossible the true transcendence of that which exceeds consciousness. For Henry there is a "precedence of phenomenology over ontology"[129] which is precisely the reverse of Merleau-Ponty's notion, from as early as the preface to *Phenomenology of Perception*, that "the most important lesson of the reduction is the impossibility of a complete reduction,"[130] which works itself out in his later work in the move towards the priority of

125. Henry, "Phenomenology of Life," 97.

126. Henry, *I Am the Truth*, 30.

127. Ibid., 30.

128. Merleau-Ponty, *Sense and Non-sense*, 174.

129. Henry, "Phenomenology of Life," 100.

130. Merleau-Ponty, *Phenomenology of Perception*, lxxvii.

ontology over phenomenology. For Henry, the fundamental reversibility of perception, and the intertwining that emerges from it, is denied. "The possibility of vision resides in this setting at a distance of that which is placed in front of the seeing, and is thereby seen by it,"[131] and so the invisible is located not in the world and the subject's chiasmatic intertwining with it, but purely in "life," which begins to look like the unexplained presence of the mind in the human observer. He remains, fundamentally, Cartesian. Rudolf Bernet, in "Christianity and Philosophy," a short article on Henry's thought, brings some critical questions to bear, and in a crucial passage shows how Henry's thought cannot make sense of the incarnation.

> M. Henry's hyper-transcendentalism and his theological conception of Life does not lead only to the abandonment of the world, but also to a devaluation of everything that makes the concretion of human life. We have seen how M. Henry disinterests [sic, read "divests"] himself of all that comes from the contingency or the facticity of human existence, that is, social, cultural, sexual, etc., differences, in the name of the condition of man as Son of God. [. . .] It is as if the fact of being born of a woman and a man, of *this* woman and *this* man, it is as if our debt with respect to the past generations and our responsibility for the future generations were to be deprived of any transcendental signification. It is as if one had to choose between divine generativity and human generativity, instead of them illuminating one another mutually. Is it a matter of indifference that the Archi-Son was born a Jew, that he took flesh in the body of Mary, and that he died on the cross at Golgotha? And this Incarnation of Christ, having become man among men (despite what M. Henry says), had it not completely changed the meaning of human fecundity without taking from it anything of its carnal character?[132]

Thus, Henry's Manichaeism implies a Docetism. As Mauro Carbone points out, Henry rejects Tertullian's understanding that the incarnation means that in Christ God was joined to the "mud," the earthly soil of which all flesh is made. For Henry, human flesh (and the incarnation in which God is made flesh) can have nothing to do with those roots in the humus, and in humility, which Old Testament tradition has always ascribed to it. Carbone observes "Not from mud, but from the Word—Henry interprets—comes the flesh that unites mankind to Christ: therefore [. . .] flesh proves in his opinion to be incomparable both with 'inert bodies of material nature' and

131. Henry, "Phenomenology of Life," 101.

132. Bernet, "Christianity and Philosophy," 338–39.

with 'living beings other than mankind.'"[133] Henry's phenomenology, here, does us the service of showing more clearly, by its own failure, the terms in which Merleau-Ponty's ontology can think the incarnation of the classical Christian understanding, of the ontological significance of the idea that God took flesh in a particular human body, was born to a human mother, with all the danger, dirtiness, and difficulty that this involves, that Christ was not only born in flesh, but died there. This point of doctrine must lead to an absolute refusal to denigrate the bodily as bodily, and the material world as material, and even the animality that the body of the incarnate Son of God shared with the beasts in whose trough he slept as a baby.

The Ambiguity of "Flesh"

Renaud Barbaras lays out an admirably clear objection to Merleau-Ponty's late ontology in his article "The Ambiguity of the Flesh."[134] For Barbaras, Merleau-Ponty's ontology of flesh and of incarnation is a transcendental anthropomorphism, a humanizing of the whole of reality, and this transcendental anthropomorphism is incompatible with the ontological anthropomorphism "for which the lived body is a privileged sample of the meaning of being."[135] Barbaras develops the tension between these two kinds of anthropomorphism in dialogue with Hans Jonas's work in *The Phenomenon of Life*,[136] for whom a certain kind of anthropomorphism must be granted; for Jonas "the organic body signifies the latent crisis of every known ontology and the criterion of "any future one which will be able to come forward as a science.""[137] And so "Perhaps, rightly understood, man *is* after all the measure of all things—not indeed through the legislation of his reason but through the exemplar of his psychophysical totality which represents the maximum of concrete ontological completeness known to us."[138] Jonas's philosophy, like that of Merleau-Ponty, seeks to develop an ontology that takes the living body as its point of entry. But as Barbaras sees it, Merleau-Ponty fails, as he does not just start with the body, but absolutizes it in the ontological notion of "flesh." Barbaras questions Merleau-Ponty's adherence to the vocabulary, in terms such as "seer" and "visible," of the ontological duality that he is attempting to overcome. Barbaras asks of the incarnation:

133. Carbone, "Flesh: Towards the History of a Misunderstanding," 53.
134. Barbaras, "The Ambiguity of the Flesh."
135. Ibid., 20.
136. Jonas, *The Phenomenon of Life*.
137. Ibid., 19.
138. Ibid., 23.

"the incarnation of vision and of consciousness that would lead us to call into question the transcendental point of view—how is it possible that the constituting subject as such is on the side of that which he constitutes?"[139] This problem leads to "a gap between the reality of incarnation, as irreducible dimension of being and the vocabulary through which Merleau-Ponty approaches it: the interiority of our body is thought as perception, as vision, and its exteriority is characterised as visibility, perceptibility."[140]

The implication is that there are two countervailing meanings of flesh at work in Merleau-Ponty's ontology, meanings that are irreconcilable and that it seems to me adhere to the two notions of the body. The first is that of my body as a body, that notion that we have called the anonymous body, which shows me that I am a thing among things, that other bodies are like my body. This body is both material and sensitive, and as such evades any duality between *res extensa* and *res cogitans*. Insofar as other bodies are like mine, they also escape this duality and cannot be reduced to the *bloße sachen* of Husserlian nature. But to speak of the flesh of the world is in fact to speak of the world as *living*, insofar as flesh translates the German *Leib*, derived from *leben* (to live) and meaning the living body as opposed to the *Körper* of the anonymous body. In Barbaras's words "Merleau-Ponty uses the concept of Flesh to define the external world."[141] Now, this is perhaps not straightforwardly the case; Merleau-Ponty never says that everything is flesh. He does speak, however, in ambiguous terms, of "the flesh of the world," and if Barbaras's critique is correct, then we might think that such an idea has to remain ambiguous because to make it clear would be to make a nonsense of it, to highlight these two incompatible meanings of flesh. For Barbaras, "to say that the world is Flesh amounts to saying that, like our flesh, its exteriority involves a kind of interiority, which means that there is *no longer an ontological difference between matter and organic beings.*"[142] This is why Merleau-Ponty's philosophy has seemed, in certain of its moments, to suggest a panpsychism, or at least a panexperientialism (which would introduce a whole slew of philosophical problems), as in *Eye and Mind* when he speaks of the painter saying "in a forest, I have felt many times over that it was not I who looked at the forest. Some days I felt that the trees were looking at me, were speaking to me,"[143] and similarly, in *The Visible and the Invisible*,

---

139. Barbaras, "The Ambiguity of the Flesh," 21.

140. Ibid., 22.

141. Ibid.

142. Ibid., 23, italics original.

143. Merleau-Ponty, "Eye and Mind," 167. The citation is from G. Charbonnier, *Le monologue du peintre* (Paris, 1959), 143–45.

"I feel myself looked at by the things."[144] For Merleau-Ponty the possibility of things looking at me is expressed, not by their seeing me and recognizing me, but by my feeling that they might. The point is not that subjectivity is distributed throughout the world, but that experience spreads out across a world in which all kinds of meaningful things are drawn into the domain of flesh, are encrusted into sensing bodies. "The flesh of the world is not *self-sensing* (*se sentir*) as is my flesh—it is sensible and not sentient—I call it flesh, nonetheless [. . .] in order to say that it is a pregnancy of possibles [. . . ,] that it is therefore absolutely not an ob-ject, that the *bloße sache* mode of being is but a partial and second expression of it."[145] This, Barbaras claims, leads to an equivocation over the meaning of flesh that makes a nonsense of its use as a foundation for his ontology. For Barbaras, "Merleau-Ponty misses the genuine unity of the body and this is why he cannot acknowledge the ontological consequences of incarnation."[146] For Barbaras, Merleau-Ponty's philosophy remains a philosophy of the insertion of consciousness into the world, and as such remains a philosophy of consciousness.

It is certainly the case that Merleau-Ponty's early distinction between the objective, anonymous body, and the lived body, the *corps propre* or one's own body, in some ways focuses the problem of the Cartesian pineal gland on the surface of the body—how do "inner" and "outer" world communicate? But it seems that Barbaras misunderstands Merleau-Ponty's project from the first when he identifies the crossing of the body and the world as the constituting subject who is on the side of what he constitutes. The logic of institution points to a route beyond this impasse precisely by showing us the way in which acts of institution are sedimented in the world. We have, here, a problem of language. How will we speak of the agents who perform these acts of institution? Merleau-Ponty, in his earlier work, speaks of the "human level" and of the operations of consciousness. Barbaras, with Jonas, and like Michel Henry, speaks of "life" and of "organic beings." Either of these ways of speaking seem already to imply a whole philosophy. By the time he is writing the extant chapters of *The Visible and the Invisible*, Merleau-Ponty leaves talk of "consciousness" behind, for the most part, speaking only of "we" or "he" used as impersonal pronouns, ultimately, of *on* (one), the perceiver.

Barbaras's critique—that Merleau-Ponty confuses two ways of speaking of flesh, and that this makes his notion of "the Flesh of the world" as the basis of ontology an equivocation—strikes at the heart of the confusions

---

144. Merleau-Ponty, *The Visible and the Invisible*, 139.

145. Ibid., 250.

146. Barbaras, "The Ambiguity of Flesh," 24.

latent in Merleau-Ponty's later ontology. In the extant form of *The Visible and the Invisible*, the four full drafted chapters and extensive working notes, there is scant mention of "institution" or of the Husserlian *Stiftung* that it translates, but it seems that with the use of this notion as he developed it in the earlier lecture course Barbaras' objections can be overcome.

Barbaras interprets the "flesh of the world" in terms of what he calls "transcendental flesh"; in this sense, the world is flesh insofar as it is the object of the operation of constitution for the transcendental subject; here we are thrown back into idealism. But this is not the only way to understand Merleau-Ponty's notion of flesh. On the basis of the logic of institution, we understand that to speak of the flesh of the world is to speak of the world as sedimented with human meanings; and these are not sedimented as "psychic" substance, nor do they belong only to the perceiver as a form of interpretation of things. Rather, the world is made flesh, prototypically, in culture: traditions of eating are bound up with traditions of agriculture, so the treatment of animals, and the condition of soil, ecosystems, and human biology are all affected by the ways people eat. There is not a chasm between the facts of the world and people's absolutely free choices; rather, the condition of the Earth is bound up with, constantly affecting and affected by, our mode of life, which consists not in a series of acts of free choice but in our inheritance of habits as they are sedimented in culture and the institution of new ones. The same is true of our traditions of building, of architecture and planning, our social relations as they organize human power and the ways in which we make use of natural resources; the institution of money and the ways it determines human relations being amongst the most powerful.

Philosophers of mind and of technology, inspired by Merleau-Ponty, have spoken of "extended cognition" in those cases where their use of extra-bodily systems has played a determinative role in the thought of given individuals. For example, Clark and Chalmers cite the example of Otto,[147] who suffers from Alzheimer's disease, and who relies on a notebook that he carries with him, and in which he writes down information. This notebook serves as a significant part of his memory, and the information in it serves for him as a normal person's latent beliefs do, at least with regards to the kind of information it contains. Thus, cognition is extended, depending not only on the mind in the brain but on Otto's extended, bodily life. Komarine Romdenh-Romluc argues that, *mutatis mutandis*, Otto could write his

---

147. Clark and Chalmers, "The Extended Mind," 12–19. This example was brought to my attention by Komarine Romdenh-Romluc, and discussed in her paper "Agency and Embodied Cognition."

intentions down in a notebook, and that these writings could serve effectively for him as intentions, which therefore need not be mental states.[148]

These examples show at the most basic level the way in which thought and matter are entwined in bodily habit. We could deepen the example with reference to Richard Wrangham's work *Catching Fire: How Cooking Made Us Human*, in which he shows how human evolution has made use of the development of cooking to outsource much of the work of digestion and thus to enable humans to make available the surplus of energy and of time required for thinking and for the large brains that support it.[149] Here is an example of "extended digestion" that shows how not only our ability to eat but also our ability to think belongs to a tradition, a culture that is bound up with our biology, our agriculture, our use of fuel, our division of labor, and so much else. Our whole bodily situation is meaningful, and our whole world participates in *flesh through us.*

Clark and Chalmers alert us to the persistent Cartesian assumptions of philosophy when they note of Otto's unusual case that "like many Alzheimer's patients, he relies on information in the environment to help structure his life."[150] Should it not be obvious to us that we all constantly rely on information in our environments to structure our lives and even to think in the most basic ways? In his reflection on animality in the second nature course, Merleau-Ponty writes

> Consciousness is only one of the varied forms of behavior; it must not be defined from within, from its own point of view, but such as we grasp it across the bodies of others; not as a centrifugal form, but as a closed world where external stimulations appear to it as outside of it. *Consciousness must appear as institution, as a type of behavior.* Behavior includes elementary organization (embryology), and physiological, instinctive organization, or behavior properly called. We must allow for an *Umwelt* at the level of the organ, at the level of the embryo, just as it is necessary to allow for activities of consciousness.[151]

Contrast this to Barbaras's view: "Merleau-Ponty's philosophy is not a philosophy of flesh but a philosophy of the *incarnation*, as the insertion of consciousness in the world, that is, a philosophy of consciousness." Barbaras

---

148. Romdenh-Romluc, "Agency and Embodied Cognition." (Note that we use "intention" here in the everyday sense of "a plan to do *x*" and not in the sense of the *intentionality* of Brentano and the phenomenologists).

149. Wrangham, *Catching Fire.*

150. Clark and Chalmers, "The Extended Mind," 12.

151. Merleau-Ponty, *Nature*, 167–68, my emphasis.

repeats this understanding of incarnation a few lines later, saying that in Merleau-Ponty "our body is described on the basis of the incarnation, as the insertion of a consciousness in the world, that is, as the unity of a vision and a visibility."[152] Here the question of theology returns forcefully, with the notion of incarnation. For Barbaras, incarnation means the insertion of transcendence into nature, of the elsewhere in the here, of the foreign in the native. But this is not what it means for Merleau-Ponty. Similarly, the geometrical view of nature, in which God is the absolute perceiver, has fostered an understanding of incarnation as that of a totally "outside" God entering the world, as though the viewer "stepped in" to the painting. But perhaps this is not the most cogent theological view.

In this chapter, I have developed an account of Merleau-Ponty's ontology of flesh, building on the account of vision developed in chapter 4, and supplemented by our investigation of eating in chapter 2. I have argued that the perceived world is characterized by a "depth" in which it always exceeds itself, that there is a necessary transcendence by which meaningful *logoi* are grounded in the soil of nature by the instituting processes of history. I have developed an account of Merleau-Ponty's notion of institution through a close reading of his lecture course on the subject, and argued that an instituted understanding of human knowledge will place a high value on science, not as a solely descriptive enterprise discovering timeless truths, but as a creator of meaning and a significant creative element of a shared world, which liberates new possibilities for culture (which is not a layer superimposed on nature but the entwined development of it). All this is grounded in the prepersonal nature of the bodily subject, which makes itself flesh, in so transforming the ontological situation of the whole world.

In the next chapter I will bring this ontology into dialogue with Christian theology, showing their fundamental resources and the potential discordances, and asking whether Christian theology may have anything to learn from the theology of flesh, and vice versa.

---

152. Barbaras, "The Ambiguity of Flesh," 24.

6

Incarnation, Existence, and *Musterion*

I<small>N</small> "T<small>HE</small> P<small>HILOSOPHY OF</small> Existence," originally a 1959 article in the journal *Dialogue*,[1] Merleau-Ponty discusses existentialist thought in France. For him, existentialism begins after 1930 in reaction to the dominant Kantian idealism of Brunschvicg, and "is primarily explicable by the importance of a completely different theme, that of *incarnation*."[2] He takes Gabriel Marcel as an example. The philosophy that Merleau-Ponty, Sartre, and others of their generation knew had considered the body, one's own body, to be an object in the same way that others' bodies, animals, and "ordinary objects" (i.e., tables and suchlike) are objects, and that the subject is a *mind*, an essentially thinking thing that is not an object at all, "and opposite me there is, therefore, this body which is an object."[3] Marcel opposed this view, and showed that attention to my body reveals that it is not simply an object; it is in some sense *myself*. Through this attention to the body, the general reduction of existence to objectivity is brought into question. Philosophy, then, is to attend not to scientific objects but to sensible things, to that which exists. For Marcel, this establishes an important distinction between philosophy and other disciplines: "it deals with mysteries, not problems."[4] Merleau-Ponty explains this distinction as it appears in Marcel:

---

1. Merleau-Ponty, "The Philosophy of Existence," 129–39.
2. Ibid., 132.
3. Ibid.
4. Ibid., 133.

A problem is a question which I pose to myself and then resolve by considering different givens which are external to me. For example, if I wish to know how to construct a bridge or how to solve an equation, I consider the givens of the problem and then try to find the unknown. In philosophy it is an entirely different phenomenon, because, as Marcel said, in philosophy we must work out a very singular type of problem. In these problems, the one who poses them is also engaged. This person is not a spectator in relation to the problem, but is rather caught up in the matter, which for him defines the mystery.[5]

This notion of incarnation emerged with Marcel, amongst others, during the editorship of the Catholic personalist Emmanuel Mounier at the journal *Esprit*, at the center of a circle of broadly Catholic thinkers of which Merleau-Ponty was a part as a young scholar. His concept of incarnation has, then, a definite *theological* genesis, although it here takes on philosophical shape. Nonetheless, there seems no doubt that these reflections on the body have their roots in a Catholic framework, and perhaps of the questions posed by the notion that God could become human. The opening to mystery, which for this group had significant political implications, arises directly from the reality of being embodied, of being a subject-object, or in other words, from my own mystery, from the mystery of existence. Merleau-Ponty claims that the question of existence, and of conducting an investigation without being able to take up a spectatorial position (Marcel's logic of incarnation), was broached by his own early work, because the sensible knowledge of the world is "completely paradoxical, in the sense that it always appears to me as already complete at the very instant that I pay attention to it."[6] The early existentialism characteristic of Marcel also introduced the theme of one's relations to the other, a theme to which Merleau-Ponty often returned, and which developed into the logic of intersubjectivity and of history that we have been discussing: Merleau-Ponty claims, here, in 1959, that "the theme of history [. . .] is essentially the same as the theme of the other." For him,

What simultaneously attracts and scandalizes philosophers about history is precisely man's given condition of not being alone, of always being considered in the presence of others, in an extraordinarily complex relationship with them. The result is that we are no longer concerned simply with juxtaposed

5. Ibid.
6. Ibid.

individuals, but with a sort of human tissue which is sometimes called "collectivity."[7]

Here we see how, for Marcel and for Merleau-Ponty following him, the theme of incarnation suggests a series of priorities for philosophy that dualisms tend to ignore: the problem of the other, both in the form of the basic question of the existence of other minds and then in the more nuanced form of the question about my relation to the other. This leads us to a consideration of intersubjectivity and of history. The importance of *time* in this regard comes to Merleau-Ponty from his inheritance from Bergson (rather than from early existentialism) as the most basic form of subjectivity, but the logic of duration is in fact crucial in his investigations of all these themes. If philosophy is to live up to Marcel's conception, to wrestle with mysteries, it must re-enter its ancient dialogue with theology, and it is to theology's engagement with these questions that I now turn.

Incarnation and Sacramentality

For the Orthodox theologian Alexander Schmemann, "time is the only reality of life," and like Marcel he offers a suggestion that Christian thought on time cannot offer a solution to a philosophical problem but a *gift*, which engages with the mystery of time.[8] For Schmemann

> Christians [have been] tempted to reject time altogether and replace it with mysticism and "spiritual" pursuits, to live as Christians out of time and thereby escape its frustrations; to insist that time has no real meaning from the point of view of the Kingdom which is "beyond time." And they finally succeeded. They left time meaningless indeed, although full of Christian "symbols." And today they themselves do not know what to do with these symbols. For it is impossible to "put Christ back into Christmas" if he has not redeemed—that is, made meaningful—time itself.[9]

On Schmemann's understanding, Christianity is responsible for the pathological modern approach to time because, on the one hand, it "made it impossible for man to live in the old natural time, broke beyond repair the cycle of the eternal return,"[10] revealing time as history, but, having done so, it has abandoned it, inviting Christians to reject time and history in favor

7. Ibid., 133.

8. Schmemann, *The World as Sacrament*, 56–57.

9. Ibid., 59.

10. Ibid.

of the hope of eternal rest. For John Inge, drawing on Timothy Gorringe, an understanding of time in this context is related to sacramental action. Inge explains that the word sacrament derives from the Latin *sacramentum*, and as such is not present in the New Testament.[11] That Latin word is a rendering of the Greek μυστεριον, which, as Rowan Williams shows, derives from the word μυω, meaning to conceal, and carrying the sense of showing something in its hiddenness. It is used in this sense to speak of the rites of the Greek mystery-cults.[12] While in Christ God's mystery has been made known in its fullness, at the same time there is still ambiguity, the secret is not simply laid bare; on Williams's understanding this is because human "motivations and desires do not display themselves unambiguously."[13]

This notion of sacrament or μυστεριον must be understood in relation to the logic of the incarnation, with all its attendant ambiguity, which we are developing here: "The incarnation is the primary and determining Christian *musterion.*"[14] For Aquinas, in the sacraments, "the word is joined to a sensible sign, just as in the mystery of Incarnation the Word of God is united to sensible flesh."[15] In the sacraments, the invisible *logos* of things is encountered through their visible form; Aquinas cites Augustine on this point that the sacrament is the visible sign of the invisible truth of things.[16] Aquinas makes it clear at the beginning of his discussion of the sacraments that there is a general sense of this word that refers to a thing's "hidden sanctity," and he for the most part limits his use of this word to a more restricted special sense, that of the specific signification of the seven sacraments; nevertheless for him "every sign of a sacred thing is a sacrament,"[17] and it is in this sense that theology has extended the notion to Christ himself, the church, and to the world, as evidenced by the titles of the texts under discussion here.[18] For Schmemann, "the sacrament is the manifestation of the Word,"[19] and the limitation of the sacramental in this broad sense is an effect of the fall: "The fall is not that [man] preferred [the] world to God, distorted the balance between the spiritual and material, but that he made

---

11. Inge, *A Christian Theology of Place,* 59.

12. Williams, "The Church as Sacrament," 116.

13. Ibid., 116.

14. Ibid., 118.

15. Aquinas, *Summa Theologica* III.60.6

16. Ibid., III.60.1, citing Augustine, *The City of God,* Book X, ch.v.

17. Ibid., III.60.2

18. Cf. Inge, *A Christian Theology of Place,* 60–61.

19. Schmemann, *The World as Sacrament,* 38.

the world *material*, whereas he was to have transformed it into 'life in God', filled it with meaning and spirit."[20]

As a sign, then, the sacramental depends on perception, on the intertwining of "consciousness" and "nature" that Merleau-Ponty's ontology of flesh has made thinkable. Schmemann reminds us that the human is a hungry being, and that although "all that exists lives by 'eating,'"[21] which is determined by what we earlier called *appetite*, there is a development of this which can be seen in the human being: "he alone is to *bless* God for the food and the life he receives from Him. He alone is to respond to God's blessing with his blessing."[22] The significance of humankind's ability to bless, of course, depends on being able to withhold blessing, to refuse thankfulness, which is to say that it depends on that same freedom that makes the human not just appetitive, but *hungry*. The human being's relationship to God is not one of the mechanical return of gratitude or acknowledgement to God, rather it depends on the creative expressivity of her ability not just to return God's blessing but to "recirculate" it in the world, extending the sacramental moment in unforeseen ways.

This freedom, this lability of his bodily life, is thus fundamental to what we have called sacramentality, and it is in this connection that Schmemann writes in *For the Life of the World*, "The first, the most basic definition of man is that he is *the priest*."[23] For Schmemann there is a sense in which the human act of blessing God unifies the world. Perhaps this can help us to form a better understanding of Maximus's notion of man as microcosm: Humans do not, and cannot, "unify the world" by participating in the pre-existing and separated worlds of the rational, spiritual, or mental and the natural, material, or extended. Rather, they participate in the emergence of this duality in the mode of intertwining; as capable of expressive love, he is, as participant in a greater "we," able to continue this action and to make a world.

Graham Ward relates this movement to the complex moment of the *fracture* in the liturgy of the Eucharist: the priest, acting and speaking on behalf of the gathered church proclaims, "We break this bread to share in the body of Christ," the people responding, "Though we are many, we are one body, because we all share in one bread."[24] At the very moment that the church is gathered together, and ready to receive, its breaking apart again is

20. Ibid., 20.

21. Ibid., 15.

22. Ibid.

23. Schmemann, *For the Life of the World*, 15.

24. Ward, *Cities of God*, 152–54.

begun, because the Eucharistic binding-together demands that this "we," to maintain its unity, must always remain open; that those who receive do so in view of being sent out, as they "go in peace to love and serve the Lord." Ward writes elsewhere, "the Church is now the body of Christ, broken like the bread, to be food dispersed throughout the world."[25] Thus Inge refers to Timothy Gorringe's notion that the sacraments are "extroverted." "Having been fed with the sacramental elements of bread and wine, through which Christ nourishes us with his body and blood, we are to go out to find Christ in the people and places of our everyday life." So "the physicality of [. . .] the sacraments are 'an affirmation of the material, as the assertion, consonant with the incarnation, that you cannot go round, or beyond, matter, but that you must go through it.'"[26] For Schmemann, "the Church is mission, and [. . .] to be mission is its very essence, its very life."[27]

For Timothy Fry, then, commenting on the rule of St. Benedict, "Material things are *sacramenta*, symbols that reveal the goodness and beauty of the creator,"[28] and for Graham Ward, "to desire or love God is to invest the world with significance, a significance which deepens the mysterious presence of things."[29] This Benedictine logic of an everyday sacramentality, the denial of a rupture between matter and meaning, between the sacred and the profane, the temporal and the eternal, stems from the same root as Merleau-Ponty's ontology of flesh, from the basic understanding that gives him to claim that "sensation is, literally, a communion."[30] This conviction that the *logos* is made known in and through things roots perception in history and in the logic of institution in Merleau-Ponty's ontology and in sacramental thought. Williams emphasizes that the church is bound up with God's self-revelation in history, and that, "The Church is a mystery *as a whole*: not only in its praying and feeding but in its vulnerable historical actuality."[31] For Schmemann, the idea of the sacramental is a fundamental intuition that the world "is an *epiphany* of God, a means of his revelation, presence, and power,"[32] not only "in its totality as *cosmos*" but also "in its life and

25. Ward, "Bodies," 176.

26. Inge, *A Christian Theology of Place*, 62, citing Gorringe, "Sacraments," 168.

27. Schmemann, *For the Life of the World*, 107.

28. Fry, *RB80*, cited in Inge, *A Christian Theology of Place*, 61.

29. Ward, *Cities of God*, 173.

30. Merleau-Ponty, *Phenomenology of Perception*, 219. Cf. Kearney, "Merleau-Ponty and the Sacramentality of the Flesh."

31. Williams, "The Church as Sacrament," 119.

32. Schmemann, *For the Life of the World*, 120.

becoming as time and history."[33] Williams warns that to think the church as sacrament in this sense "leads us not towards a static picture of the Church as a simple epiphany of the 'sacred,'" and against any notion of the church as an idealized, perfect spiritual entity, but rather to an understanding of the realization of the *logos* of God in the midst of contingency, in a church whose life is "still in formation, still subject to change and suffering."[34] This ambiguity would call into question a lazy pan-sacramentalism. For Gorringe, "if everything is a sign, nothing is," and Inge cites his claim that sacraments are "those rents in the opacity of history where God's concrete engagement to change the world becomes visible."[35] These can be "rents" on a world-historical scale, as at Pentecost or when God called to Moses from the burning bush. But, as Inge suggests, the most everyday of events can be sacramentally transfigured.

> Sacramentality is not simply an affirmation of the world as it is, but of the fact that Christ is in the world to unite the broken fragments of life by making the material a vehicle for the spiritual. This is not, it should be emphasized, equivalent to proposing a dualistic approach: our experience may sometimes suggest such a duality, but religious experience understood sacramentally links the dualities under which the one world keeps appearing. Christ himself is the reintegration of God's original creation, and in Christ God has restored the sacramental nature of the universe.[36]

That is, God's intervention restores the world to itself. Speaking of marriage as sacramental, Schmemann writes, "for the Christian, *natural* does not mean self-sufficient—a 'nice little family'—or merely insufficient, and to be, therefore, strengthened and completed by the addition of the '*supernatural*.' The natural man thirsts and hungers for fulfilment and redemption."[37] Sacramentality, then, is not the addition to nature of the supernatural. It is rather the calling into question of the very idea of nature; it is a rejection of the idea that there could be any sufficient definition of "nature" or of "matter." Rejecting the pure presence-to-itself of nature conceived on a geometrical model, it puts into relief the idea that the being of things dwells not in pure positivity but in relation, and as such, it makes a

---

33. Ibid., 120.

34. Williams, "The Church as Sacrament," 122.

35. Gorringe, "Sacraments," 159, 165, also cited in Inge, *A Christian Theology of Place*, 66–67.

36. Inge, *A Christian Theology of Place*, 76.

37. Schmemann, *The World as Sacrament*, 109.

question of nature, not in the mode of "is nature all there is?" and "can there be anything supernatural?" but rather as the question "what is nature, and what is its relation to consciousness?"

God and Nature

In his lectures published as *Nature: Course Notes from the Collège de France,* Merleau-Ponty focused on the arrangement of the ontological problematic around "the nexus [. . .] 'Nature'–'Man'–'God.'"[38] In these three series' of lectures, as he does so often, Merleau-Ponty repeatedly takes Descartes as his starting point. Descartes and Newton posited a new idea of nature, which, as he sees it, makes possible new scientific discoveries, rather than being prompted by them. This new conception is not, as it may first seem, the rejection of Aristotelian finality, but is rather its sublimation, in God.

The new element is the idea of infinity, which derives from Judaeo-Christian monotheism, and which splits the Aristotelian nature into the pair *natura naturans,* nature considered as productive power, and *natura naturata,* inert and mute nature, nature as pure externality. Insofar as Aristotelian finality had constituted the *meaning* of things, it was expelled from nature as *naturata,* and located in God considered as the source of nature. Merleau-Ponty acknowledges the origin of the division, which the Cartesian concept of nature made concrete, of the opposition between *naturans* and *naturata* in Averroes, and suggests that it was this division that allowed Aquinas to integrate the Greek conception of nature with Christianity in his metaphysics, though it is not until Descartes that the consequences of this are realized.

In dealing with the humanist conception of nature, Merleau-Ponty takes Kant as paradigmatic. Whereas for Descartes, nature as given by God was basic, and the human was a problem (which was expressed in terms of the question about the relations of body and soul), Kant's "Copernican revolution" puts human experience at the center, so making a problem of the constitution of phenomenal nature. Kantian humanism seems to be indifferent with regard to God, although Merleau-Ponty cites Brunschvicg, finding in Kant's thought an anthropo-theology that invests the autonomy and finality of Descartes's God in humanity. Merleau-Ponty says, "in the end, by way of morality, Kant lets the old ontology subsist."[39] For him, Kant has not done away with the Cartesian ontology, or its nexus of God–Man–Nature, but has just shifted the priority of the terms. It is Schelling who

38. Merleau-Ponty, *Nature,* 204.

39. Ibid., 37.

moves on from the Kantian humanism: where for Kant nature is the abyss of human reason, that which lies beyond reason, for Schelling this abyssal element is the definition of God. Where non-knowing is the limit for Kant's epistemological ontology, for Schelling there can be some recognition of the non-known. For Schelling, being exceeds the limit of reflection. Nature is considered as both product and productivity, and the distinction between *natura naturans* and *natura naturata* is no longer simple and unidirectional. Part of what is reproduced, for example, in animal reproduction, is the productive capacity itself.

Merleau-Ponty does not, in these lectures, explicitly critique an ontology that takes God as its basic term. For him the concept of nature is always a privileged expression of ontology *in toto*, so it is that the Cartesian understanding of nature expresses an ontological complex that also must find a place for God and for humankind. He wants, then, to work over the concept of nature in an attempt to build a larger ontology, on the basis of "our experience of Nature in us and outside of us."[40] In this phrase he refers to his work on perception, which gives us a picture of reality that centers on his account of the subjective body, as developed in the vital understanding of structure in *The Structure of Behaviour* and in the intentionality of the body-subject in the *Phenomenology of Perception*.

In *The Visible and the Invisible*, Merleau-Ponty writes, "the flesh is not matter, is not mind, is not substance. To designate it, we should need the old term 'element,' in the sense it was used to speak of water, air, earth and fire, that is, in the sense of a *general thing*, midway between the spatio-temporal individual and the idea, a sort of incarnate principle."[41] Alphonso Lingis, in his *Translator's Preface* to this work, argues that *flesh* is not identical with the experienced body, which Merleau-Ponty had contrasted in *Phenomenology of Perception* to the objective, observable body. The experienced body would not seem to be correctly described as an *element* or a *general* thing; rather, it is characteristic of the lived body that it is a *specific* thing that nevertheless shapes all of, and only, my experience. There is a general reality, which ought to be basic to ontology, for Merleau-Ponty, to which the specific reality of my lived embodiment gives me access, and this general reality is flesh. Lingis writes "The flesh is the body *inasmuch as* it is the visible seer, the audible hearer, the tangible touch—the sensitive sensible: inasmuch as in it is accomplished an equivalence of sensibility and sensible thing."[42] All this

40. Ibid., 205.

41. Merleau-Ponty, *The Visible and the Invisible*, 139.

42. Lingis, "Translator's Preface" (to Merleau-Ponty, *The Visible and the Invisible*), liv.

is to say that the Merleau-Pontyan ontology of flesh is well captured by the title of his unfinished last work; the flesh is the meeting-point of the visible world of the senses and the invisible world of intelligibility, so that Merleau-Ponty's ontology of the flesh is, in the last instance, about the instantiation of meaning or intelligibility in the sensed world. It is not that flesh joins the mute, physical substance of *nature* to the meaningful, intellectual or spiritual human substance; rather Merleau-Ponty writes that, "*We must not think the flesh starting from substances, from body and spirit—for then it would be the union of contradictories—but we must think it, as we said, as an element, as the concrete emblem of a general manner of being.*"[43]

Existential Metaphysics

We have here pursued Merleau-Ponty's final ontology in response to a *philosophical* problem, that of the failure of dualistic ontologies. We found dualisms to be implied in all kinds of objective thought, and we have seen that we continue to think in ways that are more Cartesian than we realize. Merleau-Ponty's ontology of flesh resists dualisms and enables us to think human being and nature outside of them. But pursuing Merleau-Ponty's thought has reintroduced another term to the ontological nexus, that of *God*.

Where theology has been dismissed in modern thought, this has been on the basis of the "flat" ontologies of objective thought, and especially of empiricist naturalism. There the experienced world was spread out into a pure, externalized nature that reduced everything to *phusis*, or perhaps more accurately to physics in its modern sense, a sense that excludes not only the first-person perspective, not only freedom ungoverned by mechanical determinism, but also excludes all that in nature that cannot be reduced to a geometry.

Merleau-Ponty argues in his lectures on nature that Laplace's conception of nature "Is a theological affirmation, the affirmation of a view of totality capable of subtending all evolution of the world."[44] It was Laplace who first formulated the idea, belonging to classical physics, that if one knew the position and motion of every particle in the universe at an instant, one would be able, in principle, to derive the whole history and future of the world from it. Why would Merleau-Ponty claim that such a conception is *theological*? Because this understanding of the world stands in a tradition for which law-like predictability is ascribed to God, and Laplace simply

43. Merleau-Ponty, *The Visible and the Invisible*, 147, emphasis added.

44. Merleau-Ponty, *Nature*, 89.

translates this law into an absolute physical law that can in principle be known. Indeed, I would suggest that this gets closer to what Merleau-Ponty means when he uses the term "theological" in the disparaging way he does here—Laplace replaces the bad-faith pretense of the priesthood to possession of an absolute law with its scientistic equivalent. For Merleau-Ponty, this conception of God is implicit in Descartes. Cartesian philosophy makes concrete the division between mind and extended nature; this makes way for Descartes's geometrical conception of the physical world for which all behavior can be reduced to a set of axioms that are fundamental physical laws, explicable in geometrical terms. Laplace's determinist mechanism is based on this conception. But the axioms themselves, for Descartes, are not purely contingent. Rather, they are the result and outworking of God's nature: for this reason, as God (axiomatically) is unchanging, so we can be sure that the fundamental physical laws of nature are eternally unchanging. In Spinoza's Cartesianism, the absolute divide between *res cogitans* and *res extensa* is collapsed; the two are modes of one underlying substance. Descartes's conception demands that we would ask the question how exactly the laws of nature are grounded in God, a parallel question to that of how the two substances are connected in the human being. Spinoza's picture is an improvement on Descartes's insofar as it removes this problem: God just *is* the laws of nature. "For all things follow from God's eternal decree by the same necessity as it follows from the essence of a triangle that its three angles are equal to two right angles."[45] Ultimately, God was dismissed on the basis of this geometrism because "I have no need of that hypothesis;" and as such science became theological in the sense Merleau-Ponty associates with the Stoics as well as Laplace.

For Merleau-Ponty, metaphysics is not a matter of that which is detached from the visible world, but of that which is visible in it but is not of it; of the *invisible*, in the sense we have developed, following Merleau-Ponty, of the self-transcending depth of the visible world. We are not speaking here of a metaphysics of total transcendence but of the metaphysical that is made known in the world. In an article originally published in July 1947, Merleau-Ponty was content to speak of "The Metaphysical in Man," as opposed to the metaphysics "which Kantianism reduced to the system of principles employed by reason in constituting knowledge or the moral universe,"[46] writing

> Metaphysics is the deliberate intention to describe this paradox
> of consciousness and truth, exchange and communication,

45. Spinoza, *Ethics*, 100 (*Ethics* Sch. Pr. 49, II).
46. Merleau-Ponty, "The Metaphysical in Man," 83.

in which science lives and which it encounters in the guise of vanquished difficulties or failures to be made good but which it does not thematize. From the moment I recognize that my experience, precisely insofar as it is my own, makes me accessible to what is not myself, that I am sensitive to the world and to others, all the beings which objective thought placed at a distance draw singularly nearer to me.[47]

Merleau-Ponty ends the passage cited here with a footnote that refers to a planned work to be called *The Origin of Truth*. This work was never completed, but became what we now have as *The Visible and the Invisible*; thus the affirmation of this sense of metaphysics is an immediate progenitor of the Merleau-Pontyan ontology of flesh. Albert Rabil tells us that, for Merleau-Ponty,

metaphysics no longer means a philosophy of first principles; now it refers to a philosophy of being-in-the-world, a *philosophy of finitude*. [. . .] Metaphysics no longer concerns itself with that which transcends the world (God, Being, consciousness), but only with experience, "this world, other people, human history, truth, culture."[48]

What are the implications of a fleshly ontology for metaphysics? First of all, it is clear that metaphysics must always begin with the perceived world, with the sensible. In the preliminary summary of the argument in "The Primacy of Perception," Merleau-Ponty states his conclusion thus: "The perceived world is the always presupposed foundation of all rationality, all value and all existence. This thesis does not destroy either rationality or the absolute. It only tries to bring them down to earth."[49] The perceived world must be the always presupposed foundation for metaphysics, for Christianity, and for any possible understanding of God.

Second, this metaphysics will not see necessity behind all that happens; the contingency of the perceived world is not held to be unreal in comparison to some ideal necessity. There is reason and necessity in the course of things, but only *de facto*, not *de jure*. Merleau-Ponty claims that "the contingency of all that exists and all that has value is not a little truth for which we have somehow or other to make room in some nook or cranny of the system: it is the condition of the metaphysical view of the world." And "such a metaphysics cannot be reconciled with the manifest content of religion

47. Ibid., 94.

48. Rabil, *Merleau-Ponty*, 84; he refers to "The Metaphysical in Man," the final quote being taken from p. 94.

49. Merleau-Ponty, "The Primacy of Perception," 13.

and with the positing of an absolute thinker of the world."[50] Merleau-Ponty sees religion as bound up with a metaphysics of necessity: indeed this lies at the heart of his critique of Christianity. But he does glimpse (and continually returns to) the possibility that the theological notion of the incarnation in Christ suggests a different kind of God. In "Faith and Good Faith," originally published a year earlier than this essay, he outlined the possibility, at least, of a true "religion of the incarnation," which does not posit God as absolute thinker of the world. Time is not the unfolding of a course already given in immanent laws working themselves out mechanically; nor is it the procession of things toward a teleological goal given "from the outside." Rather, there is an immanent teleology of things that proceeds from their depths, that does not determine their behavior but precisely makes possible "behavior" properly speaking, that is the result not of mechanism but of the power of agents to structure the world, to bring it to expression and as such to sediment their own meanings within it.

Thirdly, the *invisible* meanings of things can be made known in the world; the invisible is made known in the visible. This institution of invisible meanings, of the *logos* at work in things, is not once and for all, but is a living tradition; that is, what is sedimented there must be recuperated. The tradition does not need to be wholly reactivated, down to its primordial roots, to be reconstituted as a whole in thought; but its sedimentation does not exhaust it, since a tradition is never pure sedimentation but also living expression; where tradition is not recuperated in this way it is sedimented as a dead expression no longer to be taken up. The non-recuperation of the tradition does continue to express the tradition; but it expresses it as no longer livable, as a fossilized tradition of dead history, as a tradition that is already on the way to being lost.

If we are to suppose a God, God must be seen *in things*. If this God is known in human history, this knowledge will depend on its historical mediation, and thus on an invisible that not only appears in the sensible but that is *instituted* there. For a God to be encountered, especially a God who is in some way related to humanity, we would need a God to whom witness is borne in nature and history, as instituting and instituted. God is here the silent ground of nature in which he institutes himself as a sign.

Galen Johnson notes that

> the pregnancy of the Flesh with expression renders this new ontological term as a correlative of the old term, Logos. Together, Flesh and Logos are icons of a Biblical theme—"and the Word became Flesh and dwelt among us," and these two

---

50. Merleau-Ponty, "The Metaphysical in Man," 96.

words suggest to us an inquiry regarding depth and spirituality in Merleau-Ponty. We recall the range of the word *esprit* in the title of "Eye and Mind"—consciousness, wit, spirit. This is the term chosen by Jean Hyppolite, French translator of Hegel, as the closest available French term to convey the sense even of Hegel's *Geist*. The attentive reader must also wonder about the pervasive sacramental language of "transubstantiation" found in "Eye and Mind," so readily related to the creedal phrase, "maker of all things visible and invisible," found in the title of Merleau-Ponty's last work.[51]

As Johnson notes, the title of *The Visible and the Invisible* is an allusion to the formula of the Nicene Creed: "We believe in one God, the Father, the Almighty, maker of heaven and earth, of all that is, seen and unseen." We can see here the consonance between Merleau-Ponty's recognition of a distinction between the sensible and the intelligible, even as this distinction is grounded in the notion of "flesh," and the visible and invisible universe of the creed, which alike encompass both terms. In the *Phenomenology of Perception*, Merleau-Ponty makes use of a metaphor of transubstantiation to convey this elemental unity of the *in-itself* and the *for-itself*, writing "just as the sacrament does not merely symbolize, in a sensible way, an operation of Grace, but is the real presence of God and makes this presence occupy a fragment of space and to communicate it to those who eat the bread, given that they are inwardly prepared. In the same way, the sensible does not merely have a motor and vital signification, but is rather nothing other than a certain manner of being in the world that is proposed to us from a point in space, that our body takes up and adopts if it is capable, and *sensation is, literally, a communion*."[52]

Merleau-Ponty rejected any notion of an entirely sufficient analogical relation between the sensible and intelligible worlds. In an interview with Maurice Fleurent he explicitly repudiates the view that the realm of the visible is systematically grounded in and points to a higher world of eternal truths, saying: "Husserl contends that western philosophy has for centuries been founded on a rationalist dogma whose origin is theological: the world is entirely rational."[53] What exactly can he mean by this? It is, it seems, a challenge to any notion of God that implies a purely necessitarian conception of the world, that denies freedom. (In "Faith and Good Faith" Merleau-Ponty writes, thinking of that religion that Hegel called "the reign

51. Johnson, "Desire and Invisibility," 90.

52. Merleau-Ponty, *Phenomenology of Perception*, 219, emphasis added.

53. Merleau-Ponty, "The Contemporary Philosophical Movement," 86.

of the Father," "There is always an element of Stoicism in the idea of God: if God exists, then perfection has already been achieved outside this world; since perfection cannot be increased, there is, strictly speaking, nothing to do.")[54] By way of explaining Husserl's contention, Merleau-Ponty says "the nineteenth century understood this for the first time, even though we cannot affirm it *a priori*, which does not authorise us to abandon reason but obligates us to redefine the human situation in order to see reason's tasks more clearly. There is reason and logic in the course of things, but only *de facto*, not *de jure*, and we have to describe the human condition with this mixture of chance and reason that defines it."[55] Like many other modern thinkers, Merleau-Ponty did not understand that the transcendence of God does not need to operate along rationalist and necessitarian lines.

Merleau-Ponty's Doubt

Merleau-Ponty's critique of Christianity is presented in terms of a critique of the ontology of the object and of God as *ens realissimum*. In "Man and Adversity," based on a lecture given in Geneva in 1951, he claims that "fear of contingency is everywhere," rightly noting that while "Catholicism, particularly in France, is being crossed by a vigorous movement of inquiry next to which the Modernism of the beginning of the century seems sentimental and vague," the church hierarchy censured and restrained the new theology. He mentions with favor an article by Francois Mauriac, for whom Christian faith would side with atheism against "the God of philosophers and scientists, God in idea," but finds such interrogative thinking falling flat in the church's thinking. For Merleau-Ponty, "the return to an explanatory theology and the compulsive reaffirmation of the *Ens realissimum* drag back all the consequences of a massive transcendence that religious reflection was trying to escape."[56] This is not simply a matter of intellectual debate but of the workings of real institutions. And, writing just a few years after the publication of the last edition of the *Index Librorum Prohibitorum* in 1948 and the reactionary censure of the new theologians in Pius XII's papal encyclical *Humani Generis* in 1950, Merleau-Ponty was well aware of what was happening to many of the great Catholic minds of his time. This is the context of these furious words:

---

54. Merleau-Ponty, "Faith and Good Faith," 174.
55. Merleau-Ponty, "The Contemporary Philosophical Movement," 85.
56. Merleau-Ponty, "Man and Adversity," 242.

Once again the Church, its sacred depository, its unverifiable secret beyond the visible, separates itself from actual society. Once more the Heaven of principles and the earth of existence are sundered. Once more philosophic doubt is only a formality. Once more adversity is called Satan and the war against it is already won. Occult thought scores a point.[57]

Merleau-Ponty took the institutional church's adherence to a neo-scholastic vision of theology and an objectivist understanding of Thomas Aquinas's ontology at face value. He took theology to be necessarily "explanatory" and objectivist, always militating against liberation, and always functioning to justify suffering, refusing the "wild" principle of *Logos* at work in the world and a "brute" being that always escapes explanation. In a 1959 note he writes "the *Theodicy* of Leibniz sums up the effort of Christian theology to find a route between the necessitarian conception of Being, alone possible, and the unmotivated upsurge of brute Being, which latter is finally linked up with the first by a compromise, and, to this extent, the hidden god sacrificed to the *Ens realissimum*."[58] And by 1960, Merleau-Ponty's antipathy to Catholicism had hardened somewhat. Asked whether he thought the new ontology is atheistic, he answered:

I would prefer not to *define* it that way, not out of a false spirit of reconciliation or in order to equivocate, but because it is unworthy of philosophy to begin with a negation. Yet, having said this, it is nonetheless true that Catholicism, for example, is closely tied to the ontology of the object. Frankly, I do not believe that another ontology could be compatible with traditional forms of theology. But what good is it to defend these [forms] when one knows that all that is alive in Christian philosophy is in fact rather alien to an ontology of *ens realissimum*?[59]

Merleau-Ponty's understanding of Christian faith was deeply formed in his juvenile experience—and it is on the basis of this experience that he retains a fondness for Catholicism and an open ear to what is alive in Christian philosophy. But, rightly or wrongly, he makes his judgments about theology on the basis of the *actually existing Thomism* of the Catholic Church of his time, which reduced mysteries to philosophical problems with scholastic explanations. As Merleau-Ponty himself saw, "We never get away from our life. We never see our ideas or our freedom face to face."[60]

57. Ibid., 242.
58. Merleau-Ponty, *The Visible and the Invisible*, 211.
59. Merleau-Ponty, "Merleau-Ponty in Person," 11.
60. Merleau-Ponty, "Cézanne's Doubt," 25. I am grateful to Simon Ravenscroft for

Where faith ceases to be able to wrestle with philosophical mystery, it also fails to address the complex problems of political life, problems that must be addressed, like Marcel's philosophical "mysteries" and the traditional mysteries of theology, without admitting of a geometrical solution.

But "traditional theology" does not think of God as *ens realissimum*. This notion comes not from St. Thomas, but from Kant. In the *Critique of Pure Reason*, it forms a part of his attack on the ontological argument, on the basis that existence is not a predicate. It proceeds from a rational theology that has little to do with traditional theology. Kant makes God a supreme individual thing, "possessing all realities or perfections and thus also grounding all the possibilities realized by other particular things."[61] The *ens realissimum* is the possessor of the fullest substantive conceptual content— it is, in a sense, the most knowable thing: "Thus it is a transcendental ideal which is the ground of the thoroughgoing determination that is necessarily encountered in everything existing, and which constitutes the supreme and complete material condition of its possibility, to which all thinking of objects in general must, as regards the content of that thinking, be traced back."[62] That is to say, God as *ens realissimum* is fullness of essence, and of possibility. This conception of God belongs thoroughly to modernity, although its sources are theological. As Adrian Pabst has argued at length, "in the West at least, late scholastic theology established the hegemony of the possible over the actual, a hegemony perpetuated by modern philosophy."[63] This scholastic theology, which Pabst traces from Avicenna, through Gilbert of Poretta, Duns Scotus, and William of Ockham, to Wolff, Kant, and Descartes, and into postmodernity, turns away from the analogical ontology of Aquinas in its embrace of the doctrine of univocity of being. As John Caputo has put it,

> God as St. Thomas conceives him is not some *ens realissimum*. Indeed, [. . .] God is not an *ens* at all for St. Thomas, in the strict sense, but *ipsum esse subsistens*, the pure subsistent act-of-being itself. St. Thomas' metaphysics does not terminate in a first being causing other beings, but in pure Being itself whose Being is communicated by participation to created beings. It is a metaphysics of *esse* throughout, not of *ens*.[64]

pointing out the significance of these words of Merleau-Ponty for his relation to Christian faith.

61. Guyer and Wood, "Introduction to the *Critique of Pure Reason*," in Kant, *Critique of Pure Reason,* 17.

62. Kant, *Critique of Pure Reason,* 556.

63. Pabst, *Metaphysics,* 198.

64. Caputo, *Heidegger and Aquinas,* 119.

Merleau-Ponty misunderstands the Thomist position—as if God had always been understood as *ens realissimum*. But Aquinas, and the Catholic tradition, has understood God rather as *ipsum esse subsistens*, subsisting Being itself. And, far from a necessitarian picture of God, Aquinas' understanding of God guarantees the contingency of things. Rather than the "massive transcendence" that stands over against existence, it conceives God's transcendence in very different terms, and in fact, I will argue, fulfills the Merleau-Pontyan search for a transcendence of depth, which refuses to domesticate "wild being" but which motivates the ongoing interrogation of the created world, and a political engagement that refuses to explain away suffering and oppression.

Aquinas' account of God begins with question 2 of the *Summa Theologiae*. The proofs of the existence of God insist that there are some questions that cannot be answered in causal terms. All regional investigations, every attempt to show why things are as they are, may be open to causal investigation. But Aquinas, with much of the Christian tradition, wants to preserve the notion that there is a further question that can be asked, a question that makes sense and yet cannot (by definition) be answered in the same terms. This is a question, not about *how* the world is, but about *the fact* that it is. In the classical formulation, "why is there something rather than nothing?" As Herbert McCabe puts it, "this is the question I call the God-question, because whatever the answer is, whatever the thing or state of affairs, whatever the existing reality that answers it we call 'God.'"[65] And to ask this question is also to ask about my own existence, to insist that the world is not simply arrayed before sight but is the medium of all life, that "the world is not what I think, but what I live."[66] It is to recognize my own implication in a world that exceeds me, to know myself as a hungry animal. Herbert McCabe draws the link between this mysterious metaphysical question and the ontology of flesh, of the human being as hungry animal, when he writes:

> To invite a guest to a meal is to invite her or him into the family circle, into a relationship defined by that first and most primitive act of hospitality; hence the deep relationship between food and gift. Our first experience of gift is the gift of food from our mother's body; it is the closest thing to the gift of life itself. Now in a certain way we are giving life to our guests when we give them food. This is true partly because to give them food is not merely to give them something they can use, but to give them their own bodies, which the food becomes. It is also true because

65. McCabe, *God Matters*, 5.
66. Merleau-Ponty, *Phenomenology of Perception*, lxxx.

all such giving goes back to, and is a kind of imitation of, the primary giving. [. . .] In and through and beyond our host, all our food and all our life comes from an ultimately mysterious source of life and this we call "God" (*et hoc omnes dicunt Deum*, as Aquinas used to say at the end of each of the Five Ways; a meal can be a reaching into mystery just as the Five Ways are.)[67]

As Ted Toadvine points out, it is not often noticed that Merleau-Ponty's notion of flesh has its foundations in Sartre's use of that term in his account of desire in *Being and Nothingness*. For Sartre, the flesh, as the site of the often insatiate and distracting or destructive impulse of sexual desire, is a blockage, a factical obstacle to the existential freedom of a human being. Sartre's notion of flesh here is reminiscent of St. Paul's *sarx*, a principle of dissipation against which the human spirit must struggle, and of Augustine's thinking of the flesh in terms of concupiscence. For Sartre, the flesh is tragic. But for Merleau-Ponty, flesh is not an obstacle at all. Indeed, as his earlier thought made clear, embodiment is not the obstacle of freedom, but its very condition. The flesh does not, for Merleau-Ponty, oppose the spirit, but is its incarnate ground. The flesh is the site of generativity.

We have already seen that in the Cartesian-Spinozist conception of nature, nature mirrors God; God is the source of the laws of nature or is in fact those laws themselves. This always leads to an insistence that there can be no hiatus, no "gap" between God and nature. There is no possibility, in this case, of God completing nature through grace, since nature either is God (under a different mode) or is the outworking of God's own nature. Neither is there a possibility of God intervening in nature, for the same reason. It seems that Cartesian thought accepts, implicitly, that matter might have been created *ex nihilo*, as a totally alien substance to its creator. But for Descartes, thought, reason, or *res cogitans* is not truly new; it must proceed from God on the basis of his nature, it must be the creation of God *ex Deo*. Spinoza does not accept any *creatio ex nihilo*; for his geometrical understanding, there is no creation in that sense. All that is is simply the outworking of what has been; the origin of things is obscured.

Creation and Participation

Andreas Nordlander has shown that Merleau-Ponty's antipathy to a certain kind of theology is based on a misapprehension about the meaning of creation. He "takes the presumed productive power of God and the productive power of nature to operate on the same level and to be antithetical: if God is

---

67. McCabe, *God Matters*, 85.

a productive power, nature cannot be."[68] Creation is still often understood in this or similar ways in popular discourse: God sets a world going, then either "tinkers" with it along the way (via Humean "miracles") or leaves it well alone. Creation here is always taken to be an explanation of the world, rather than the basis of the continual interrogation of existence, a "reaching into mystery." And this misunderstanding leads to the simplistic opposition between science and Christian faith. For all that I have sought to challenge an ontology that begins and ends with science and all its presuppositions, we must insist that science, and all its lower-level discourses, are integral to the pursuit of knowledge. As Nordlander proposes, "contemporary theology stands in need of development" when it comes to building an understanding of "human participation in the unfolding sense of the world."[69] Natural causes, as Merleau-Ponty insists, are themselves no longer seen as subject to a mechanistic model built on the presuppositions of modernity: "today, even science has stopped looking for inspiration in this secularized god, namely, Laplace's ideal physicist."[70]

The God of the Bible and of Christian tradition has little to do with this model. God as *ipsum esse subsistens* is not the Aristotelian "prime mover," nor is God the idealist absolute. Brian Davies explains that "[i]n Aquinas's view, to call God *ipsum esse subsistens* is primarily to assert that, whatever else we say about God, we should deny that he is something the existence of which is caused by what is not God. Aquinas, of course, does not mean that God's existence is caused by God himself. He means that God is not caused to exist by anything."[71] *Ipsum esse subsistens* is not offered as a description of God that identifies God amongst other things. It is in this sense a negative claim, intended to show what God is *not*, as is clearly shown by its first appearance in the *Summa Theologiae* amongst the denials that God is composed of extended parts, of form and matter, essence and existence, genus and difference, substance and accidents, and other things, in Question 3 of the first part.

The God who, as *ipsum esse subsistens*, is the uncaused plenitude of subsisting existence that holds all things in being by giving *esse*, stands in a relation to creation quite different to that of the conceptual God of *ens realissimum*. Everything that is not God receives its being from God, and so all created existence is in some sense being towards, an existence that stands

---

68. Nordlander, "Wonder of Immanence," 122.

69. Ibid., 122.

70. Merleau-Ponty, "Merleau-Ponty in Person," 11.

71. Davies, *Thomas Aquinas on God and Evil*, 49.

in relation to its source.[72] As Pabst argues, relation takes ontological priority over substance—things exist as the things they are in virtue of their relation to God and to all other things.[73] This is the ultimate conclusion of the logic of depth—grounded in the phenomenological insistence on the primacy of perception that Merleau-Ponty shares with Thomas Aquinas.

For Michael Hoonhout

> At the very beginning of the treatise on creation (*ST* I, q. 44, a. 1), Aquinas explicitly reminds the reader of the foundational point of his theology: God is *ipsum esse per se subsistens*. What grounds his theology of God will ground his theological under-standing of the world. In marked contrast to God's subsistent existence, created reality is *participant esse*, or *esse per participa-tionem*. When a thing possesses some characteristic that it does not have on account of its own essence, it must receive it by an act of participation in another being that does have it as proper to its own essence. Participation occurs by the patient sharing in what the agent is essentially.[74]

The notion of participation derives from a Platonic tradition in which it has been conceived in a variety of ways. In the Middle Platonism of the second and early third centuries, which combined Stoic, Platonic, and Aris-totelian elements, God's transcendence was preserved through a hierarchi-cal distancing in which God is conceived in terms of an uneasy synthesis between the Aristotelian unmoved mover, the highest Good (to which the soul ascends) of the *Republic*, and the supreme One of the *Parmenides*. For Kathryn Tanner, "The transcendence of God is imaged here [in Middle Pla-tonism] as distance; transcendence is understood spatially, as a distance or spatial interval occupied by intermediary divinities. And one finds much the same thing in a more straightforwardly Aristotelian cosmology that talks about the first God as simply the unmoved mover."[75]

As the ordering principle of the highest God is divorced from the pro-ductive principle of immanent divinity, the emanationist schema enforces a hierarchy that, even when conceived in terms of the ascent of the soul, leads to the denigration of the body and the insistence that the productive capac-ity of the created world submit to a discipline that is not that of its relation to its creative and sustaining source, but to the manipulative and repressive

---

72. Burrell, "*Creation ex Nihilo* Recovered," especially 8–9.

73. Pabst, *Metaphysics*, especially 104–5.

74. Hoonhout, "Aquinas' Theology of the God Who Is," 47–48.

75. Tanner, "*Creatio ex Nihilo* as Mixed Metaphor," 144.

discipline of the putative hierarchy of creation—it serves to justify the *status quo* of human oppression.

> God's involvement in the world—particularly as a productive principle—should have an unlimited scope and be utterly direct in manner. That, I take it, is the point of creation *ex nihilo*. [. . .] Emanationist imagery [. . .] is often retained in creation *ex nihilo* accounts [. . .], but with significant warping. [. . .] The practical resonances of these radicalized claims about God's transcendence and creative agency need have very little to do, therefore, with support for a principle of coercive domination or for dualistic hierarchies among creatures. When seen as a modification of the Greco-Roman problematic, radicalized transcendence seems designed to prevent the divinizing of any this-worldly status quo, while relativizing the significance of differences among creatures: none of those differences makes any difference to intimacy to God. [. . .] [T]he given order and reason of things in this world (both natural and socio-political) are not likened to the divine and due respect as such.[76]

As such the logic of creation, fulfilled by incarnation, refuses any simple hierarchy. The God beneath us is not a Kantian *ens realissimum*, subjecting alien matter to hierarchical order. Rather, God is the creator of matter and the one who grants *esse* to all material beings, compounded of form and matter. For McCabe,

> Material substances exist (as does everything other than God) by being some kind of thing, and exist over against the possibility of changing into other kinds of things—for this is what being "material" implies. They are contingent, not in the later rationalist sense (that we can conceive them not being) but in the medieval sense of being contingent on how they will be affected by the other things in the universe.[77]

The logic of participatory ontology, in its Christian modification, cannot imply that things participate in God if this means that they tend toward and realize ideas already conceived in the mind of God. Aquinas is ambiguous on this point, claiming that the plurality of divine ideas can be reconciled with divine simplicity—"to attribute an idea to God, however, is to refer to that *which* God knows. But God by one act knows many things, not only as they are in themselves, but also as they are known."[78] The

76. Tanner, "*Creatio ex Nihilo* as Mixed Metaphor," 148.

77. McCabe, *God Still Matters*, 125.

78. Aquinas, *Summa Theologiae* (ed. Davies and Leftow), 204 (*ST* 1a.15.2 *ad* 1).

manifestation of *logos* in the depths of creation in relational terms explored in chapter 4 thus casts the notion of the recognition of the Forms (in the Platonic sense) or divine ideas into properly Thomist-existentialist terms. For John Hughes

> David Burrell is surely correct when he wishes that Aquinas had taken the analogy of the artisan to its radical conclusion and rejected the residual Aristotelian priority of speculative over practical reason. For an artist does not "choose" from a set of options whether to create this work of art or that one, "like a jury in an architectural contest," as Burrell puts it. Rather those other possibilities which were never realized have at most a shadowy, virtual existence, merely "penumbral" to this practical knowledge which creates. It is not that the ideas are the problem which must be abandoned, but rather that they must be understood in this more integral, intentional, practical way.[79]

The ongoing work of creation is here seen in terms of Merleau-Ponty's understanding of expression in the context of a logic of institution, which is not to see God as inscribed within these terms, but to insist on the createdness of God's created works. So

> For Aquinas, the divine ideas are clearly not some hangover from Platonic demiurgic or emanationist schemes of creation, but rather, understood according to the logic of the Trinity, are crucial to understanding creation as truly free and personal rather than proceeding from natural necessity, but also in accordance with the intrinsic order of divine goodness and wisdom rather than simply formless, random, and arbitrary.[80]

For Merleau-Ponty, then, my intuition of essences, my knowledge of the world, is implicated in those essences and that world, and implicates me in things—so the reduction can never be made complete. This is not a Husserlian attempt at philosophy as a rigorous science, nor is it an attempt to discover the meaning of being as it necessarily is in itself. Mary Rose Barral claims that for Merleau-Ponty, the Thomist real distinction between essence and existence cannot be maintained, because my access to essences depends on my own existence, and my essential nature as a thinking thing. For Barral, Merleau-Ponty's "phenomenology is also a philosophy which puts essences back into existence and does not claim to arrive at an understanding of men and of the world except from the basic starting point of

79. Hughes, "*Creatio ex Nihilo* and the Divine Ideas in Aquinas," 135.

80. Ibid., 136.

their facticity."[81] So "Man's particular point of view provides science with its subject matter." But this is a misunderstanding of Thomas, for whom, as we have seen, essence is always subordinate to existence. For Merleau-Ponty, it is simply a fact that

> I am not a "living being," a "man," nor again even a "conscious-ness," possessing all of the characteristics that zoology, social anatomy and inductive psychology acknowledge in these prod-ucts of nature or history. Rather, I am the absolute source. My existence does not come from my antecedents, nor from my physical and social surroundings; it moves out toward them and sustains them. For I am the one who brings into being for myself—and thus into being in the only sense that word could have for me—this tradition that I choose to take up or this ho-rizon whose distance from me would collapse were I not there to sustain it with my gaze (since this distance does not belong to the horizon as one of its properties).[82]

There is, in this sense, a fundamental narcissism in Merleau-Ponty. And it is this idealistic trap from which Merleau-Ponty is trying to find his way back when he writes "The problems posed in *Ph. P.* are insoluble because I start there from the 'consciousness'–'object' distinction." So "the common stuff of which all the structures are made is the *visible*, which, for its part, is nowise of the objective, of the in itself, but is of the transcen-dent—which is not opposed to the for Itself, which has cohesion only for a Self—the Self to be understood not as nothingness, not as something, but as the unity by transgression or by correlative encroachment of 'thing' and 'world' (the time-thing, the time-being)."[83]

In Merleau-Ponty's later thought, the "narcissistic" perceiving self finds itself entwined with a reality that *does* precede it, the "anonymous body," that material existence that in some sense precedes it, but that also anticipates that which retroactively founds it. Metaphysics, then, for Merleau-Ponty, is not a matter of an abstract system—rather, it is a matter of the structure of the perceived world. "Metaphysical consciousness has no other objects than those of experience: this world, other people, human history, truth, culture. But instead of taking them as all settled, as consequences with no premises, as if they were self evident, it rediscovers their fundamental strangeness to me and the miracle of their appearing."[84]

---

81. Barral, "Thomas Aquinas and Merleau-Ponty," 207.

82. Merleau-Ponty, *Phenomenology of Perception*, lxxii.

83. Merleau-Ponty, *The Visible and the Invisible*, 200.

84. Merleau-Ponty, "The Metaphysical in Man," 94.

The theological significance of all this is that knowledge of God cannot be contained in an abstract system but must relate the divine absolute to the situated "I" who seeks it, to *me*. The invisible source of *esse*, at work in the depths of the visible, must be made visible. The revelation of the "image of the invisible God" in Jesus Christ, then, does not simply overthrow all worldly knowledge; rather, it completes it. While no natural theology can make the Christian God visible, the revelation of God in Jesus Christ is not divorced from our experience of the world—it makes visible the invisible of this world, the divine depths of things, which is to say, their character as made by and for God, and as knowing their being by participation in God. A metaphysics of participation is known as a response to the revelation of Christ in a world I know (which is not to say I understand, or can explain) without reference to God. The universal is known not in pure abstraction but as it mediates itself in the very particularity of beings.

Creation and Contingency

An ontology of participation does not mean that things simply work out an extrinsic *telos* already conceived in the mind of God. There is something of the logic of embodied thought here: things participate in God's creative work by playing their part in the generation of those ideas, as the site of God's creative ideation.

When creation is properly understood as the work of God who is *ipsum esse subsistens*, theology demands "a philosophy that places essences back within existence and thinks that the only way to understand man and the world is by beginning from their 'facticity.'"[85] Such a theology will fulfill the philosophical anthropology of human being as "the hungry animal" that we developed in chapter 2, as in the theology of Meister Eckhart:

> Every created being is analogically ordered to God in existence, truth, and goodness. [. . .] Therefore every created being radically and positively possesses existence, life, and wisdom from and in God, not in itself as a created being. And thus, [commenting on Sirach 24:29], it always "eats" as something produced and created, but it always hungers because it is always from another and not from itself. [. . .] So he is inside all things in that he is existence, and thus every being feeds on him. He is also on the outside because he is above all and thus outside all. Therefore all

85. Merleau-Ponty, *Phenomenology of Perception*, lxx.

things feed on him because he is totally within; they hunger for him because he is totally without.[86]

Such a theology will also fulfill the demand of Merleau-Ponty's ontology of flesh that the fundamental contingency of the world, the wildness of brute being, is recognized in all its generativity, and not domesticated by facile explanation. As Rudi te Velde explains, "What characterizes Thomas's understanding of God's providential government is that it includes the operations of all the secondary causes."[87] God's providential activity does not operate in competition with natural causation, because God and the created order are not two entities in a shared field. The affirmation of contingency does not mean that God ceases to be immutable; providence operates through both primary and secondary causes, and thus human actions play their part in the exercise of providence.

> This means that providence, as Thomas points out in full detail, does not entirely exclude the existence of evil [In the *Summa Contra Gentiles*, Book III] (c.71), contingency (c.72), free will, (c.73), fortune and chance (c.74). These four are all essential characteristics of the world in which we live; they mark the open and unpredictable character of the human world, open and unpredictable not in spite of God's providence, but rather as the dimension in which God's providence will be fulfilled. Hence, providence, being the rule of reason (wisdom) in all things, does not remove contingency from our world.[88]

So, again, as free, desiring, hungry animals, we shape our own labile essence and those of the things around us, and participate in providence. For McCabe, "We create the ways in which we live together—they are only in the very broadest sense laid down by nature. [. . .] What, you may ask, about God? [. . .] [W]e can only make sense of God (in the Christian sense) as the centre of our freedom and not as a constraint upon it, not as setting 'natural' limits to it. As man becomes more and more self-creative God does not fade out of the picture, he fades in."[89] This modifies Aquinas' inherited metaphysical starting point in Augustine's divine ideas in light of his rigorous working out of divine simplicity, insisting that essences are not "eternal" but labile and bound up with the ongoing work of creation. That there are *entia per se* (i.e., naturally-occurring things with stable essences)

---

86. Eckhart, *Meister Eckhart: Teacher and Preacher*, ed. Bernard McGinn, 178–79, cited in Burrell, "*Creatio ex Nihilo* Recovered," 16.

87. Velde, "Aquinas, Prayer, and *Creation ex Nihilo*," 53.

88. Ibid., 54.

89. McCabe, *God Matters*, 170.

cannot be taken for granted in a univocal mode. Individuation depends on the continuous creative involvement of God as primary cause and source of existence. There is an autopoeisis at the level of secondary causes that is genuinely creative and spontaneous—but only as created, and always dependent on its ultimate cause, the final realization of the new creation, of the kingdom of God, which is inaugurated but not completed. This grounds the possibility of redemption—not just that bad things can be made good, but that bad things can become new kinds of things, and so good.

As McCabe has argued, the inevitability of hierarchical order in fallen political life does not serve to justify such hierarchy. The God who is *ipsum esse subsistens* is radically related to every existent, and this is the significance that Merleau-Ponty gave to the notion of incarnation. To speak of the God beneath us is not to claim ontological equality with God. But it is to claim that creation and incarnation are ordered towards a love that is predicated on equality, grounded in the mutual love of the Trinity. And this making-equal lies at the heart of Christian understanding. God conceived as "the creator and manipulator of the world, cannot himself, it seems, be other than a vast omnipotent baby, unable to grow up, unable to abandon himself in love."[90] But "Love begins and ends in equality. In a sense to love just is to see the equality of another."[91] This equality is not proper to things, but is given in the life and death of Jesus Christ. So "it is only the doctrine of the divinity of Christ (and thus the doctrine of the Trinity) that makes possible the astounding and daring idea that God can after all genuinely love."[92]

The Logic of Incarnation

We have developed, with Merleau-Ponty, an account of "incarnation" as the heart of human bodily existence. This thought of "general" incarnation begins with a critique of Cartesian ontology, in which an absolute distance isolates the *res cogitans* of the perceiver from the *res extensa* of the world of objects. When I understand my incarnate nature, I overcome the distance of this separation. Love becomes possible, because there is an in-principle reversibility of subject and object. I am no longer a subject installed in (and against) a world of objects, but a "member" of the world. The fact that my body precedes me, that I am in a sense given to myself, underscores this possibility.

90. McCabe, *God Still Matters*, 6.

91. Ibid., 4.

92. Ibid., 7.

Do we mean something similar when we speak of the incarnation of the Son of God? Just as the ontology of the object reifies an ontological understanding that separates us from the world and actually reinforces our alienation, so idolatrous pictures of God as the "Top Man" or most powerful inhabitant of the universe harden the difference between creator and creation into an absolute distance. Such a distance is, in the end, not a matter of too much transcendence and too little immanence in our conception of the relationship between God and the world, but a failure of transcendence and a failure of immanence—a failure to realize that God's transcendence is closely related to the fact that God also stands at the center of things, holding them in being—to what we have called *depth*. For John Webster, "Every element of creaturely being and action is what it is in 'the very dependency of the created act of being upon the principle from which it is produced.' [Aquinas, *Summa Contra Gentiles*, II.18.2.] There is, therefore, a *depth* to created things. To consider them, we have to understand not only their finite causes but the first cause, tracing them back to God, their *principium*."[93]

In the incarnation of the Son of God, God does not compromise God's own logic and abrogate God's own nature. Rather, God offends human idolatry and disrupts our hardened picture of creation, showing that God is not first of all to be characterized as creator (to create, *ex nihilo*, is a matter of freedom for God) but rather as *lover*. As the "general" notion of incarnation overcomes an ossified subject-object divide, so the particular incarnation shows how our understanding of creation can become corrupted. It does not, of course, show that God is a "member" of the world—precisely because the created order in no sense precedes God. It is *not* given to God; God is the giver. What is shown is that the Son receives himself from the Father, that God is from the first a life of love from which creation is born and into which creation can be received. For McCabe,

> this notion of our divinisation is already implicit in the Hebrew conviction that God speaks with us, that we are in communication with God. This already says something more than that we are his creatures, for in the end communication itself demands equality, in the end communication itself demands love. [. . .] I am maintaining, then, that the Christian gospel is that we are given equality with God. It is important not to lose sight of either of those words: we are *given equality*. What we are given is the *divine* life itself, the Holy Spirit—if we lose sight of that we will be speaking merely of some created gift, like moral excellence or some other human thing, and this could not be the foundation

93. Webster, "*Creatio ex Nihilo* and Creaturely Goodness," 165.

and implication of love, it is only if we really have equality with
God that there can be love between God and us. At the same
time it is an equality that is *given*. To lose sight of that would be
to make ourselves God, to divinise ourselves.[94]

In Merleau-Ponty's general sense, "incarnation" describes the logic of
our intimate and immanent relation to a world on which we depend for
our existence, a world that precedes us and that guarantees the possibilities of communication, communion, and reconciliation. In the particular
sense, the logic of the incarnation of the Son of God describes an intimate
and immanent relation to a world that ultimately depends on God, and that
grounds the communication between creator and creation, present communion and ultimate reconciliation, assuming the priority of love over
creation.

We must return here to Merleau-Ponty's claim: nature is *soil*. It is a
productive capacity that is grounded in substantial reality. It is the potency
of "Vibrant Matter," as Jane Bennett calls it.[95] In *The Structure of Behaviour*,
Merleau-Ponty wrote of the relation of the soul to the body:

> it is not a duality of substances; or, in other words, the notions
> of soul and body must be relativized: there is the body as mass
> of chemical components in interaction, the body as dialectic of
> living being and its biological milieu, and the body as dialec-
> tic of social subject and his group; even all our habits are an
> impalpable body for the ego of each moment. Each of these
> degrees is soul with respect to the preceding one, body with
> respect to the following one. The body in general is an ensemble
> of paths already traced, of powers already constituted; the body
> is the acquired dialectical soil upon which a higher "forma-
> tion" is accomplished, and the soul the meaning which is then
> established.[96]

The notion of soul is found in Merleau-Ponty's earliest work, and it
serves, I contend, the same function: although Merleau-Ponty's work here
is concerned with the problem of the body, and not with nature, the point
is the same. The body is not simply an analogue of nature; it *is* nature as
the human being. "Nature," like "body," names neither a substance nor a
process, but a material site of generativity. If what we usually denote by the
term "nature" is something like the organic world, then this is because it is

94. McCabe, *God Matters*, 21.
95. Bennett, *Vibrant Matter*.
96. Merleau-Ponty, *The Structure of Behaviour*, 210.

the world that we most obviously depend on for our sustenance, which is the ground of our very possibility. The term is ambiguous because its meaning must derive from its structural relation to its other, to what we mean to mark out as "not nature" when we call everything else "nature." Thus nature can be the opposite of the unnatural, art, artifice, humanity, the supernatural, grace, freedom, and so on. There is an inorganic, mineral world that constitutes nature with respect to the organic world, and looked at in this perspective human beings are not distinct from that organic world. But the organic world is also transformed by the effects of human action, as we have argued: making nightmarish as well as fecund situations possible—in this regard humanity is "nature" with respect to the organic world; human action is the "soil" from which a transformed world grows. This is to say that all is nature and all is non-nature; that the human-nature distinction is a structural distinction that must be made if we are to think humanity against the background of the conditions that make it possible. And this helps us to understand why "nature loves to hide":[97] because thought is prone to forget its dependence on a set of conditions, that their "figure" exists against a "background." When life is endangered, its dependence on the nature which is its ground returns very much into view, and we see the figure against its background.

Felix Culpa

Christianity insists, then, on the lived earth, the created world, as fundamentally good, as freely created, and as blessed with an analogous freedom, so that when God creates he allows for the genuine freedom of his creation, granting the created world power to generate what is radically new. This creative dimension of the created world demands the radical contingency of things to make possible the appearance of the unanticipated. Merleau-Ponty speaks of this in terms of the doctrine of *felix culpa*. "The Christian teaching that the Fall is fortunate, that a world without fault would be less good, and, finally, that the creation, which made being fall from its original perfection and sufficiency, is nevertheless more or was all to the good makes Christianity the most resolute negation of the conceived infinite"[98] (that is to say, of God as the great geometer). Contingency and freedom are inevitable if a

---

97. This quote from Heraclitus, the translation of which is highly disputed, is the theme of Hadot's *The Veil of Isis*.

98. Merleau-Ponty, "The Metaphysical in Man," 96–97.

God of love created a world for the sake of the genuine expression that can only come from others. In "Faith and Good Faith" Merleau-Ponty writes

> Hegel said that the Incarnation is "the hinge of universal history" and that all history thereafter has only developed its consequences. And the God-man and the Death of God do, in effect, transform spirit and religion. As if the infinite God were no longer sufficient, as if something moved in Him, as if the world and man became the necessary moments of a greater perfection instead of being a useless decline from the originating perfection. God can no longer be fully God, and Creation cannot be completed unless man freely recognizes God and returns Creation to Him through Faith. Something is happening; the world is not futile, there is something to be done. Man could not return to God unless he had been separated from Him. "Fortunate the fault which merited such a Redeemer."[99]

This last line is a quotation from the Latin phrase, used in the Exsultet of the Easter Vigil Mass, cited by Aquinas and alluded to by both Augustine and Aquinas, "*O felix culpa quae talem ac tantum meruit habere Redemptorem*," "O Happy fault! That merited such and so great a Redeemer."[100] This religion of the incarnation, then, re-articulates the problem of how God might make Godself known in the world without compromising human freedom: there is no contradiction here, indeed human freedom proceeds, in a sense, from God. "Our redemption will not just be the successful end of a journey, the triumphant culmination of the history of man, but in some utterly mysterious way we will be freed from our history, or *our history will be taken up into some totally new pattern in which even our sins become part of our holiness*. We will somehow be able to accept them as God accepts them."[101]

Incarnation and Transubstantiation

God is made known in the flesh, in nature and history, with the incarnation; this is communicated in the traditions we might associate with *word* and *table*: as the linguistic expression of a set of invisible truths, most obviously in the traditions of Scripture, liturgy, and theology (understood as the

---

99. Merleau-Ponty, "Faith and Good Faith," 175.

100. Aquinas, *Summa Theologiae* III, 1, 3 ad. 3. Cf. Milton, *Paradise Lost*, XII, lines 469–478; Augustine, *City of God*, XII.6.

101. McCabe, *God Matters*, 214 (my emphasis).

reflexive element of continued expression of these, that is, as the reflection on Scripture and liturgical tradition, which is incorporated into them). But this linguistic sedimentation is not all; there is also a tradition of sacramentality. This involves a focused expression of the truth at the heart of things in the bodily practices of worship and prayer.

"Sensation is, literally, a communion."[102] This is to say that the sensed thing, the visible, has a reality that is like that of the host in the Eucharist. This raises the question of transubstantiation, the question of what it would mean for the substance of a thing (which is invisible) to change while its (visible) accidents remain the same. Conor Cunningham points out that "according to Aquinas, we do not comprehend the substantial form of any being. We learn of a thing, instead, by its proper accidents. [. . .] 'The essential grounds of things are unknown to us.'"[103] This leads us to the sixteenth-century Anglican theologian Richard Hooker's proposal that, as Anthony Thiselton puts it, "'real presence' derived not from the consecrated elements of bread and wine, but from the Christian believer's *understanding, reception and appropriation* of the *promissory word* of God *through the elements*."[104] This might at first look like a nominalism that would deny the bodily reality of the Eucharist. But we can read it in another way. Perhaps the importance of this is that the host is transformed not in the mode of the *bloße sachen* but in the fullness of its materiality; it is not that the physical atoms of which it is made change, but that its whole being, in its relation to the oriented being of humanity, is transformed. Merleau-Ponty's analysis of perception showed us that the sensible thing is not an aggregation of accidents; its substance is not the blank that supports a collection of accidents, nor is it mathematizable form determined from an absolute perspective, but is rather its "flesh," its resistant and productive intertwining with nature and history. The host appears no longer as a brute *in-itself* but *sub specie regni*, under the aspect of the kingdom of God and the remaking of heaven and earth. "The bread does not turn into the body by acquiring a new form in its matter; the whole existence of the bread becomes the existence of the living body of Christ. It is not that the bread has become a new kind of thing in this world: it now belongs to a new world."[105]

Thiselton notes that "the 1662 English Book of Common Prayer defines a sacrament in its *Catechism* as 'an outward and visible sign of an

102. Merleau-Ponty, *Phenomenology of Perception*, 219.

103. Cunningham, "The Difference *of* Theology," 293, citing Aquinas's *Commentary on De Anima*, 1, 1.15.

104. Thiselton, *Hermeneutics of Doctrine*, 535.

105. McCabe, *God Still Matters*, 119.

inward and spiritual grace unto us, ordained by Christ himself as a means whereby we received the same and a pledge to assure us thereof.' To the next catechetical question, 'How many parts are there in a sacrament?' The answer given is 'Two: the outward visible sign and the inward spiritual grace.'"[106] Again this sounds like a dualism, and could be contrasted to John Milbank's insistence that "as Christians we have to view the world as God's creation and therefore we have to view the world sacramentally: this means that everything in the world is at once a thing and a sign."[107] Again, a non-dualistic reading is demanded: the host is not ontologically divided, because the outward and inward parts are not substances but *dimensions* of the thing; they are *not* separable. If the "inward spiritual grace" was given without the "outward visible sign," it would not be the same grace. The bread considered as mere matter is not the same thing as the host, because it is not understood in its instituted thickness, but the practice of using bread as this sign transforms not only the bread used as sacrament but announces and points to a yet-to-come reality in which *all* bread is recognized as a means of God's grace. And indeed the bread considered as mere matter is not the same as *any* real bread, which, as thick with instituted meaning, as deeply significant for human life, is always more than matter.

This is also to say that there is no simple divide between substantiality and intelligibility. The knowledge of the *logos* of things is not gained by referring them to a God who perceives all. The end of things does not lie in God conceived as the ultimate *explanation* for existence. Remy Kwant thinks Merleau-Ponty's "denial of the absolute and his conception of metaphysical consciousness, clearly presaged his atheism."[108] But Kwant is not quite right to say that Merleau-Ponty denies the absolute; Merleau-Ponty's claim is that "the absolute which [Pascal] looks for beyond our experience is implied in it. Just as I grasp time through my present and by being present, I perceive others through my individual life, in the tension of an experience which transcends itself." So it is that, as we saw earlier, "Christianity consists in replacing the separated absolute by the absolute in men."[109] In a footnote Kwant explains: "The thesis that intelligibility belongs to the order of facts indissolubly connected with man implicitly contains the germ of atheism. For God is always conceived as the one who understands all reality. If there is a God, then, reality must be intelligible and, reversely, there cannot be

---

106. Thiselton, *Hermeneutics of Doctrine*, 519.

107. Milbank, "The Moral Market is a Freer Market."

108. Kwant, *Phenomenological Philosophy*, 128.

109. Merleau-Ponty, "The Primacy of Perception," 27.

a God if intelligibility is a fact indissolubly connected with man."[110] But this would seem to impose a much too rigid divide between nature and grace, between substantiality and intelligibility. Merleau-Ponty's position is not that intelligibility belongs to the order of facts. From the beginning his philosophy militates against the idea that there is a simple plane of facts or of sensation.

Rather, intelligibility belongs to the lived world as the present belongs to time; the human perceiver does not have a status *somewhere between* the created world and God conceived as pure thought, nor as a conjunction of the two. To ask whether (and on what terms) creation is intelligible without reference to a human perceiver is to ask not about the general intelligibility of things but to enquire about the meaning of a world severed from itself. I concur with Merleau-Ponty's claim that "God needs human history," not in any sense that would imply that human history precedes God, nor that God could not exist without it, but that it is an integral part of the world God has created and in which he became incarnate; "God ceases to be an external object in order to mingle in human life, *and this life is not simply a return to a non-temporal conclusion.*"[111] For McCabe,

> Very frequently the man who sees himself as an atheist is not denying the existence of some answer to the mystery of how come there is anything instead of nothing, he is denying what he thinks or has been told is a *religious* answer to this question. He thinks or has been told that religious people, and especially Christians, claim to have discovered what the answer is, that there is some grand architect of the universe who designed it, just like Basil Spence only bigger and less visible, that there is a Top Person in the universe who issues arbitrary decrees for the rest of the persons and enforces them because he is the most powerful being around. Now if denying this claim makes you an atheist, then I and Thomas Aquinas and a whole Christian tradition are atheistic too.
>
> But a genuine atheist is one who simply does not see that there is any problem or mystery here, one who is content to ask questions within the world, but cannot see that the world itself raises a question.[112]

110. Kwant, *Phenomenological Philosophy*, 128 n. 1.

111. Merleau-Ponty, "The Primacy of Perception," 27, emphasis added.

112. McCabe, *God Matters*, 7.

While mystery may be refused, and a person may oppose the claims of Christianity if they are willing to stake their claim on the basis that the question of why there is anything at all is not a real question, this was not Merleau-Ponty's position. His putative atheism was not a refusal of mystery, but an attempt to preserve it in the face of what he saw as a necessitarian theology. Where God is understood as *ipsum esse subsistens*, Merleau-Ponty's ontology of flesh does not demand or even suggest an atheism. Rather, it takes seriously the notion that God is not the final referent of all intelligibility as an explanation for things; the question "why is there something rather than nothing?" is not an attempt to explain the world in a theological grand unified theory, but the question that lies behind an ongoing interrogation of the world. God is not the explanation for nature. Rather, God is nature's ultimate ground. To expect that the world would be intelligible if we excise human being and history from the picture is to fail to see that intelligibility belongs to nature as a graced whole rather than to its atomic elements. Creation is not a plane of pure positivity, and as Emmanuel de Saint Aubert puts it, in an article entitled "L'incarnation change tout," "Merleau-Ponty seeks the 'positive signification of negativity,' that which [. . .] belongs to 'the essence of Christianity.' Yet it is this same fecund negativity that the theology he has called 'explanatory' has ignored. That theology is thus stopped in its tracks in a tentative thought of the central mysteries of Christianity, and does not respond to the dual requirement of contesting false absolutes and thinking the Incarnation through to its end."[113] In "Faith and Good Faith," Merleau-Ponty's accusation had been that Christianity compromises with political conservatism or with liberalism because "The Incarnation is not followed out in all its consequences. [. . .] And so love changes to cruelty, the reconciliation of men with each other and with the world will come to naught, the Incarnation turns into suffering because it is incomplete, and Christianity becomes a new form of guilty conscience."[114]

Finally, Creation is abandoned to evil and the goodness of God is thought of as outside the world. Saint Aubert cites Merleau-Ponty's unpublished manuscripts from the *Bibliotèque Nationale*, in which he writes, "There is a 'milieu,' not infinite greatness, not infinite smallness, which is the place of meaning [*sens*]. The infinity of God is sought on this side and not with the bad infinity of magnitude."[115]

---

113. Saint Aubert, "L'incarnation change tout," 374, my translation. The citation is from Merleau-Ponty, *Éloge de le philosophie*, 49–50. English translation: Merleau-Ponty, *In Praise of Philosophy*, 47.

114. Merleau-Ponty, "Faith and Good Faith," 176–77.

115. Saint Aubert, "L'incarnation change tout," 394, my translation.

The "bad infinite," of "calculability," as Saint Aubert has it, which is aligned with what we have called the geometrical conception of nature and its implicit theology, is contrasted to the good infinite, which for Saint Aubert is linked to the knowledge of intuition rather than of mathematics.[116] God is not derived like a mathematical law but intuited like a sensible idea, heard like a melody, from the depths of things. Saint Aubert again cites an unpublished note: "This infinity [. . .] belongs for me to the visible thing or to the sea no less than to God. For, in some ways or in all ways, its richness is no less, it is in every case inexhaustible. [. . .] We say that we see the sea because there is in it this carnal and invisible infinity. Just the same, we say that we see ~~God~~ Being because there is within this carnal infinity."[117] "Thus," for Saint Aubert,

> In opposition to the model of knowledge, transposed into Man, as a cyclopean God who sees everything, all at once, Merleau-Ponty takes as a model the thought of the vision of the sea and of horizons, building up the implicit model of a beatific vision. For the inexhaustible God in a vision without flesh, he substitutes another absolute, in which the inexhaustibility of depth is the durable core of being, just as being is the condition of possibility of this vision. For the secret ontology informed by the generalization, of being and of God, of being because of God, of an imaginary omnipotence which represses the corporeal modalities of our opening to the world, the philosopher of the flesh is in a quest for another ontology, where the negativity intrudes into the force of being, where it is the condition of the possibility of donation. Thus seeking the sole absolute which does not bridle the inexhaustibility of desire, this phenomenology affirms that it is in the flesh that we see being, whose infinity is not of another nature than the inexhaustible which is expressed in our relation to the sensible world.[118]

Sacramentality, to retain its meaning, must transform the world of which it itself is a part as a sign of the greater transformation in which it participates, must follow the logic of incarnation in the work of reconciliation, in Merleau-Ponty's terms. Those who are fed in the Eucharist must continue the expression of the work of love as they "go in peace to love and serve the Lord," which derives from the Latin phrase that gives the Mass its name: *Ite, Missa Est.* The Mass is not Mass without mission, but by the same token,

116. Ibid., 394.

117. Ibid., 400–401.

118. Ibid., 401.

mission depends on and begins with Mass.[119] As (and when) Christians feed the poor and heal the sick, expressing the love of this God of love in action, it is instituted as a *tradition of transformation*. This tradition must always be prepared to submit itself to its own logic of transformation, to work out and bring to expression its own implications in its institutional forms.

Transcendence and Transformation

In this book I have presented a series of concentric conceptions of transcendence. Beginning with perceptual faith, we turned to desire and its imaginative development, to the transcendence of visual depth, the voluminosity of things, and their intelligible depth, which we called *logos*, revealed, finally, in the sacramental understanding of flesh. The central motif that unites these forms of transcendence is the possibility for transformation that they make available:—the perceptual faith is the ground of the emergence of perception from the indistinct field of sensation; the voluminosity of things completes this transformation by installing the perceiver in an inexhaustible world that is resistant to his investigations; the possibility of hunger allows for the imaginative transformation of given desires, and the intelligible *depth* of *logos* and the sacramentality of the flesh call us toward the possibilities for transformation in intersubjective sociality, in the pursuit of understanding and of wisdom, and to the transformation of our relation to the world, which comes from understanding it in relation to the God who is its source. What all these transformations share is that they lead us into a deeper engagement with the lived world *and not* to a detached ascent from the world to a different, higher realm.

God in himself must remain beyond determination, in this ontology. God cannot be known as if he were submitted to a gaze that could take in both Godself and the world; God must be known as the invisible *in* the visible, in and through the world.

> A God who would not be simply for us but for Himself, could [. . .] be sought by metaphysics only behind consciousness, beyond our ideas, as the anonymous force which sustains each of our thoughts and experiences. At this point religion ceases to be a conceptual construct or an ideology and once more becomes part of the experience of interhuman life. The originality of Christianity as the religion of the death of God is its rejection

---

119. This point is made by Inge in *A Christian Theology of Place*, 62; He cites Gorringe, "Sacraments," 168.

of the God of the philosophers and its heralding of a God who takes on the human condition.[120]

Merleau-Ponty was not a supporter of Christianity. There can be no doubt that his thought was deeply shaped by his Catholic intellectual inheritance. But what he describes here is a Christianity hoped for but not seen. Merleau-Ponty's writings on religion and comments on the church bear witness to a certain crisis of faith, a crisis that remained unresolved. It may be that the acceptance of such a crisis is the most intellectually honest way of responding to the challenge of Christianity in light of certain of the church's failures. But to remain honest would also require that such a crisis does not prevent us from acting: indeed, it would require that we *do* act.

Albert Rabil, Jr., in *Merleau-Ponty: Existentialist of the Social World*, understands Merleau-Ponty differently. For him, "Merleau-Ponty does not say, though he implies, that the only way for Christianity to rejoin human experience is to abandon the idea of transcendence."[121] This claim is not unreasonable in light of the passages Rabil cites, but it seems hard to resolve with Merleau-Ponty's continued attempts to present a this-worldly transcendence, a position to which he still seems committed in *The Visible and the Invisible*. Rabil does recognize that the later Merleau-Ponty allows for a distinction between subordinating "vertical" transcendence and a liberating "horizontal transcendence." But this does not quite get things right, because it is the logic of depth, not of planar horizontality, that is developed into a new notion of transcendence, and this logic grows out of Merleau-Ponty's thought. It does not arise from any sudden change around 1950, as Rabil suggests.[122] Similarly, in "The Soul of Reciprocity" John Milbank engages Merleau-Ponty's ontology to develop an Aristotelian account of the soul, and although he characterizes Merleau-Ponty in broadly positive terms, he finally suggests that his model is "a decapitated Catholic theology in which God incarnate is *only* incarnate and incarnate everywhere."[123] I have shown that we do not need to read Merleau-Ponty in this way: though his understanding of the Christian notion of God was mistaken, his thought does not imply a denial of transcendence. Philosophy begins in immanence, but it cannot remain there; immanence cannot be made complete. Merleau-Ponty's phenomenology, I have shown, ultimately "reaches beyond" itself to an ontology, because phenomenological appearance is constituted by an ontological "depth" against which it will always come up. As we make this

120. Merleau-Ponty, "The Metaphysical in Man," 96.

121. Rabil, *Merleau-Ponty*, 224.

122. Ibid., 225.

123. Milbank, "The Soul of Reciprocity Part Two," 504.

ontology explicit, we find that it in turn points outside of the domain of ontology towards that of metaphysics. Such a leap is anticipated in Merleau-Ponty's anthropology, in his critical engagements with what he took to be Christian thought, and his suggestions that the logic of incarnation points to an ontology that goes beyond objectivism, and a God who is not *ens realissimum*. Transcendence appears in the perceptual faith that is basic to our encounter with the world, and in the imaginative excess of our perceptual desire. Transcendence is revealed in depth, in the simple sense that what *is* is always in excess of my perspective. My existential relation to the world reveals things in their inexhaustible voluminosity, and in their intelligibility discovers the *logoi* of things at the heart of the world. This transcendence is necessarily ambiguous; in Cunningham's terms, God is *known* without being comprehended, just as the objects of perception are known while remaining partly comprehended.[124] God is the ultimate voluminosity, the inexhaustibility at the source of all that is. Of course this knowledge of transcendence is brought to expression in theology, not proceeding directly from the thought of flesh but rather from the history, from the institutions, from the living stories that the philosophy of flesh makes way for and demands, but that it cannot complete. This is no decapitated theology, but it is true to say that the "head" is excluded from its purview because its focus is elsewhere.

Spirit and Transformation

On Rabil's understanding, "Merleau-Ponty's interpretation of the Christian doctrine of God is Sabellian."[125] It is true that Merleau-Ponty opposes the "religion of the Father" to the "religion of the Son" and of the Spirit. But this is no modalism; the point is that the incarnation *actually changes things*, that Christ necessarily transforms our understanding of God. For Merleau-Ponty,

> The Incarnation is not followed out in all its consequences. The first Christians felt abandoned after the death of Christ and looked everywhere for a trace of him. Centuries later the Crusaders plunged into the search for an empty tomb. And this was because they worshiped the Son in the spirit of the religion of the Father. They had not yet understood that God was with them now and forever. The meaning of the Pentecost is that the

124. Cunningham, "The Difference *of* Theology," 294.
125. Rabil, *Merleau-Ponty*, 221.

religion of both the Father and the Son are to be fulfilled in the religion of the Spirit. [. . .] Christ's stay on earth was only the beginning of his presence, which is continued by the Church. Christians [. . .] should live out the marriage of the Spirit and human history which began with the Incarnation.[126]

Both Rabil and Milbank assume that the "reign of the Father" must be done away with in Merleau-Ponty's thought (because, for him, it is incompatible with incarnationalism) and object to this. But "Faith and Good Faith" suggests something different: that in view of the incarnation, a liberal "religion of the Son" is not to be balanced against a conservative "reign of the Father"; rather the two undergo a radical transformation. The God of grace is no longer posited in thought as existing in a kind of unknowable clarity, distinct yet separated from us by an epistemic chasm that can only be crossed by a blind leap of faith. Rather, the world as created becomes a milieu for such action, for our interrogation which discovers the ground and source of things in God who is mediated to us through nature, who instituted himself in the world. This implies an earthliness of theology, taking seriously the notion that God is revealed amongst the outcast, interrogating the world with an expectation, or at least an openness to the possibility, that such interrogation draws us into to grace. McCabe casts this in Thomist terms when he writes

> The Christian holds that in so far as the world receives the Spirit, in so far as it lets itself be destroyed and re-born in grace, the distance between God and man disappears. And this means that in the kingdom to which he looks forward when the love of God for mankind is fully revealed, when all are taken up into the divine life, not only will there, of course, be no religion, no sacraments, no cult, no sacred activity set aside from human life, but there will be no God in the sense of what is set above or apart from man. God will simply be the life of mankind.
>
> Then, but only then, we shall be able to blow the dust off all those books written by the atheists and humanists and even some of the curious works written by the God-is-dead theologians, and find that at last they have come true in an odd way. They all thought that talk of God was just a convoluted and misleading way of talking about man; what we will come to see when we come to the kingdom of divine love is that talk about

126. Merleau-Ponty, "Faith and Good Faith," 176–77.

man is then the only clear and luminous way of talking about God.[127]

Another way to say this would be to insist that theology, if she is the queen of the sciences, will become their servant, since her logic is that of the incarnation, of the kenosis of God. Theology itself, we may say, must have "the same mind [. . .] that was in Christ Jesus,"

> Who, being in very nature God,
>> did not consider equality with God something to be grasped,
> but made himself nothing,
>> taking the very nature of a servant.[128]

Merleau-Ponty's thought alone cannot get us here. But, far from foreclosing on transcendence, Merleau-Ponty's philosophy awaits theological completion, and cries out for the logic of incarnation in all its consequences.

Flesh and Nature

Merleau-Ponty's ontology of flesh does not only seek a way beyond the impasses of the "philosophy of consciousness." It also anticipates, and seeks to avoid, the problems of a too crude or reductionist "philosophy of nature." This notion of transcendence, which is essential to the sense of Merleau-Ponty's ontology of flesh, as we have seen, problematizes and pluralizes the notion of nature, as we see in his three courses on nature, which engage with a great breadth of thought on nature but which find no monolithic account, no final definition, even while each engagement with a particular thought of nature generates insights. For the ontology of flesh, nature exceeds itself, insofar as that which exceeds nature, the more-than-natural, appears in and through the natural in perception, through intersubjectivity, through institution. Humankind does not act in total freedom. Indeed, this would make its freedom utterly meaningless. Rather we have not just freedom from constraint but freedom to *do something*, to change the world. Acts of love, the creation of art, the generation of new knowledge, and political action in the arena of public history all produce new situations whose efficacy lasts, which go on determining the possible. Institution rejoins nature, and such instituted acts can ossify and go forgotten or can be remembered and take on new life, but this latter is only possible as they are developed, as they

127. McCabe, *God Matters*, 24.
128. Phil 2:6–7 (NIV).

encounter the world anew and are taken up into new acts of institution. All life is this paradox between the thrown-ness, the given-ness, the natality of its situatedness in positivity, and the creativity, the generativity, the indeterminacy of its negative freedom. But the two poles only make sense at all in light of the paradox we describe: givenness *can only be* givenness to the freedom that encounters it as its limit; freedom can only be freedom to act in a world if it is situated within something that is resistant to it. There can be no "nature" without "consciousness," to remain with these old terms; and no "consciousness" without "nature."

The depths we meet in the situated encounter of perceiving nature transcend nature in any normal sense, and all the more so as perception is drawn into intersubjectivity: I see the other hungering, loving, thinking, and I see the other perceiving, even perceiving *myself*. All these operations are instituted in the sense that they arise from a natural ground, from the living system of the earth as soil; and they return to that soil, making it ever new, insofar as the effects of hungers, loves, thoughts, and perceptions do not "float free" from the perceived world but remain attached to it, having their own consequences there. Naturalism, then, can never understand nature, since nature exceeds itself in depth, in intersubjectivity, and in institution. Merleau-Ponty sought to avoid the "philosophy of consciousness," which fails to account for consciousness' grounding in nature, and so to account for either nature or consciousness. Today some are striving for a philosophy of nature, to address the natural problems created by our failure to properly think our relation to nature; the real, pressing problems of resource depletion, climate instability caused by human effects on the biosphere and global inequality. The answer is emphatically not to turn to a "philosophy of nature" in any straightforward sense, since such a philosophy would repeat the mistake: in failing to think the relation between consciousness and nature, it would fail to account for either. Seventy years after *The Structure of Behaviour*, to "understand the relations of consciousness and nature"[129] remains our task.

A "philosophy of life" repeats the failings of a philosophy of consciousness if it divorces life and truth from the world, as we saw in Michel Henry. We would be inclined to assert a materialism, insofar as all that we can speak of arises from a material soil in nature. But, as we have constantly emphasized, nature exceeds itself. And we can too easily become Cartesian again, can collapse all that is into one side of the dualistic divide. We have affirmed the metaphysical in matter, but this makes of matter a question rather than a given; to use Marcel's terms, matter has become a *mystery*, because it is

---

129. Merleau-Ponty, *The Structure of Behaviour*, 3.

not a world from which we can separate ourselves. We are matter. And as such, we do not yet know what matter can be. On this point, both Spinoza and Deleuze were assuredly correct.[130] For this reason we have refused to lay claim to a naturalist or materialist determination of this ontology of flesh; the truth is that we do not have a sufficient definition of "nature" or of "matter" to make such a claim.

Merleau-Ponty's Faith

Christian faith, and the story it tells about human origins and human ends, about the *sens* of existence and the last things, about the meaning of the created world and the nature of the God who created it, is thus not an attempt to construct an adequate model of the world in thought. It is not an attempt to re-present reality in the mind. Rather, it must be an attempt to live with a fuller orientation to reality and to the world in which we find ourselves. We cannot know what God is like from a standpoint outside of the world; no such standpoint is available to us. While, of course, we cannot know before the fact how God may make Godself known to us, we know that we can only attain to a vision of God on the basis of the world we know. Christian faith does not seek to make known the God who is *penseur absolu du monde*, who is the ultimate perspective on things, the God who is perceiver of all, as if we could share this knowledge or this perspective. Rather it seeks to make known the God who is in all things and through all things and to all things, "visible and invisible,"[131] who is revealed from the depths of perception as the truth of the world.

> The human soul can signal God's place at the origin of the world, but it can neither see nor understand Him and cannot therefore be centered in Him. The world ceases to be like a flaw in the great eternal diamond. It is no longer a matter of rediscovering the transparence of God outside the world but a matter of entering body and soul into an enigmatic life, the obscurities of which cannot be dissipated but can only be concentrated in a few mysteries where man contemplates the enlarged image of his own condition.[132]

130. "[N]obody as yet has determined the limits of the body's capabilities: that is, nobody as yet has learned from experience what the body can and cannot do." Spinoza, *Ethics*, 105 (III.2.Sch); Deleuze regularly alludes to Spinoza's point here; for example, in *Cinema 2: The Time Image*, 182: "We do not even know what a body can do."

131. Col 1:16 (NRSV).

132. Merleau-Ponty, "Faith and Good Faith," 175.

We may think that the Christian tradition does not fully agree with Merleau-Ponty here. If the human soul cannot be centered in Him, what would be the point of Christianity? It seems to me that Merleau-Ponty's point here is not to deny that the soul is the basis of the human's relation to God, but rather that this "soul" (Merleau-Ponty is not at all shy about using the word *esprit* in this sense) cannot see God in a purely perspicuous vision. Rather, the soul is thoroughly embodied, it is not something separate or detachable from the body, and its access to God is always mediated by its bodily condition. The notion of the "flaw in the great diamond" is taken from Paul Valéry's poem *Le Cimetière marin*, to which he alludes in *Phenomenology of Perception*[133] and elsewhere; Merleau-Ponty uses it as a cipher for the unexplainable fact, that which gives the lie to any great systematic explanation of the world. In *Phenomenology* he uses it to speak of the fact of perception, that fact of which objective thought cannot give account. Here, he is speaking of the Christian acosmism that he has opposed, the Manichaean thought that cannot understand why God would have compromised his perfection by creating a world. A Christianity that understood this would, then, cease to be a metaphysics in the rationalist sense. Rather than looking up into the sky, it would focus on the "few mysteries" of which he speaks. This is almost certainly another appeal to sacramentality. For Merleau-Ponty, here the human being contemplates "the enlarged image of his own condition." This might be read as an understanding of Christianity as a humanism writ large, as a case of humanity making God in its own image. Such a reading fails to attend to Merleau-Ponty's real concern in the passage, and his appeal to sacramentality as an example. Rather, I read Merleau-Ponty here as claiming that the incarnation of the Son of God on which Christianity reflects gives us a symbol to think through what it is to be human. That the logic of mystery applies not only to humans but also to God, who acts in and on a world of which He has become a part, into which He has arisen from its depths.

And sacramentality does not and cannot constitute a discrete moment in the life of the believer and of the church. The sacraments are cultural

133. "Mes repentirs, mes doutes, mes contraintes / Sont le défaut de ton grand diamant" Paul Valéry, *Le Cimetière marin.* "My penitence, my doubts, my limitations / are the flaw in your great diamond" (my translation). Merleau-Ponty does not give a reference for this allusion, but Colin Smith provides it in his translation of *Phenomenology of Perception* (2002), 241. Landes, in his translation, offers a citation for the bilingual version of the poem: "Le cimetière marin / The Graveyard by the Sea," in *Poems*, trans. David Paul, Bollingen Series XLV-1 (Princeton, NJ: Princeton University Press, 1971), 216–17. Merleau-Ponty, *Phenomenology of Perception* (2012), 215 n. 1, the endnote being on p. 534.

forces, transformative not only in what they do for the individual believer or for the local community of believers. They also form a part of the broader culture in which they are situated. This is true both of the sacraments properly speaking, which sediment and express the internal cultural memory of Christianity and continually form and reform its imaginary. It is also true of the broader sacramental action that is involved in the making-known of the God who is posited as "the other side of things" by enacting the love that God *is*, a love biased towards the poor, the broken, the hungry, the disenfranchised, the lonely and the sick.

Merleau-Ponty's final ontology was left incomplete as a consequence of his untimely death, just as he was preparing to write what might have been a text that gave his renewed and developed ontology of the flesh as full an expression as the *Phenomenology of Perception* gave to his early philosophy of embodiment, the philosophy out of which all his further work grew. We have attempted, here, to bring the ontology of flesh to expression by tracing it from these roots, through his essays and lecture courses, to the extant work towards the project of *The Visible and the Invisible*. We have pursued the implications of embodiment for perception broadly conceived in the example of eating, by situating these implications within a developed account of vision and of visibility, and finally by showing how this ontology may be understood as uniquely consistent with elements of Christian practice, with the logic of God's appearance in the world he created at the incarnation, and of the sedimentation and continued expression of the God revealed there in sacramental celebration and action.

Merleau-Ponty's ontology of flesh, to be brought to full expression, demands to be "fleshed out" in the concrete terms of a living tradition. To make full sense, it must complete the joining of abstract thought to the understanding of a culture and a set of lived expressions, and ultimately to be *lived*, though we accept that such a task lies outside the domain of academic philosophy. This general philosophical account of perception, of seeing, of God, of humankind, of culture, and of history must work itself out in relation to particularities in these fields of thought. It is for this reason that, in an attempt to work out the internal logic of Merleau-Ponty's thought, we have brought it into contact with Christian experience and with the Christian tradition.

While Merleau-Ponty's position *does not* imply an approval of all the contents of Christian belief and experience; perhaps it would be right to say that Christian theology *does* imply an ontology that is something like the fleshly ontology we have developed here. It seems clear that Merleau-Ponty's thought is at least in part inspired by his deep understanding, an understanding developed on the basis of a lived engagement with them as a believer until his late twenties,[134] of the theological concepts of sacramentality and incarnation, and their philosophical implications.

134. Merleau-Ponty alludes in "Faith and Good Faith" to the Austrian Christian Socialist Chancellor Engelbert Dolfuss (a Catholic who had suspended and seized power from the Austrian Parliament) shelling buildings in "working-class sections of Vienna," inside which Austrian Socialist rebels has barricaded themselves. This happened in February 1934, when Merleau-Ponty was approaching his twenty-sixth birthday. Merleau-Ponty recalls the story of Pierre Hervé, who was shocked when some monks with whom he had been invited to eat refused to condemn Dollfuss, as he was the established power in the nation, despite their being members of a progressive order which had supported the workers' cause in Austria. Merleau-Ponty seems to identify with Hervé when he says that "the young man never forgot this moment," and it seems these events played a significant part in his own rejection of Catholicism. "Faith and Good Faith," 172.

CONCLUSION

The Logic of Incarnation
in Merleau-Ponty's Ontology

I SET OUT, IN this book, to bring to expression Merleau-Ponty's ontology of flesh, to develop a logic of incarnation that we found latent in that ontology, and to draw out those aspects of this ontology that carry significance for Christian theology.

In the first chapter, I argued that perception depends on the perceiver being situated at the heart of things, actively engaged in a world on which he depends. Drawing on Merleau-Ponty's *Phenomenology of Perception*, I emphasized the reversibility that overturns the idea of perception as an observation from outside, as well as emphasizing that there is a fundamental perceptual faith that is demanded of us if we are to live: our most basic encounter with the world already depends on faith, a faith that is our assent to our own incarnation. We acknowledged there the inevitability of a certain kind of duality in our ontology of the flesh, and the pervasiveness of Cartesianism in our own thought, which must be overcome from within and cannot be excised from our thinking by a wholesale rejection of philosophy. The perceiver is a body-subject—engaged, interested in his world, and, indeed, hungry. She mediates desire and flesh, self and world, thought and things.

In the second chapter, I argued for a distinction between animal appetites and properly human hunger, making the case that to be the sort of thing that perceives is also to be the sort of thing that desires. The movement of perception is mirrored by that of imagination in expression. Taste is not a matter of cultivated disinterest but of our fundamental perceptual investment in the world. The human being, the hungry animal, transforms her desire and thus makes way for the transformation of the world.

Conclusion

In the third chapter, I brought the old ontology, which Merleau-Ponty seeks to overcome, to a clearer expression. Where a pervasive Cartesianism has been criticized, Descartes's fundamentally geometrical paradigm has been countered in modern thought with an anti-ocularcentric ontology that reverses the hierarchy of the senses, often giving priority to touch. Such ontologies fail because sight is not opposed to touch, but rather rooted a fundamental synaesthesia, which integrates the other senses into the basic existential dimension of depth within which it situates us.

I also established here that the Cartesian visual ontology enshrines a theological position. The dualistic position grounds a naturalistic approach to the world in a conception of God as *penseur absolu du monde*, as the highest principle and absolute that stands utterly outside of the world and divorced from it. Merleau-Ponty counters this dualism with an ontology that implicitly opposes this theology, with a position that has an utterly different theological genesis, a radical theology that springs from an incarnational source. This theology posits us not as abstract consciousnesses but as concrete bodily subjects, entwined with the world, shaped by it and shaping it, labile and dependent, perceptive and expressive.

Thus a non-dualistic ontology requires a recovery of vision as central to ontology, a recovery that we rehearsed and developed in chapter 4. Movement is central to sight as we experience it; the sight of Hockney's "paralyzed Cyclops," the immobilized subject of Plato's cave, is not in fact sight at all. Perception offers us not atomic sense data but a world. Our seeing involves us in a world whose significance for us is not superimposed on it but arises from its depths. The world is thick with sexual meanings, with desire and love in general, with hunger and thirst; this basic insight has been obscured by a dualistic Sartrean theology of the negative freedom of humanity installed in the pure plane of positivity, arrayed before God conceived as the highest point of view on things.

By replacing this conception of sight as representation of things spread out in three-dimensional space, with one of the relation of the perceiver to her world in the fundamental dimension of depth which carries her involvement with that world, we liberate the conception of God from its Cartesian determination and the negation of that determination in modern atheism.

This liberation prepares the ground for an incarnated conception of God. The Cartesian god is *anthropomorphic* in this sense—that god is the infinitization of human perspectives who is required to guarantee human knowledge. The God who is liberated by the ontology of flesh is understood in "incarnational" terms on the basis of our own incarnation: God is not posited as the highest axiom from which all existence derives but as the most basic existential soil from which nature and humanity grow. This is not

God as determining first cause but God as the fecund source of all that is; God does not determine all things, but rather makes possible all things. My originary relation to God is not one of alienation; but of dependence and involvement. Transcendence emerges as a possibility of this world. Perception is incarnational insofar as it is both passive and active; we become both subject to the world and responsible in part for the world, as agents able to shape it. Perception is not here a matter of illumination but of interrogation, and transcendence appears, not as the "beyond" of ultimate height, as with the god beyond the heavens, but in depth, as the God who is in all things, who is transforming nature and making Godself known amongst the poor, in the dirt and sweat of the earth. This transcendence does not fill space but rather permeates places; this would not be God as the ultimate geometer but the God who dwells with us.

In the fifth chapter, I began by arguing that place is constitutive of the world; nature must be understood as the "soil" of existential *place* rather than as a spatiotemporal container. We are already *involved in* nature, it could not be what it is for us without our involvement in it. The nature of nature is not divorced from the nature of human beings but is bound up with it in a relationship of mutual implication. This is another way of saying that the world is given to us not as brute matter nor as a pure upsurge of being but as instituted, which is to say that the soil of nature gives rise to the genuinely human, which both exceeds it as the advent of something genuinely new, but that does not take flight from nature and create a *world* divorced from it (this is the situation of Husserl's sciences in crisis), but re-joins nature, transforms it, and is sedimented within it. We are returned, in the logic of institution, to Merleau-Ponty's basic, incarnational insight. I am thoroughly entwined with the world, and I emerge from that intertwining; it does not emerge from me and my junction with the world. The classical Christian understanding of the incarnation affirms the significance of a particular human body, born in poverty and killed by torture, as the center of human history. The Cartesian ontology makes a nonsense of this; but for Merleau-Ponty's ontology the incarnation of God in Christ is the icon of incarnation as a general structure of the world; it is the blooming of a transcendence always already present at the depths of the world. Incarnation is not the insertion of divinity in the world, the insertion of consciousness in nature, but the flowering of what is contained within the depths of nature, which is not simply "natural," but which is neither opposed to nature, which is rather its completion.

It is this flowering of grace, of the divine, which confirms nature as soil, just as the emergence of humanity "naturalizes" nature. There is a "mystery" encountered where I wrestle with problems from which I cannot distance myself; such a situation arises in my encounter with the world of inter-subjectivity and of history. These mysteries, which arise in my perceptual encounter with things, form the basis for a sacramental conception of the world. It is in interrogation that the invisible *logos* of things is encountered in the world, that transcendence is revealed at the depths of matter.

This transforms our idea of nature insofar as there can be no bifurcation between nature and grace (or the supernatural). Rather, the appearance of *logos* in the perceived world makes our relationship to that world one of interrogation, and makes of nature a question and a fecund mystery. This interrogation opens the domain of metaphysics—not as the question of what is outside *phusis*, but as the question of what emerges within it, of what is unknown in nature. But this metaphysics must always begin with the perceived world and the ways in which it exceeds itself. This metaphysics would not found a necessitarianism or a rationalism but would come to terms with the mixing-up of *logos* in the world of contingency, its incarnate emergence there.

In the final chapter, I argued that Merleau-Ponty's refusal of Christianity was based on a common misunderstanding of the Christian view of God. He found the god of *ens realissimum* represented in the life of the actually existing church of his time; but his understanding of the incarnation suggested to him that the fullness of Christian understanding implied something rather different. While modern thought insists on the absolute distance between God and the world, between creator and creation, Merleau-Ponty's philosophy helps us to recover an understanding of incarnation at its heart. I then offered a brief account of God as *ipsum esse subsistens*. What do we mean by this? The absolute difference between creator and creation is not a matter of distance. Ultimately, the failure of modernity to grasp the Christian distinction, the absolute difference between God and the world, leads to a notion of God installed at the apex of a worldly geometry whose depths he cannot traverse. The God of Christian tradition, the God who creates *ex nihilo*, is not closer to the world by being more like it, but by being absolutely removed from competition with it. God *is* subsistent existence, and thus preserves things in being, in *esse*, from moment to moment.[1] God makes His transcendence known *à la profondeur, ex profundis*, from the depths of things—we see the divine at work in the world as we learn to see things not as brute objects but as a part of a larger scheme. Merleau-Ponty's ontology, and his critique of Christianity, cry out for such an account, but, having not discovered it, he remained an atheist.

---

1. Thomas Aquinas, *Summa Contra Gentiles* III.65.

Bibliography

Abram, David. "Merleau-Ponty and the Voice of the Earth." *Environmental Ethics* 10 (1988) 101–20.

———. *The Spell of the Sensuous: Perception and Language in a More-Than-Human World.* New York: Vintage, 1997.

Allhof, Fritz, and Dave Monroe, eds. *Food and Philosophy: Eat, Think, and Be Merry.* Malden, MA: Blackwell, 2007.

Al-Saji, Alia. "The Temporality of Life: Merleau-Ponty, Bergson, and the Immemorial Past." *The Southern Journal of Philosophy* 45 (2007) 177–206.

Aristotle. *De Anima (On The Soul).* Translated by Hugh Lawson-Tancred. London: Penguin, 1986.

———. *Metaphysics.* Translated by W. D. Ross. Stilwell, KS: Digireads.com, 2006.

———. *The Metaphysics.* Translated by Hugh Lawson-Tancred. London: Penguin, 2004.

Arnould, Jacques. "*Theologians Wanted!* Some Reflections about the Creation/Evolution Debate." *Theology and Science* 8 (2010) 357–70.

Aquinas, Thomas. *Summa Theologica.* 2nd and rev. ed. Translated by Fathers of the English Dominican Province. 1920. Online: http://www.newadvent.org/summa/.

———. *Summa Theologiae, Questions on God.* Edited by Brian Davies and Brian Leftow. Cambridge: Cambridge University Press, 2006.

Augustine. *Confessions.* Translated by Henry Chadwick. Oxford: Oxford University Press, 1998.

———. *On the Trinity, Books 8–15.* Edited by Gareth B. Matthews. Translated by Stephen McKenna. Cambridge: Cambridge University Press, 2002.

Bannan, John F. "Merleau-Ponty on God." *International Philosophical Quarterly* 6 (1966) 341–65.

Barbaras, Renaud. "The Ambiguity of the Flesh." *Chiasmi International* 4 (2002) 19–25.

———. *The Being of the Phenomenon: Merleau-Ponty's Ontology.* Translated by Ted Toadvine and Leonard Lawlor. Bloomington, IN: Indiana University Press, 2004.

———. "The Turn of Experience: Merleau-Ponty and Bergson." In *Merleau-Ponty and the Possibilities of Philosophy: Transforming the Tradition,* edited by Bernard Flynn et al., 33–60. Albany, NY: State University of New York Press, 2009.

Barral, Mary Rose. "Thomas Aquinas and Merleau-Ponty." *Philosophy Today* 26 (1982) 204–16.

Bennett, Jane. *Vibrant Matter: A Political Ecology of Things.* Durham, NC: Duke University Press, 2010.

Bergson, Henri. *Introduction to Metaphysics*. Translated by T. E. Hulme. London: Macmillan, 1913.

———. *Matter and Memory*. Translated by Nancy Margaret Paul and W. Scott Palmer. Mineola, NY: Dover, 2004.

Bernet, Rudolf. "Christianity and Philosophy." Translated by Gregory B. Sadler. *Continental Philosophy Review* 32 (1999) 325–42.

———. "The Subject in Nature: Reflections on Merleau-Ponty's *Phenomenology of Perception*." Translated by R. P. Buckley and S. Spileers. In *Merleau-Ponty in Contemporary Perspective*, edited by Patrick Burke and Jan Van Der Veken, 53–68. Dordrecht: Kluwer Academic, 1993.

Biernoff, Suzannah. "Carnal Relations: Embodied Sight in Merleau-Ponty, Roger Bacon and St Francis." *Journal of Visual Culture* 4 (2005) 39–52.

———. *Sight and Embodiment in the Middle Ages*. London: Palgrave, 2002.

Biran, Maine de. *The Influence of Habit on the Faculty of Thinking*. Translated by Margaret Donaldson Boehm. Westport, CT: Greenwood, 1970.

Blond, Philip. "Theology and Perception." *Modern Theology* 14 (1998) 523–34.

Bolla, Peter de. "The Visibility of Visuality." In *Vision in Context: Historical and Contemporary Perspectives on Sight*, edited by Teresa Brennan and Martin Jay, 63–81. New York: Routledge, 1996.

Boulnois, Olivier. "Reading Duns Scotus: From History to Philosophy." *Modern Theology* 21 (2005) 603–608.

Brennan, Teresa, and Martin Jay, eds. *Vision in Context: Historical and Contemporary Perspectives on Sight*. New York: Routledge, 1996.

Brillat-Savarin, Jean-Anthelme. *The Physiology of Taste*. Translated by Anne Drayton. London: Penguin, 1994.

Brown, Charles S. "The Real and the Good." In *Eco-Phenomenology: Back to the Earth Itself*, edited by Ted Toadvine and Charles S. Brown, 3–18. Albany, NY: State University of New York Press, 2003.

Burke, Patrick, and Jan van der Veken, eds. *Merleau-Ponty in Contemporary Perspective*. Dordrecht: Kluwer Academic, 1993.

Burrell, David B. "*Creation Ex Nihilo* Recovered." *Modern Theology* 29 (2013) 5–21.

Caputo, John D. *Heidegger and Aquinas: An Essay on Overcoming Metaphysics*. New York: Fordham University Press, 1982.

Carbone, Mauro. "Flesh: Towards the History of a Misunderstanding." Translated by Andrea Zhok, revised by Duane H. Davis and Leonard Lawlor. *Chiasmi International* 4 (2002) 49–64.

———. *The Thinking of the Sensible: Merleau-Ponty's A-Philosophy*. Evanston, IL: Northwestern University Press, 2004.

Casey, Ed. "Taking a Glance at the Environment: Preliminary Thoughts on a Promising Topic." In *Eco-Phenomenology: Back to the Earth Itself*, edited by Ted Toadvine and Charles S. Brown, 187–210. Albany, NY: State University of New York Press, 2003.

———. *The World at a Glance*. Bloomington, IN: Indiana University Press, 2007.

Cataldi, Suzanne L., and William S. Hamrick, eds. *Merleau-Ponty and Environmental Philosophy: Dwelling on the Landscapes of Thought*. Albany, NY: State University of New York Press, 2007.

Clark, Andy, and David Chalmers. "The Extended Mind." *Analysis* 58 (1998) 7–19.

Coole, Diana. *Merleau-Ponty and Modern Politics after Anti-Humanism*. Lanham, MD: Rowman & Littlefield, 2007.

Cox, Harvey. *The Secular City: A Celebration of Its Liberties and an Invitation to Its Discipline.* New York: Macmillan, 1965.

Curtin, Deane W., and Lisa M. Heldke, eds. *Cooking, Eating, Thinking: Transformative Philosophies of Food.* Bloomington, IN: Indiana University Press, 1992.

Cunningham, Conor. "The Difference *of* Theology and Some Philosophies of Nothing." *Modern Theology* 17 (2001) 289–312.

Dastur, Françoise. "World, Flesh, Vision." In *Chiasms: Merleau-Ponty's Notion of Flesh*, edited by Fred Evans and Leonard Lawlor, 23–50. Albany, NY: State University of New York Press, 2000.

Davies, Brian. *Thomas Aquinas on God and Evil.* New York: Oxford University Press, 2011.

Deleuze, Gilles. *Bergsonism.* Translated by Hugh Tomlinson and Barbara Habberjam. New York: Zone, 2001.

———. *Cinema 2: The Time Image.* Translated by Robert Galeta and Hugh Tomlinson. London: Continuum, 1989.

Descartes, René. *Meditations on First Philosophy.* Translated by John Cottingham. Cambridge: Cambridge University Press, 1996.

———. *Optics.* In *Discourse on Method, Optics, Geometry and Meteorology*, translated by Paul J. Olscamp, 63–173. Rev. ed. Indianapolis: Hackett, 2001.

Dillon, M. C. *Merleau-Ponty's Ontology.* 2nd ed. Evanston, IL: Northwestern University Press, 1997.

Dreyfus, Hubert L. "Todes's Account of Nonconceptual Perceptual Knowledge and Its Relation to Thought." In *Body and World*, xv–xxvii. Cambridge: MIT, 2001.

Dreyfus, Hubert L., and Patricia Allen Dreyfus. "Translator's Introduction." In Maurice Merleau-Ponty, *Sense and Non-Sense*, translated by Hubert L. Dreyfus and Patricia Allen Dreyfus, ix–xxvii. Evanston IL: Northwestern University Press, 1964.

Elkins, James. *The Object Stares Back: On the Nature of Seeing.* San Diego: Harcourt & Brace, 1996.

Evans, Fred, and Leonard Lawlor. *Chiasms: Merleau-Ponty's Notion of Flesh.* Albany, NY: State University of New York Press, 2000.

Flynn, Bernard. "Merleau-Ponty and the Philosophical Position of Skepticism." In *Merleau-Ponty and the Possibilities of Philosophy: Transforming the Tradition*, edited by Bernard Flynn, Wayne Froman and Robert Vallier, 117–28. Albany, NY: State University of New York Press, 2009.

Flynn, Bernard, and Wayne J. Froman. "Introduction." In *Merleau-Ponty and the Possibilities of Philosophy: Transforming the Tradition*, edited by Bernard Flynn et al., 1–16. Albany, NY: State University of New York Press, 2009.

Flynn, Bernard, et al., eds. *Merleau-Ponty and the Possibilities of Philosophy: Transforming the Tradition.* Albany, NY: State University of New York Press, 2009.

Gasché, Rodolphe. *The Tain of the Mirror: Derrida and the Philosophy of Reflection.* Cambridge: Harvard University Press, 1997.

Gibson, James J. *The Ecological Approach to Visual Perception.* Hillsdale, NJ: Lawrence Erlbaum, 1986.

Gorringe, Timothy. *The Education of Desire: Towards a Theology of the Senses.* London: SCM, 2001.

———. "Sacraments." In *The Religion of the Incarnation: Anglican Essays in Commemoration of Lux Mundi*, edited by Robert Morgan, 158–71. Bristol, UK: Bristol Classical, 1989.

Goudge, Thomas. "Editor's Introduction." In Henri Bergson, *An Introduction to Metaphysics*, translated by T. E. Hulme, 9–20. London: Macmillan, 1913.

Hadot, Pierre. *The Veil of Isis: An Essay on the History of the Idea of Nature*. Translated by Michael Chase. Cambridge: Harvard University Press, 2008.

Hamrick, William, and Jan Van der Veken. *Nature and Logos: A Whiteheadian Key to Merleau-Ponty's Fundamental Thought*. Albany, NY: State University of New York Press, 2011.

Hegel, G. W. F. *Phenomenology of Spirit*. Translated by A. V. Miller. Oxford: Oxford University Press, 1977.

Heldke, Lisa M. "Foodmaking as a Thoughtful Practice." In *Cooking, Eating, Thinking: Transformative Philosophies of Food*, edited by Deane W. Curtin and Lisa M. Heldke, 203–29. Bloomington, IN: Indiana University Press, 1992.

Henry, Michel. *I Am the Truth: Toward a Philosophy of Christianity*. Translated by Susan Emanuel. Stanford: Stanford University Press, 2003.

———. "Phenomenology of Life." Translated by Nick Hanlon. *Angelaki* 8 (2003) 97–110.

Hoonhout, Michael A. "Aquinas' Theology of the God Who Is: The Significance of *Ipsum Esse Subsistens* in the *Summa theologiae*." *Seat of Wisdom* 1 (2010) 27–57.

Hooker, Richard. *Of the Laws of Ecclesiastical Polity*. Book V. Edited by W. Speed Hill. Cambridge: Belknap, 1977.

Hughes, John. "*Creatio ex Nihilo* and the Divine Ideas in Aquinas." *Modern Theology* 29 (2013) 124–37.

Hume, David. "Of the Standard of Taste." In *Essays Moral, Political and Literary*, edited by Eugene F. Miller. Indianapolis: Liberty Fund, 1985.

Husserl, Edmund. "Foundational Investigations of the Phenomenological Origin of the Spatiality of Nature: The Originary Ark, the Earth, Does Not Move." Translated by Fred Kersten; revised by Leonard Lawlor. In Maurice Merleau-Ponty, *Husserl at the Limits of Phenomenology*, edited by Leonard Lawlor and Bettina Bergo, 117–31. Evanston, IL: Northwestern University Press, 2002.

———. "The Origin of Geometry." Translated by David Carr. In Maurice Merleau-Ponty, *Husserl at the Limits of Phenomenology*, edited by Leonard Lawlor and Bettina Bergo, 93–116. Evanston, IL: Northwestern University Press, 2002.

Inge, John. *A Christian Theology of Place*. Aldershot, UK: Ashgate, 2003.

Jackson, Gabrielle Bennet. "Skill and the Critique of Descartes in Gilbert Ryle and Maurice Merleau-Ponty." In *Merleau-Ponty at the Limits of Art, Religion and Perception*, edited by Kascha Semonovitch and Neal DeRoo, 63–78. London: Continuum, 2010.

Jay, Martin. *Downcast Eyes: The Denigration of Vision in Twentieth-Century French Thought*. Berkeley: University of California Press, 1993.

John of Damascus. St. *On the Divine Images: Three Apologies against Those Who Attack the Divine Images*. Translated by David Anderson. Crestwood, NY: St. Vladimir's Seminary Press, 1980.

Johnson, Galen A. "Desire and Invisibility in 'Eye and Mind': Some Remarks on Merleau-Ponty's Spirituality." In *Merleau-Ponty in Contemporary Perspective*, edited by Patrick Burke Jan van der Veken, 85–96. Dordrecht: Kluwer Academic, 1993.

Jonas, Hans. *The Phenomenon of Life: Toward a Philosophical Biology*. Evanston, IL: Northwestern University Press, 2001.

Jung, Hwa Yol. "Merleau-Ponty's Transversal Geophilosophy and Sinic Aesthetics of Nature." In *Merleau-Ponty and Environmental Philosophy: Dwelling On the Landscapes of Thought*, edited by Suzanne L. Cataldi and William S. Hamrick, 235–58. Albany, NY: State University of New York Press, 2007.

Kant, Immanuel. *Critique of Pure Reason.* Edited and translated by Paul Guyer and Allen W. Wood. Cambridge: Cambridge University Press, 1998.

Kass, Leon R. *The Hungry Soul: Eating and the Perfecting of Our Nature.* Chicago: University of Chicago Press, 1999.

Kearney, Richard. *Anatheism: Returning to God after God.* New York: Columbia University Press, 2010.

———. "Merleau-Ponty and the Sacramentality of the Flesh." In *Merleau-Ponty at the Limits of Art, Religion, and Perception*, edited by Kascha Semonovitch and Neal DeRoo, 147–66. London: Continuum, 2010.

Korsmeyer, Carolyn. *Making Sense of Taste: Food & Philosophy.* Ithaca, NY: Cornell University Press, 1999.

Kwant, Remy C. *The Phenomenological Philosophy of Merleau-Ponty.* Pittsburgh: Duquesne University Press, 1963.

Lacan, Jacques. *The Four Fundamental Concepts of Psychoanalysis.* Translated by Alan Sheridan. Harmondsworth, UK: Penguin, 1977.

Ladd, George Eldon. *The Gospel of the Kingdom: Scriptural Studies in the Kingdom of God.* Grand Rapids: Eerdmans, 1959.

Lakoff, George, and Mark Johnson. *Philosophy in the Flesh: The Embodied Mind and Its Challenge to Western Thought.* New York: Basic, 1999.

Lawlor, Leonard. "The Chiasm and the Fold: An Introduction to the Philosophical Concept of Archeology." *Chiasmi International* 4 (2002) 105–16.

———. *Derrida and Husserl.* Bloomington, IN: Indiana University Press, 2002.

———. "Foreword—*Verflectung*: The Triple Significance of Merleau-Ponty's Course Notes on Husserl's 'The Origin of Geometry.'" In Maurice Merleau-Ponty, *Husserl at the Limits of Phenomenology*, edited by Leonard Lawlor and Bettina Bergo, ix–xxxvii. Evanston, IL: Northwestern University Press, 2002.

———. *The Implications of Immanence: Toward a New Concept of Life.* New York: Fordham University Press, 2006.

Levinas, Emmanuel. *Totality and Infinity.* Translated by Alphonso Lingis. Pittsburgh: Duquesne University Press, 1994.

Lingis, Alphonso. "Translator's Preface." In Merleau-Ponty, *The Visible and the Invisible*, translated by Alphonso Lingis, xl–lvi. Evanston, IL: Northwestern University Press, 1968.

Maldiney, Henri. "Flesh and Verb in the Philosophy of Merleau-Ponty." In *Chiasms: Merleau-Ponty's Notion of Flesh*, edited by Fred Evans and Leonard Lawlor, 51–76. Albany, NY: State University of New York Press, 2000.

Maximus the Confessor. *Selected Writings.* Translated by George C. Berthold. Mahwah, NJ: Paulist, 1985.

Mazis, Glen A. "Time at the Depth of the World." In *Merleau-Ponty at the Limits of Art, Religion and Perception*, edited by Kascha Semonovitch and Neal DeRoo, 120–44. London: Continuum, 2010.

McCabe, Herbert. *God Matters.* London: Continuum, 2010.

———. *God Still Matters.* London: Continuum, 2005.

McCullough, Lissa. "Prayer and Incarnation: A Homiletical Reflection." In *The Phenomenology of Prayer*, edited by Bruce Ellis Benson and Norman Wirzba, 209–16. New York: Fordham University Press, 2005.

Meacham, Darian. "Faith Is in Things Not Seen: Merleau-Ponty on Faith, *Virtù*, and the Perception of Style." In *Merleau-Ponty at the Limits of Art, Religion and Perception*, edited by Kascha Semonovitch and Neal DeRoo, 185–207. London: Continuum, 2010.

Melville, Stephen. "Division of the Gaze, or, Remarks on the Color and Tenor of Contemporary 'Theory.'" In *Vision in Context: Historical and Contemporary Perspectives on Sight*, edited by Teresa Brennan and Martin Jay, 101–16. New York: Routledge, 1996.

Merchant, Carolyn. "Reinventing Eden: Western Culture as a Recovery Narrative." In *Uncommon Ground: Rethinking the Human Place in Nature*, edited by William Cronon, 132–59. New York: Norton, 1995.

Merleau-Ponty, Maurice. "Cézanne's Doubt." In *Sense and Non-Sense*, translated by Hubert L. Dreyfus and Patricia Allen Dreyfus, 9–25. Evanston, IL: Northwestern University Press, 1964.

———. "The Child's Relation with Others." Translated by William Cobb. In Merleau-Ponty, *The Primacy of Perception*, edited by James M. Edie, 96–158. Evanston, IL: Northwestern University Press, 1964.

———. "The Contemporary Philosophical Movement." Interview conducted with Maurice Fleurent. *Carrefour* 92, May 23, 1946, 6. Reprinted in *The Merleau-Ponty Reader*, edited by Ted Toadvine and Leonard Lawlor, 85–87. Evanston, IL: Northwestern University Press, 2007.

———. "The Discovery of History." Translated by Michael B. Smith. In *Texts and Dialogues*, edited by Hugh Silverman and James Barry, Jr., 126–28. Atlantic Highlands, NJ: Humanities, 1992.

———. "Eye and Mind." Translated by Carleton Dallery. In *The Primacy of Perception*, edited by James M. Edie, 159–90. Evanston, IL: Northwestern University Press, 1964.

———. "Faith and Good Faith." In *Sense and Non-Sense*, translated by Hubert L. Dreyfus and Patricia Allen Dreyfus, 172–81. Evanston, IL: Northwestern University Press, 1964.

———. *Humanism and Terror: The Communist Problem*. Translated by John O'Neill. Boston: Beacon, 1969.

———. *Husserl at the Limits of Phenomenology: Including Texts by Edmund Husserl*. Edited by Leonard Lawlor and Bettina Bergo. Evanston, IL: Northwestern University Press, 2002.

———. *In Praise of Philosophy and Other Essays*. Translated by John O'Neill. Evanston, IL: Northwestern University Press, 1988.

———. *The Incarnate Subject: Malebranche, Biran and Bergson on the Union of Body and Soul*. Translated by Paul B. Milan. New York: Prometheus, 2001.

———. "The Indirect Language." In *The Prose of the World*, edited by Claude Lefort, translated by John O'Neill, 47–113. London: Heinemann, 1969.

———. "Indirect Language and the Voices of Silence." In *Signs*, translated by Richard C. McCleary, 39–83. Evanston, IL: Northwestern University Press, 1964.

———. *Institution and Passivity: Course Notes from the Collège de France (1954–1955)*. Edited by Dominic Darmaillacq, Claude Lefort, and Stéphanie Ménasé. Translated by Leonard Lawlor and Heath Massey. Evanston, IL: Northwestern University Press, 2010.

———. "Man and Adversity." In *Signs*, translated by Richard C. McCleary, 224–43. Evanston, IL: Northwestern University Press, 1964.

———. "Merleau-Ponty in Person (An Interview with Madeleine Chapsal, 1960)." Translated by James Barry Jr. In *Texts and Dialogues*, edited by Hugh Silverman and James Barry Jr., 2–13. Atlantic Highlands, NJ: Humanities, 1992.

———. "The Metaphysical in Man." In *Sense and Non-Sense*, translated by Hubert L. Dreyfus and Patricia Allen Dreyfus, 83–98. Evanston, IL: Northwestern University Press, 1964.

———. *Nature: Course Notes from the Collège de France*. Compiled with notes by Dominique Séglard. Translated by Robert Vallier. Evanston, IL: Northwestern University Press, 2003.

———. "On the Phenomenology of Language." In *Signs*, translated by Richard C. McCleary, 84–97. Evanston, IL: Northwestern University Press, 1964.

———. *Phénoménologie de la perception*. Paris: Gallimard, 1945.

———. *Phenomenology of Perception*. Translated by Colin Smith. London: Routledge & Kegan Paul, 1962.

———. *Phenomenology of Perception*. Translated by Colin Smith. Reprint, London: Routledge, 2002.

———. *Phenomenology of Perception*. Translated by Donald Landes. New York: Routledge, 2012.

———. "The Philosophy of Existence (1959)." Translated by Allen S. Weiss. In *Texts and Dialogues*, edited by Hugh Silverman and James Barry Jr., 129–39. Atlantic Highlands, NJ: Humanities, 1992.

———. "The Primacy of Perception and Its Philosophical Consequences." Translated by James M. Edie. In Merleau-Ponty, *The Primacy of Perception and Other Essays*, edited by James M. Edie, 12–42. Evanston, IL: Northwestern University Press, 1964.

———. *The Primacy of Perception*. Edited by James M. Edie. Evanston, IL: Northwestern University Press, 1964.

———. *The Prose of the World*. Edited by Claude Lefort. Translated by John O'Neill. London: Heinemann, 1969.

———. "Science and the Experience of Expression." In *The Prose of the World*, edited by Claude Lefort, translated by John O'Neill, 9–46. London: Heinemann, 1969.

———. *Sense and Non-Sense*. Translated by Hubert L. Dreyfus and Patricia Allen Dreyfus. Evanston, IL: Northwestern University Press, 1964.

———. *Signs*. Translated by Richard C. McCleary. Evanston, IL: Northwestern University Press, 1964.

———. *The Structure of Behaviour*. Translated by Alden L. Fisher. London: Methuen, 1965.

———. *Themes from the Lectures at the Collège de France 1952–1960*. Translated by John O'Neill. Evanston, IL: Northwestern University Press, 1970.

———. *Texts and Dialogues: On Philosophy, Politics, and Culture*. Edited by Hugh J. Silverman and James Barry Jr. Translated by Michael B. Smith et al. Atlantic Highlands, NJ: Humanities, 1992.

———. *The Visible and the Invisible*. Translated by Alphonso Lingis. Evanston, IL: Northwestern University Press, 1968.

Midgley, Mary. *Beast and Man: The Roots of Human Nature*. New York: Routledge, 2002.

Milbank, John. "Beauty and the Soul." In John Milbank et al., *Theological Perspectives on God and Beauty*, 1–34. Harrisburg, PA: Trinity, 2003.

———. "The Moral Market is a Freer Market." Paper presented at *Back to Basics or Business as Usual? Responsible Lending, Responsible Borrowing and the Christian Response to the Great Recession*, London, December 12, 2010. Transcript available at http://www.kcl.ac.uk/content/1/c6/01/92/46/JohnMibankTalk. FreeMarketsMoralEconomies.pdf.

———. "The Soul of Reciprocity Part Two: Reciprocity Granted." *Modern Theology* 17 (2001) 485–507.

Miles, Margaret. *The Word Made Flesh: A History of Christian Thought*. Oxford: Blackwell, 2005.

Milton, John. *Paradise Lost: A Poem in Twelve Books*. 2nd ed. Vol. 2. London: printed for J. and R. Tonson and S. Draper; and for S. Birt et al., 1750. Online: https://play. google.com/store/books/details?id=j1MCAAAAQAAJ.

Morris, David. *The Sense of Space*. Albany, NY: State University of New York Press, 2004.

Mounier, Emmanuel. *Personalism*. Translated by Philip Mairet. London: Routledge & Kegan Paul, 1952.

Naess, Arne. "Reflection on Gestalt Ontology." *The Trumpeter* 21 (2005) 119–28.

Nietzsche, Friedrich. *The Gay Science*. Translated by Walter Kaufmann. New York: Vintage, 1974.

———. *Twilight of the Idols*. Translated by Duncan Large. Oxford: Oxford University Press, 1998.

Noë, Alva. *Action in Perception*. Cambridge: MIT, 2004.

Nordlander, Andreas. "Figuring Flesh in Creation: Merleau-Ponty in Conversation with Philosophical Theology." PhD diss., Lund University, 2011.

———. "The Wonder of Immanence: Merleau-Ponty and the Problem of Creation." *Modern Theology* 29 (2013) 104–23.

Pabst, Adrian. *Metaphysics: The Creation of Hierarchy*. Grand Rapids: Eerdmans, 2012.

Panofsky, Erwin. *Perspective as Symbolic Form*. Translated by Christopher S. Wood. New York: Zone, 1997.

Peres, Michael R., ed. *Focal Encyclopedia of Photography: Digital Imaging, Theory and Applications*. Burlington, MA: Focal, 2007.

Picard, Max. *The World of Silence*. Wichita, KS: Eighth Day, 2002.

Pickstock, Catherine. *After Writing: On the Liturgical Consummation of Philosophy*. Oxford: Blackwell, 1998.

———. "Duns Scotus: His Historical and Contemporary Significance." *Modern Theology* 21 (2005) 543–74.

Plato. *The Republic*. Translated by Desmond Lee. London: Penguin, 1987.

———. *Symposium*. Translated by Robin Waterfield. Oxford: Oxford University Press 1994.

———. *Timaeus and Critias*. Translated by Desmond Lee. London: Penguin, 1977.

Pollan, Michael. *In Defence of Food*. London: Allen Lane, 2008.

Priest, Stephen. *Merleau-Ponty*. London: Routledge, 2003.

Prokes, Mary Timothy. *Toward a Theology of the Body*. Grand Rapids: Eerdmans, 1996.

Proust, Marcel. *In Search of Lost Time I: Swann's Way*. Translated by C. K. Scott Moncrieff and Terence Kilmartin, Revised by D. J. Enright. London: Vintage, 1996.

Rabil, Albert. *Merleau-Ponty: Existentialist of the Social World.* New York: Columbia University Press, 1970.

Robinson, J. A. T. *The Body: A Study in Pauline Theology.* London: SCM, 1952.

Romdenh-Romluc, Komarine. "Agency and Embodied Cognition." *Proceedings of the Aristotelian Society* 111 (2011) 79–95.

———. *Routledge Philosophy Guidebook to Merleau-Ponty and Phenomenology of Perception.* London: Routledge, 2010.

Saint Aubert, Emmanuel de. "'L'incarnation change tout.' Merleau-Ponty critique de la 'théologie explicative.'" *Archives de Philosophie* 71 (2008) 371–405.

Sartre, Jean-Paul. *Being and Nothingness.* Translated by Hazel E. Barnes. New York: Citadel, 2001.

———. *Situations.* Translated by Benita Eisler. New York: Braziller, 1965.

Schmemann, Alexander. *For the Life of the World: Sacraments and Orthodoxy.* 2nd ed. Crestwood, NY: St. Vladimir's Seminary Press, 1973.

———. *The World as Sacrament.* London: Darton, Longman and Todd, 1966.

Semonovitch, Kascha, and Neal DeRoo, eds. *Merleau-Ponty at the Limits of Art, Religion and Perception.* London: Continuum, 2010.

Shaffer, Michael. "Taste, Gastronomic Expertise, and Objectivity." In *Food & Philosophy: Eat, Think and Be Merry*, edited by Fritz Allhoff and Dave Monroe, 73–77. Oxford: Blackwell, 2007.

Sheffield, Frisbee C. C. *Plato's* Symposium: *The Ethics of Desire.* Oxford: Oxford University Press, 2006.

Simpson, Christopher Ben. *Merleau-Ponty and Theology.* London: Bloomsbury, 2014.

Soper, Kate. *What Is Nature? Culture, Politics and the Non-Human.* Oxford: Blackwell, 1995.

Soskice, Janet. "Sight and Vision in Medieval Christian Thought." In *Vision in Context: Historical and Contemporary Perspectives on Sight*, edited by Teresa Brennan and Martin Jay, 29–44. New York: Routledge, 1996.

Spinoza, Baruch. *The Ethics; Treatise on the Emendation of the Intellect; Selected Letters.* Translated by Samuel Shirley. Edited by Seymour Feldman. Indianapolis: Hackett, 1992.

Stein, Edith. "On The Problem of Empathy." Translated by Waltraut Stein. In *The Phenomenology Reader*, edited by Dermot Moran and Timothy Mooney, 231–41. Abingdon, UK: Routledge, 2002.

Tallis, Raymond. *Hunger.* Stocksfield, UK: Acumen, 2008.

Tanner, Kathryn. "*Creatio ex Nihilo* as Mixed Metaphor." *Modern Theology* 29 (2013) 138–55.

Taylor, Charles. *Hegel and Modern Society.* Cambridge: Cambridge University Press, 1979.

———. "Merleau-Ponty and the Epistemological Picture." In *The Cambridge Companion to Merleau-Ponty*, edited by Taylor Carman and Mark B. N. Hansen, 26–49. Cambridge: Cambridge University Press, 2004.

Tilliette, Xavier. "Husserl's Concept of Nature (Merleau-Ponty's 1957–58 Lectures)." Translated by Drew Leder. In Merleau-Ponty, *Texts and Dialogues*, edited by Hugh J. Silverman and James Barry Jr., 162–68. Atlantic Highlands, NJ: Humanities, 1992.

Toadvine, Ted. *Merleau-Ponty's Philosophy of Nature.* Evanston, IL: Northwestern University Press, 2009.

———. "Maurice Merleau-Ponty and Lifeworldly Naturalism." In *Husserl's Ideen*, edited by Lester Embree and Thomas Nenon, 365–80. Dordrecht: Springer, 2013.

———. "'Strange Kinship': Merleau-Ponty on the Human-Animal Relation." In *Analecta Husserliana: The Yearbook of Phenomenological Research XCIII / Phenomenology of Life—From the Animal Soul to the Human Mind: Book I*, edited by Anna-Teresa Tymieniecka, 17–32. Dordrecht: Springer, 2007.

Todes, Samuel. *Body and World*. Cambridge: MIT, 2001.

Velde, Rudi te. "Aquinas, Prayer, and *Creation ex Nihilo*." *Modern Theology* 29 (2013) 49–61.

Ward, Graham. "Bodies: The Displaced Body of Jesus Christ." In *Radical Orthodoxy: A New Theology*, edited by John Milbank et al., 163–81. London: Routledge, 1999.

———. *Christ and Culture*. Oxford: Blackwell, 2005.

———. *Cities of God*. London: Routledge, 2000.

Webster, John. "*Creatio ex Nihilo* and Creaturely Goodness." *Modern Theology* 29.2 (2013) 156–71.

Whaite, Richard Patrick. "'Suspending the Material': Materiality, Incarnation and the Christian Doctrine of Creation." PhD thesis, University of Manchester, 2006.

Whitehead, Alfred North. *The Concept of Nature*. New York: Prometheus, 2004.

Williams, Forrest W. "Appendix 1: Merleau-Ponty's Early Project concerning Perception." In Maurice Merleau-Ponty, *Texts and Dialogues: On Philosophy, Politics and Culture*, edited by Hugh J. Silverman and James Barry Jr., 146–49. Atlantic Highlands, NJ: Humanities, 1992.

Williams, Rowan. "The Church as Sacrament." *International Journal for the Study of the Christian Church* 11 (2011) 116–22.

Wood, David. "What Is Eco-Phenomenology?" In *Eco-Phenomenology: Back to the Earth Itself*, edited by Ted Toadvine and Charles S. Brown, 211–33. Albany, NY: State University of New York Press, 2003.

Wrangham, Richard. *Catching Fire: How Cooking Made Us Human*. London: Profile, 2010.

Žižek, Slavoj. *The Parallax View*. Cambridge: MIT, 2009.

Index

Index

Index

Made in the USA
Lexington, KY
06 April 2017